# QUESTIONS & ANSWERS:
## Taxation of Business Entities

# QUESTIONS & ANSWERS:
# Taxation of Business Entities

*Multiple-Choice and Short-Answer Questions and Answers*

**KRISTOFER C. NESLUND**
Associate Professor
Golden Gate University

**NANCY G. NESLUND**
Visiting Professor of Law
University of New Hampshire
School of Law

ISBN: 978-1-4224-8034-2

NOTE TO USERS
To ensure that you are using the latest materials available in this area, please be sure to periodically check the LexisNexis Law School web site for downloadable updates and supplements at www.lexisnexis.com/lawschool.

Editorial Offices
121 Chanlon Rd., New Providence, NJ 07974 (908) 464-6800
201 Mission St., San Francisco, CA 94105-1831 (415) 908-3200
www.lexisnexis.com

MATTHEW◆BENDER

(2011–Pub.3309)

# TABLE OF CONTENTS

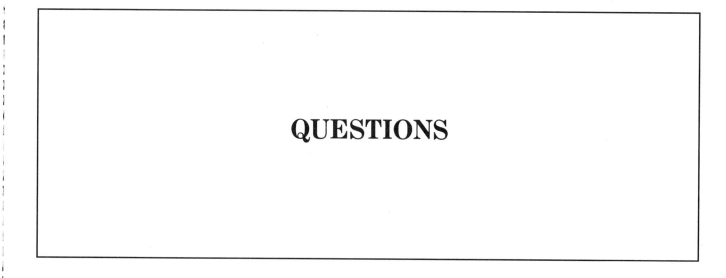

QUESTIONS

*Unless expressly stated otherwise, throughout this volume it should be assumed that all corporations are Subchapter C corporations, all business entities are domestic, and all individuals are U.S. citizens or residents.*

*Subchapter C corporations may be referred to as "C corporations"; Subchapter S corporations may be referred to as "S corporations." Limited liability companies may be referred to as "LLCs."*

*Unless otherwise indicated, all authorities using a format such as "§ 1001(a)" are references to the Internal Revenue Code, which may be referred to as the "Code." Similarly, all authorities using a format such as "§ 1.1001-1(a)" are references to the Treasury Regulations, which may be referred to as the "Regulations." The Internal Revenue Service may be referred to as the "IRS."*

*Although the focus of this volume is on business entities, it is important to understand certain tax consequences encountered by equity holders in their relationships with their entities. Among the issues are related-party losses, the characterization of recognized gains on sales or exchanges between related parties, losses on worthless stock, and losses on § 1244 stock.*

1. Lori Rebel owns 70% (by vote and value) of the Corporation. She owns raw land purchased six years ago which Corporation buys at its fair market value to use as a warehouse site. Lori's basis in the land at the time of sale is $1,300,000 and its value at that time is $1,000,000.

   Three years later Corporation is forced to abandon its warehouse plan and sells the raw land to an independent party for $1,400,000.

   What are the tax consequences to Lori in the original sale and to Corporation on the later sale?

   A. Lori will not recognize any loss and Corporation will recognize a gain of $100,000.

   B. Lori will have a recognized loss of $300,000 and Corporation will recognize a gain of $400,000.

   C. Lori will not recognize any loss and Madison will recognize a gain of $400,000.

   D. Lori will have a realized loss of $300,000 and Corporation will have a realized gain of $400,000.

2. Gwen Boone is the sole shareholder of Marcus, Inc. She also owns an item of depreciable personalty she acquired eight years ago for $250,000. The property has been fully depreciated in one of Gwen's sole proprietorship businesses. Gwen sells the property to Marcus for its value, $300,000. Which of the following is correct?

    A. Gwen has an ordinary gain of $300,000.

    B. Gwen has a § 1245 gain of $250,000 and a § 1231 gain of $50,000.

    C. Gwen has a § 1231 gain of $300,000.

    D. Gwen has a long-term capital gain of $300,000.

3.    William Moore owns .01% of the common stock (only class) of publicly traded Shackleford, Inc. He purchased the stock for $500,000 on December 22 of Year 1. On March 5 of Year 2, a major scandal related to public safety drove Shackleford into Chapter 7 liquidation bankruptcy. Assume the stock became worthless on that day. On his tax return for Year 2, which of the following will William report?

    A. A $500,000 ordinary loss.

    B. No loss because there was no disposition of property.

    C. A $500,000 long-term capital loss.

    D. A $500,000 short-term capital loss.

4.    Elizabeth Anderson, who is single, decided to open a restaurant. She withdrew $200,000 from savings and contributed it to Comanche Restaurants, Inc., a new corporation, in exchange for all of its common stock (only class). The cost of building out and furnishing the restaurant premises was $600,000. Comanche used $100,000 of Elizabeth's cash contribution and borrowed the other $500,000. Elizabeth personally guaranteed the loan.

    The restaurant failed in its third year by which time the loan was paid down to $400,000. The lender agreed to settle the debt for $225,000 because of Elizabeth's poor personal financial condition. Having no resources, Elizabeth asked her married mother, Maria, for help. After consulting with her professional advisors, Maria decided to acquire stock constituting 99% of the corporation's value for $225,000. Her advisers had informed her that, under § 1244, $100,000 of her $225,000 loss deduction would be ordinary. Maria decided the stock-purchase approach was preferable to just making a $225,000 gift to Elizabeth.

    As soon as the debt was settled, Comanche liquidated. Which of the following is false?

    A. Elizabeth will have a $50,000 ordinary loss and a $150,000 long-term capital loss.

    B. Marie will have a $100,000 ordinary loss and a $125,000 short-term capital loss.

    C. All of the stock issued to Elizabeth and Mary satisfied the literal statutory requirements of § 1244.

    D. Section 1244 applies to both Subchapter C and Subchapter S corporations.

*C corporations are taxable entities, but this does not mean that a corporation is the taxpayer with respect to a given transaction. The corporation may be an agent, and under the law of agency the principal (which may be the controlling shareholder) is the taxpayer with respect to the transaction. It is even possible that, by not engaging in enough business activity, the corporation is entirely disregarded as a taxpayer, in derogation of the basic rule that C corporations are taxable entities. The corporation's status as "the taxpayer" is the issue at hand in this topic.*

5.     Lyle Turner, for bona fide business reasons not relevant here, transferred title to Raw Land Parcel 1 to Corinth, Inc. and transferred title to Raw Land Parcel 2 to Sylvar, Inc. The corporations held title to those properties as nominees for Lyle, with the beneficial interests in the properties at all times remaining with him. All parties dealing with Lyle, the corporations and the parcels knew of this arrangement. The only post-transfer action either corporation took with respect to the properties to which they held title was that Sylvar negotiated a loan secured by Raw Land Parcel 2.

        Will Corinth be disregarded as the taxpayer with respect to Raw Land Parcel 1? Will Sylvar be disregarded as the taxpayer with respect to Raw Land Parcel 2?

ANSWER:

6.     Kristin Dent transferred title to an 11-storey apartment building with 66 rental units to her newly formed and wholly-owned corporation, Eastmark, Inc., in exchange for all of its stock. Eastmark hired a full-time property manager to operate the complex. However, Kristin makes all of the major decisions, including approval of tenant applications, approval of capital improvements, determination of all operating policies, pricing, entering loans secured by the property, etc. Eastmark remits all net rentals (less a 5% management fee) to Kristin. An agency agreement was entered into between Kristin and Eastmark prior to her transfer of the realty to the corporation. All persons dealing with Kristin, Eastmark and the apartment building are aware that Eastmark is acting as an agent for Kristin. Based on these facts, which of the following is true?

    A.    Eastmark will be entirely disregarded as an entity for tax purposes.

    B.    Eastmark is the taxpayer with respect to the full rental net income from the apartment building.

    C.    Eastmark is the taxpayer with respect to the 5% management fee.

    D.    The net rental income paid to Kristin constitutes a dividend to her.

*There are times when an unincorporated business entity, such as a partnership, finds it advantageous to be subject to the tax laws applicable to corporations rather than to the tax laws applicable to partnerships. For example, tax-advantaged fringe benefits may require an employer-employee relationship, which a partnership generally cannot provide to its partners. Or simplicity may be desired, which could make being taxed as an S corporation attractive. Unincorporated business entities obtain corporate tax treatment by securing the status of "association." This topic considers how that status is attained and explores some of the implications of being an association.*

7.  Which of the following is false?

    A.  An association is an unincorporated entity that is structured and operated in a manner substantially similar to a corporation.

    B.  Associations are taxed like corporations.

    C.  An association may be a passthrough entity for tax purposes.

    D.  No foreign business entity is eligible for association status.

8.  Tatiana Reese is thinking about forming a limited liability company (LLC) of which she would be the sole member. She meets with her tax advisor to discuss certain issues. The advisor makes four representations. Which representation is correct?

    A.  LLCs are automatically classified as associations.

    B.  An LLC's tax consequences can never be reported on a Form 1040 Schedule C (i.e., as a sole proprietorship).

    C.  If the LLC has the status of association, Tatiana can have the status of employee and enjoy a variety of tax-free fringe benefits.

    D.  If the LLC chooses to give up its association status, it can never attain that status again.

9.  Which of the following is false?

    A.  By default partnerships are disregarded entities under the association rules.

    B.  Domestic corporations are not eligible to elect association status.

    C.  The Regulations include a list of foreign entities that are deemed to have the status of "corporation" for tax purposes.

D.  If an LLC files a Subchapter S election, it is deemed to have elected "association" status and needs to file no association election form.

# DETERMINATION OF CORPORATE INCOME TAX LIABILITY

*This topic considers the federal income tax formula in the context of a C corporation. It explores issues related to gross income and a variety of important business deductions and it surveys the tax consequences of basic property transactions. The topic is designed, in part, to identify important differences between individuals and C corporations in the determinations of taxable income and the income tax liability, including tax rates, the treatment of capital gains and losses, organizational expenses, the dividends-received deduction, the alternative minimum tax, and the general implications of the "double-taxation" regime.*

BASIC FACTS FOR THE FOLLOWING TWO QUESTIONS:

Nottoway, Inc. has a federal income tax liability of $80,750. Its marginal tax rate is 39%; its average tax rate is 32.3%.

10. Explain the difference between an average tax rate and a marginal tax rate.

ANSWER:


11. What is Nottoway's taxable income?

ANSWER:


12. The Gregg Corp. has federal taxable income of $300,000. Its federal income tax liability is:

    A.  $90,250.

    B.  $102,000.

    C.  $100,250.

    D.  Indeterminable without knowing the amount of the state income tax liability.

BASIC FACTS FOR THE FOLLOWING THREE QUESTIONS:

The Bedford Corporation has taxable income of $5,000,000 (all ordinary) before considering the facts below. In addition to its ordinary taxable income, Bedford has the following capital gains and losses:

| | |
|---|---|
| Long-term capital gain | $1,000,000 |
| Short-term capital gain | $100,000 |
| Long-term capital loss | $600,000 |
| Short-term capital loss | $150,000 |

Bedford also has a short-term capital loss carryforward of $75,000.

13. Determine Bedford's net capital gain.

ANSWER:

14. Determine Bedford's taxable income.

ANSWER:

15. Will the net capital gain be taxed at a preferential rate?

ANSWER:

BASIC FACTS FOR THE FOLLOWING TWO QUESTIONS:

The Internal Revenue Code imposes a double-taxation regime on corporate income.

16. Explain this statement.

ANSWER:

17. Why are shareholders that themselves are corporations generally less adversely impacted by the double-taxation regime?

ANSWER:

18. Accomack, Inc.'s accounting records provide the following information:

| | |
|---|---|
| Gross income from the sale of goods | $3,000,000 |
| Bona fide wages paid to employees | $700,000 |
| Rent expense | $600,000 |
| Advertising expense | $100,000 |
| Bribes paid to U.S. police officials | $60,000 |
| Meals & entertainment (full amount) | $40,000 |

The meals and entertainment all relate to business meetings with customers. Accomack's taxable income is:

A. $1,500,000.

B. $1,560,000.

C. $1,580,000.

D. $1,600,000.

19. The Cooke Co., a cash-method corporation, paid penalties to the IRS this year of $80,000. Also this year it disposed of an asset it had been using in operations and had been depreciating under the following MACRS schedule, which is correct:

| | |
|---|---|
| Year 1 | $60,000 |
| Year 2 | 96,000 |
| Year 3 (current year) | 57,600 |
| Year 4 | 34,560 |
| Year 5 | 34,560 |
| Year 6 | 17,280 |
| Cost | $300,000 |

Before considering the penalties and the depreciation deduction, Cooke had taxable income of $450,000. Cooke's taxable income is:

A. $312,400.

B. $421,200.

C. $392,400.

D. $450,000.

20. The Craig Corporation has taxable income before its charitable contribution of $1,000,000. It is an accrual-method, calendar-year taxpayer. Craig has a charitable contribution carryforward from the prior year of $45,000. The board of directors, during the current year, authorized a cash charitable contribution for the current year of $110,000. The corporation paid $30,000 of this amount on December 29 of the current year, $20,000 on March 1 of the following year, and $60,000 on May 2 of that same year. Craig's charitable contribution deduction for the current year is:

A. $155,000.

B. $100,000.

C. $95,000.

D. $75,000.

21. In Year 1 York Enterprises, Inc. had gross income from the sale of services of $1,000,000 and deductible business expenses of $300,000. In addition, in Year 1 York made a cash charitable contribution of $200,000. In Year 3 it generates a $400,000 net operating loss, which is properly carried back to Year 1, resulting in the filing of an amended return for Year 1. York is a cash-method taxpayer. What is York's amended taxable income for Year 1?

A. $230,000.

B. $270,000.

C. $100,000.

    D.  $630,000.

22.  Cash-method Geauga Corporation paid the following costs related to beginning its corporate existence:

| Legal fees: | Advising board on incorporation issues | $ 5,000 |
| | Drafting articles of incorporation | 1,000 |
| | Drafting bylaws | 2,000 |
| Accounting fees: | Advising board on incorporation issues | 3,000 |
| Cost of organizational meetings | | 6,000 |
| Cost to file articles of incorporation | | 100 |
| Cost to issue stock | | 1,500 |
| Cost to transfer shareholders' property to corporation | | 2,400 |
| | | $21,000 |

Geauga's total organizational expenditures eligible for deduction under § 248 are:

    A.  $21,000.

    B.  $17,100.

    C.  $18,600.

    D.  $18,000.

23.  Calendar-year Bandera, Ltd., which commenced business on August 1, has $53,300 in organizational expenditures. Bandera elects to expense these costs. Bandera's organizational expenditure deduction (to the nearest dollar) is:

    A.  $1,700.

    B.  $0.

    C.  $53,300.

    D.  $3,135.

24.  Titus, Ltd., a domestic corporation, owns 60% of the stock (by vote and value) of the foreign Hood Corporation. Seventy-five percent of Hood's income is sourced in the United States and is therefore subject to U.S. taxation. Titus received a $100,000 dividend from Hood. Ignore § 246(b). Titus' dividends-received deduction is:

    A.  $80,000.

B. $70,000.

C. $60,000.

D. $0.

25. The board of the Salem Corporation declares a dividend on Thursday, October 20, for shareholders of record on Wednesday, November 2. The stock goes ex-dividend on Monday, October 31. Carson, Inc. had purchased some Salem common stock on Tuesday, September 20, selling it on Thursday, November 3. Assume that all markets are closed on weekends and that no holidays occur during this period. Will Carson get a dividends-received deduction with respect to the Salem dividend?

ANSWER:


26. On January 1, Year 1, calendar-year, Cameron, Inc. acquired 25% of the common stock (only class) of Cumberland, Ltd. for $630,000. Cameron borrowed 80% of the purchase price on an interest-only loan at 12% compounded and payable each December 31, principal due in ten years. During Year 3 Cameron received a $32,000 dividend from Cumberland. Cameron's dividends-received deduction with respect to the Cumberland dividend is:

A. $25,600.

B. $22,400.

C. $4,480.

D. $5,120.

27. Page Corporation waited until Johnson Corporation declared a dividend before buying 10% of Johnson's stock for $1,150,000 (10,000 shares at $115 per share). Page received a $150,000 dividend from Johnson. Immediately before the dividend was declared, Johnson stock was selling for $100 per share. Fifty days after receiving the dividend, Page sold the stock for $1,000,000 ($100 per share), resulting in a capital loss. Page's only other capital asset transaction during the year was an entirely unrelated short-term capital gain of $200,000. Without considering any of the above facts, Page's taxable income (all ordinary) was $250,000. Which of the following is true?

A. Page reduced its taxable income by acquiring the Johnson stock.

B. Page's acquisition of the Johnson stock did not change its taxable income.

C. Page's net short-term capital gain is $50,000.

D. Page is not entitled to a dividends-received deduction because of its brief holding period.

28. With regard to the corporate alternative minimum tax, which of the following is true?

A. A minimum tax credit could arise when a corporate taxpayer takes a deduction for percentage depletion in excess of cost.

B. The adjusted current earnings adjustment is intended to reduce the likelihood that a corporation with substantial economic income, but little taxable income, pays little tax.

C. Corporations with gross receipts that have always averaged $10,000,000 or less (based on a three-year moving average) are exempt from the alternative minimum tax.

D. All corporations are entitled to an exemption amount of $40,000.

29. With regard to the corporate alternative minimum tax, which of the following is true?

A. The corporate alternative minimum tax rate is either 26% or 28%.

B. Alternative minimum tax preferences are always negative (i.e., they always lower the alternative minimum tax base).

C. S corporations are subject to the alternative minimum tax.

D. Tangible property can be depreciated no faster than MACRS 150% declining balance under the alternative minimum tax.

*This topic considers the tax accounting and procedural issues facing business entities, including the selection of a taxable year and of the overall method of accounting, and tax return filing and tax payment obligations.*

30. Which of the following is correct?

   A. A taxable year ending December 31 is a fiscal year.

   B. A taxpayer may change its taxable year at its discretion.

   C. A fiscal year for financial accounting purposes ending November 15 is acceptable as a taxable year.

   D. As a general rule a taxpayer adopts a taxable year simply by using that taxable year on its first filed return.

31. Which of the following is false?

   A. In general a taxpayer in the business of selling goods must use the accrual method of accounting (at least through the determination of gross profit).

   B. A taxpayer may change its method of accounting at its discretion once every five years.

   C. The two principal methods of accounting are cash and accrual.

   D. A taxpayer with more than one business is permitted to use a different method of accounting for each.

32. Which of the following is correct?

   A. All Subchapter C corporations are permitted to use the cash method of accounting.

   B. The IRS may reject a taxpayer's method of accounting if it fails to clearly reflect income.

   C. The term "method of accounting" includes only the overall methods (e.g., cash and accrual).

   D. A taxpayer who discovers in Year 3 a material item of gross income that should have been included in its return for Year 1 should include that income in its return for the year of discovery (i.e., Year 3).

BASIC FACTS FOR THE FOLLOWING TWO QUESTIONS:

Hartley, Inc. has the following items for the current taxable year:

| | | |
|---|---|---|
| Income: | Cash sales during current year | $3,000,000 |
| | Credit sales during current year | $4,000,000 |
| | Collections on credit sales of current year | $3,300,000 |
| | Collections on credit sales made in prior year | $800,000 |
| Expenses: | Business expenses of current year paid in cash | $200,000 |
| | Business expenses of current year charged on account | $4,700,000 |
| | Cash paid in partial satisfaction of current year's expenses charged on account | $4,100,000 |
| | Cash paid to satisfy prior year's expenses charged on account | $400,000 |

None of the expenses are subject to any deductibility limitations (e.g., meals and entertainment, costs requiring capitalization). The economic performance test is satisfied for all expenses.

33.   Determine Hartley's taxable income under the cash method of accounting.

ANSWER:

34.   Determine Hartley's taxable income under the accrual method of accounting.

ANSWER:

35.   Which of the following is false?

   A.   A corporation's tax return is due by the 15th day of the third month following the close of its taxable year, assuming that day is neither a weekend nor a holiday.

   B.   An extension of the due date for a corporation's tax payment requires a showing of undue financial hardship.

   C.   If the IRS grants an extension of the due date for filing a return, the due date for payment of the tax shown on the return is extended as well.

   D.   A corporation may receive an automatic six-month extension of the due date for filing a return simply by filing the appropriate form by the due date of the return and including a good-faith estimated payment of any tax due.

36.   Which of the following is correct?

   A.   As a general rule the IRS has two years from the date a return is filed to assess a tax deficiency.

   B.   The statute of limitations on assessment does not start to run if a nonfraudulent return is filed after the due date (with extensions) for filing.

   C.   The statute of limitations on assessment with respect to a nonfraudulent amended return that corrects an initially filed fraudulent return starts to run when the amended return is filed.

D. A corporation may file a tax refund claim within three years of filing its return or, if later, within two years of making a tax payment.

37. Which of the following is false?

A. To avoid an estimated tax penalty a corporation must make estimated tax payments in the correct amount not later than the 15th day of the fourth, sixth, ninth and twelfth months of its taxable year.

B. To avoid an estimated tax penalty a corporation estimating a taxable income for the current year of $10,000,000 may use the prior year's taxable income of $8,000,000 to determine its estimated tax.

C. A corporation is not subject to the estimated tax penalty if the tax shown on its return is less than $1,000.

D. The estimated tax penalty is, in essence, an interest charge.

*Well qualified tax practitioners and knowledgeable clients realize that, as a general rule, mere strict adherence to the language of the law is generally insufficient to obtain the sought-after tax benefits. In attempting to give effect to Congress' purpose in enacting the federal income tax laws, and in the desire to do justice, courts have developed several so-called "judicial doctrines" that, at their heart, strive to elevate substance over form. Except where the congressional intent is to have form govern, the tax rules implicitly require the parties seeking the benefit of a provision to demonstrate not only that they comply with all of the literal requirements imposed by the language of the provision, but also that they are members of the class of persons Congress intended to be the beneficiaries of the provision. This topic considers the judicial doctrines of most importance to the taxation of business entities.*

BASIC FACTS FOR THE FOLLOWING THREE QUESTIONS:

Mary Smith owns 90% of the common stock (only class) of Briscoe Corp. Briscoe needed additional financing. Smith discussed the matter with her tax adviser who explained the tax consequences of characterizing the investment as a loan or as a capital contribution. She selected loan characterization and advanced $2,000,000, which the corporation booked as a "shareholder loan." No formal loan documentation was created.

Over the next three years Briscoe repaid $1,300,000, all of which the parties treated as a return of principal. Briscoe has never had any taxable income despite its genuine efforts to make a profit.

Upon audit the IRS asserted that $350,000 of the $1,300,000 paid was interest on a below-market loan taxable to Mary. She argued that although the form was "loan," the substance was "contribution to capital," the return of which was not taxable (because Briscoe never had any earnings and profits).

38. What factors undermine Smith's characterization of the substance?

ANSWER:

39. What factors support Smith's characterization of the substance?

ANSWER:

40. Will Smith be successful disavowing the form of this transaction?

ANSWER:

41. John Williams owns 100% of the stock of Worchestershire, Inc. He has a basis in the stock of $250,000 and also has a capital loss carryforward of $400,000. Worchestershire has taxable income for the current year of ($460,000) — a tax loss — before considering the following events. Worchestershire's assets are worth $700,000 and have a built-in gain of $450,000; it has liabilities

of $100,000.

John also owns 100% of the stock of Devonshire, Inc., which has accumulated earnings and profits of $900,000 and cash not presently needed for business purposes of $650,000. If John causes Devonshire to distribute $600,000, that amount will be fully taxed to him as a dividend since Devonshire has $900,000 of earnings and profits. For this reason, John's advisers propose an alternative. Devonshire will purchase Worchestershire's assets for $700,000. Worchestershire's gain on the sale will be offset by its current tax loss. Worchestershire will then completely liquidate. After satisfying its liabilities, it will distribute $600,000 to John. John's $350,000 gain will be entirely offset by a capital loss carryforward. If the plan works neither Worchestershire, nor John will have any taxable income and $600,000 will be in John's hands.

Upon audit the IRS seeks to recharacterize the $600,000 distribution as a dividend from Devonshire, Inc. under the business purpose doctrine. Describe the IRS' business purpose argument.

ANSWER:


42.   Patricia Jones owned 100% of the common stock (only class) of Jones Flowers, Inc., which had $400,000 of assets as follows: $80,000 of operating assets (accounts receivable, inventory, equipment, cash working capital), $120,000 of real estate used in the business, and $200,000 of cash and other liquid assets in excess of the needs of the business (non-operating assets). Flowers had $300,000 of earnings and profits.

Patricia attempted to sell Flowers, but the value of the real estate and non-operating assets discouraged buyers. Therefore, on a single day, Patricia liquidated Flowers, incorporated Jones Floral Boutique, Inc., and transferred the $80,000 of operating assets and the real estate to Boutique. Patricia retained the $200,000 in liquid non-operating assets. The business continued uninterrupted and without change. Patricia reported the distribution as a liquidating distribution entitling her to long-term capital gain treatment.

Upon audit, the IRS asserts that, under the substance-over-form doctrine, the liquidation/ reincorporation should be disregarded, resulting in dividend characterization with respect to the $200,000 of liquid non-operating assets. Should the IRS' substance-over-form argument prevail?

ANSWER:


BASIC FACTS FOR THE FOLLOWING TWO QUESTIONS:

Throckmorton, Inc., a publicly traded corporation, wanted to acquire the closely held Mason Corporation. Mason's shareholders wanted a cash sale; Throckmorton wanted a merger. In a merger the acquiring corporation (Throckmorton) takes a carryover basis in the acquired corporation's (Mason) assets. As a compromise a merger was undertaken with stock not yet registered with the Securities and Exchange Commission (and which therefore could not be traded), but which would be registered within three months. It was expected that nearly all of the Mason shareholders would sell their new Throckmorton stock at the first opportunity. In fact, immediately after the stock could be traded, almost 100% of the former Mason shareholders sold their Throckmorton stock.

For tax purposes Throckmorton did not treat the transaction as a merger, reasoning that, pursuant to the step-transaction doctrine, the planned-for and actually implemented rapid sale of the Throckmorton stock by virtually all of the Mason shareholders failed a critical requirement for merger treatment under the federal income tax law: the shareholders of the acquired corporation must maintain a substantial, ongoing equity interest in the acquiring corporation. For this reason Throckmorton treated the transaction as a purchase, which stepped up to fair market value the bases of the highly appreciated assets acquired from Mason. This led to $1,000,000 more depreciation than would have resulted had the Mason assets' bases simply carried over to Throckmorton, as would have occurred had the transaction been treated as a merger for tax purposes.

Upon audit, the IRS asserts that the step-transaction doctrine does not apply, that there was a merger, that the bases in the Mason assets carry over, and that therefore the extra $1,000,000 of depreciation should be disallowed.

**43.** Identify the three forms of the step-transaction doctrine.

ANSWER:

**44.** Has Throckmorton correctly applied the step-transaction doctrine?

ANSWER:

**45.** Cori Corporation (a domestic corporation) realized mid-year that it would have a substantial tax liability. It engaged a major accounting firm to develop a plan to reduce that liability. The accounting firm procrastinated and failed to offer a firm plan until two weeks before the end of the taxable year. The firm proposed a series of steps that purported to generate a foreign tax credit. Cori implemented the plan in the manner described below.

On the last day of the taxable year: 1) Gwen, Inc., a wholly-owned Canadian subsidiary of Cori, borrowed $20,000,000 from a bank; 2) Gwen repaid a $20,000,000 loan from Cori (Cori would not otherwise have had sufficient cash to implement the plan); 3) Cori purchased all of a new class of Gwen preferred stock for $20,000,000; and 4) Gwen redeemed that preferred stock for $20,000,000.

Two days later the following occurred: 1) Cori reloaned $20,000,000 to Gwen and 2) Gwen retired the $20,000,000 bank loan.

On its tax return Cori claimed a foreign tax credit based on the preferred stock redemption. That credit reduced Cori's federal income tax liability by $5,000,000. The IRS disallowed the credit under the economic substance doctrine. Will the IRS' economic substance argument prevail?

ANSWER:

*Upon the disposition of property (which includes an exchange) § 1001(a) triggers the measurement of the realized gain or loss. Then § 1001(c) states: "Except as otherwise provided . . . , the entire [realized] gain or loss . . . shall be recognized." When a person exchanges appreciated property for corporate stock, § 1001(a) requires the gain to be measured and, by default, § 1001(c) requires the gain to be recognized. Acknowledging that this mandatory gain recognition chills business incorporations, and believing that making it easy for unincorporated business entities to become corporations and thereby enhance their growth potential was in the nation's best economic interests, Congress enacted § 351, which comes within the "Except as otherwise provided" caveat of § 1001(c). Therefore, an exchange qualifying for § 351 treatment is (generally) a nonrecognition transaction. Section 351 is the subject of this topic.*

46.  Identify the basic requirements for a § 351 transaction and explain the relationship between § 1001(c) and § 351(a).

ANSWER:

47.  What theory underlies deferral nonrecognition transactions like § 351? How is the amount of the gain or loss potential in the assets contributed to a corporation in such a transaction preserved?

ANSWER:

BASIC FACTS FOR THE FOLLOWING FOUR QUESTIONS:

All of Hillman, Inc.'s 100 shares of common stock (only class) are owned by Ian Wilkes. Zahlen Groger will contribute a large tug boat used in Zahlen's business to Hillman in exchange for the following: 1) 900 shares of newly issued Hillman stock, 2) $200,000 and 3) a small parcel of land currently used by Hillman as an employee parking lot. The parcel is worth $300,000 and has a basis of $100,000 (with an eight-year holding period). Zahlen originally paid $850,000 for the tug three years ago. It is now worth $1,250,000 and has a basis of $650,000.

48.  Based on the above facts, which of the following is true?

A.  Hillman recognizes a gain with respect to the stock issued to Zahlen.

B.  Hillman recognizes a gain with respect to the land distributed to Zahlen.

C.  Hillman has a new holding period in the tug.

D.  The stock issued to Zahlen is worth $1,250,000 and likely includes no control premium.

49.  Based on the facts above, which of the following is false?

A.   The land is a § 1231 asset in Hillman's hands.

B.   Zahlen recognizes a gain of $500,000 on the § 351 transaction.

C.   Section 351 does not apply because Zahlen did not receive "solely" stock.

D.   Zahlen has a § 1245 gain of $200,000 on the § 351 transaction.

50.   Based on the facts above, which of the following is true?

A.   Zahlen's adjusted basis in the stock is $950,000.

B.   Zahlen's holding period in the stock is new.

C.   Zahlen's basis in the land is $300,000.

D.   Zahlen's holding period in the land is three years.

51.   Based on the facts above, which of the following is true?

A.   If the parcel had been worth $500,000 and had been encumbered by a $200,000 loan that Zahlen had assumed, then the liability assumed would offset the cash received and the only boot Zahlen would have been deemed to have received would have been the parcel of raw land.

B.   If Zahlen had received only 400 shares of stock, § 351 would not have applied because the control test would have been failed.

C.   If the basis in the tug had been $1,300,000, Zahlen would have recognized a $50,000 loss.

D.   If Zahlen had received stock rights rather than stock, he would have recognized a $600,000 gain.

52.   Three shareholders (Dolf, Elaine and Fasul) simultaneously capitalize a new corporation in an attempted § 351 transaction, each receiving 120 shares of the common stock (only class). One day after the capitalization transaction all three dispose of some or all of their stock. Specifically, on the day following the capitalization transaction, Dolf is approached by a party heretofore unknown to him who, having heard of the corporation's promising business plan, wants to buy two-thirds of Dolf's stock. The offer being highly attractive, Dolf agrees and sells that amount of hiis stock on the same day. Also one day after the capitalization transaction, Elaine gives all of her stock to her son, as she had firmly promised she would four days earlier. Finally, on the day after the capitalization transaction, Fasul sells three-quarters of his stock to Gerta pursuant to a contract executed by them two weeks prior to the capitalization transaction. Will § 351 relief be available to any of the transferors?

ANSWER:

53.   A client approaches his tax advisor and says, "It is my understanding that a corporation's assumption of the liabilities encumbering appreciated assets contributed to it by a new shareholder

in a § 351 transaction is not treated as 'boot' transferred to the shareholder." How should the advisor respond?

ANSWER:

54. Which of the following is true?

    A. A person who transfers property to a corporation in exchange solely for stock rights is eligible for § 351 treatment.

    B. Stock purchased from a securities underwriter is ineligible for § 351 treatment.

    C. The receipt of stock in exchange for the cancellation of a claim against a corporation for past wages is eligible for § 351 treatment.

    D. Where a person receives stock in exchange for services, § 351 is inapplicable to such person and § 83 governs the tax consequences to the new shareholder.

55. Which of the following is false?

    A. The transfer of a Noble Corporation bond with a maturity of eight years to Noble in exchange for Noble's stock could qualify for § 351 treatment.

    B. The transferring parties need not transfer their properties simultaneously to avoid gain recognition under § 351.

    C. If a person transfers (only) property with a built-in loss to a corporation in a § 351 transaction, the loss potential doubles (i.e., the shareholder retains the loss potential in the stock received and the corporation has the same loss potential in the asset transferred to it).

    D. In a § 351 transaction loss is never recognized by a person contributing depreciated property simply because boot is received.

56. Which of the following is true?

    A. To have "control", the control group must have at least 80% of the voting power and at least 80% of the nonvoting shares by value immediately after the § 351 transaction.

    B. In a § 351 transaction in which a person transfers appreciated property and no gain is recognized, the gain potential always doubles (i.e., the gain potential resides in the shareholder's stock as well as in the property contributed to the corporation).

    C. If no boot is received, the contributing party can never recognize any gain upon the transfer of assets to a corporation in a § 351 transaction.

    D. The transfer of accounts receivable by a cash-method person to a corporation in exchange for stock as part of a § 351 transaction is treated as an assignment of income.

57. Which of the following is false?

A. If Western, Inc. capitalizes Eastern, Inc. as its sole shareholder in an attempted § 351 transaction, the control test is not failed if Western immediately distributes the Eastern stock received to Western's shareholders.

B. If a transferor contributes only inventory to a corporation in exchange solely for stock in a bona fide § 351 transaction, the stock received does not tack the holding period the transferor had in the inventory.

C. If a corporation assumes a shareholder's liability in a § 351 transaction, and the contributing shareholder recognizes gain equal to the full amount of the liability because the liability was not assumed for a *bona fide* business purpose, the corporation always increases its basis in the asset received by the full amount of the gain recognized by the transferring shareholder.

D. If an attempted § 351 transaction fails to qualify under that provision, the corporation being capitalized takes a fair-market-value basis in the assets received.

BASIC FACTS FOR THE FOLLOWING THREE QUESTIONS:

On August 1 the Phoenix Corporation, a calendar-year taxpayer, came into existence. It has only one class of stock. On the same day the four individuals below contributed the items indicated in a single, coordinated transaction:

| Individual | Item Contributed | Amount/Value | Original Cost | Adjusted Basis | Holding Period | Shares Received |
|---|---|---|---|---|---|---|
| Lincoln | Cash | $100,000 | — | — | — | 10 |
| Massey | Inventory[fn1] | $200,000 | $220,000 | $220,000 | 13 months | 20 |
| Newcomb | Machine[fn1] | $680,000 | $800,000 | $600,000 | 4 years | 68 |
| O'Hara[fn2] | Services | $20,000 | — | — | — | 2 |
| | | | | | | 100 |

[fn1] Used in transferor's business
[fn2] Attorney; provided organizational services

58. Based on the above facts, which of the following is true?

A. Massey recognizes a loss of $20,000 and Newcomb recognizes a gain of $80,000 because O'Hara's receipt of stock for services makes § 351 inapplicable.

B. Massey's stock basis is $220,000 with a holding period of 13 months.

C. Newcomb's stock basis is $600,000 with a holding period of 4 years.

D. Lincoln's contribution is considered, for tax purposes, to be an exchange.

59. Based on the above facts, which of the following is false?

A. If O'Hara had rendered services worth $300,000 in exchange for stock and all of the other facts had remained the same, Newcomb would have had a recognized gain of $80,000.

B. O'Hara's stock basis is $20,000 with a new holding period.

C. Phoenix will create a new depreciation schedule for Machine using a beginning depreciable basis of $600,000.

D. If Newcomb had secretly entered a contract to sell the stock she received to O'Hara immediately after the capitalization transaction, and if that contract was performed, the control test would have been failed and § 351 would not have applied.

60. Based on the above facts, which of the following is true?

A. Phoenix's basis in the Inventory is $200,000.

B. Phoenix has a deduction of $20,000 with respect to the organizational services provided by O'Hara.

C. If Newcomb had contributed both the Inventory and the Machine (i.e., Massey was not involved in the transaction), Phoenix would have had a basis of $200,000 in the Inventory.

D. Phoenix will treat any gain or loss on its disposition of Inventory as a long-term capital gain or loss.

BASIC FACTS FOR THE FOLLOWING FOUR QUESTIONS:

Lester Eddington created and capitalized accrual-method, calendar-year Tower, Inc. on January 8, as its sole shareholder, transferring the properties below (all of which were used in Eddington's accrual-method, calendar-year sole proprietorship) in exchange for 6,100 shares of common stock (only class).

| Item | Value | Basis | Original Cost | Holding Period | Recourse Encumbrance |
|---|---|---|---|---|---|
| Cash | $500,000 | $500,000 | — | — | — |
| Inventory | $900,000 | $840,000 | $840,000 | 11 months | $100,000[fn1] |
| Operating Asset | $1,600,000 | $1,000,000 | $1,500,000 | 4 years | $1,300,000[fn2] |
| Raw Land | $5,000,000 | $200,000 | $200,000 | 18 years | $500,000[fn3] |
| | $8,000,000 | $2,540,000 | | | $1,900,000 |

[fn1] *Conventional working capital line of credit with commercial bank*
[fn2] *Purchase money note*
[fn3] *Loan from commercial bank made three weeks prior to capitalization transaction to allow Eddington's business to settle a bona fide product-liability claim in that amount*

61. Based on these facts, which of the following is true?

A. If Eddington, on the day after the capitalization transaction, gives one-quarter of the stock to his child, the control test is failed and § 351 does not apply.

B. Eddington's stock basis is $640,000.

C. Eddington has 45 shares allocable to the Raw Land with a holding period of 18 years.

D. The corporation is deemed to have assumed the three liabilities for tax purposes only if a novation has occurred.

62. Modify the facts above as follows: 1) The encumbrance on the Inventory is $800,000, and 2) Eddington received 5,400 shares of stock. Based on these revised facts, which of the following is false?

    A. Eddington recognizes a gain of $60,000.

    B. All gain recognized is § 1231 gain.

    C. Tower takes a basis in the Inventory of $847,200.

    D. Eddington's stock basis is $0.

63. Based on the facts in Question 54, which of the following is true?

    A. The IRS would assert that a note made out to Tower by Eddington with principal of $60,000 and paying market interest would not stop the recognition of gain.

    B. Some of the gain recognized with respect to Raw Land could be unrecaptured § 1250 gain taxable at a maximum rate of 25%.

    C. Eddington's holding period in the stock is long-term.

    D. The recognized gain on the Operating Asset is § 1231 gain.

64. Return to the original facts, with the exception that the loan encumbering the Raw Land was made to consolidate Eddington's personal obligations. Which of the following is correct?

    A. Eddington still recognizes no gain on the capitalization transaction.

    B. Eddington is treated as having received $500,000 of boot in the capitalization transaction.

    C. Eddington is treated as having received $1,900,000 of boot in the capitalization transaction.

    D. Eddington's recognized gain with respect to Operating Asset is $600,000.

*Earnings and profits is the tax analog to financial accounting's retained earnings. To a financial accountant, retained earnings is essentially all of the income the corporation has ever earned less all of the dividends the corporation has ever distributed to shareholders. In other words, retained earnings is the cumulative amount of corporate income that has not yet been distributed. Earnings and profits attempts to provide the same type of information, but it employs measurement rules that take into account the unique characteristics and objectives of the federal income tax system. Understanding how to measure earnings and profits is essential because the tax definition of "dividend" under § 316(a) is "any distribution . . . made by a corporation to its shareholders . . . out of its earnings and profits." The implications of a corporate distribution being characterized as a "dividend" are considered in a later topic. This topic's focus is the determination of earnings and profits.*

65. Which of the following is true?

   A. Earnings and profits represents the amount a corporation could distribute to shareholders without reducing its beginning-of-year invested capital.

   B. Earnings and profits equals the corporation's cumulative taxable income less the cumulative amount it has paid out as dividends.

   C. A corporation could use the cash method of accounting for computing earnings and profits while concurrently using the accrual method of accounting for computing taxable income.

   D. Accumulated earnings and profits has no conceptual relationship with financial accounting's retained earnings.

66. Which of the following is true?

   A. The rules for computing earnings and profits are primarily statutory.

   B. Earnings and profits are relevant primarily for the characterization of corporate nonliquidating distributions and for the computation of the alternative minimum tax.

   C. The IRS will provide an advance ruling to assist in the computation of earnings and profits.

   D. Since earnings and profits is intended to measure a corporation's true economic ability to make distributions to shareholders without impairing invested capital, earnings and profits is always determined using the accrual method of accounting.

67. Which of the following is true?

A. Consistent with its treatment for taxable income purposes, exempt interest under § 103 is also excluded in the determination of earnings and profits.

B. The federal income tax liability for Year 1 that is actually paid by an accrual-method corporate taxpayer in Year 2 would reduce earnings and profits in Year 1.

C. When a corporation reduces the net capital gain it reports on its tax return for Year 2 through the use of a capital loss carryforward from Year 1, the corporation would also reduce its Year 2 earnings and profits by that carryforward.

D. A corporation reduces its earnings and profits by its dividends-received deduction.

68.   Which of the following is false?

A. Life insurance premiums on key persons are deductible in computing earnings and profits.

B. A cash-method corporation's payment of estimated tax during Year 2 with respect to that taxable year would reduce its earnings and profits for Year 2.

C. A corporation that files an amended return for Year 3 to utilize a net operating loss carryback from Year 4 would also reduce its Year 3 earnings and profits.

D. Where, through the use of percentage depletion, a corporation has reduced its basis in the depletable asset to zero, there will be no future earnings and profits deductions for depletion.

69.   Which of the following is true?

A. Allowing a deduction in the computation of earnings and profits for a civil tax penalty is considered contrary to public policy.

B. A cash-method corporate taxpayer's payment of a tax deficiency for taxable year Year 1 in Year 3 pursuant to an audit in Year 3 of its Year 1 tax return would reduce its earnings and profits for Year 1.

C. A corporation with taxable income before its charitable deduction of $1,000,000 would reduce its current earnings and profits by $125,000 if it makes a $125,000 charitable contribution during the year.

D. The last-in-first-out (LIFO) inventory method may be used in determining earnings and profits.

70.   Which of the following is false?

A. An accrual-method corporate taxpayer's payment of a tax deficiency for Year 1 in Year 3 pursuant to an audit in Year 3 of its Year 1 tax return will reduce its earnings and profits for Year 1.

B. A corporation that generates a net operating loss of $300,000 for the taxable year could have current earnings and profits for the year of negative $300,000.

C. A corporation with a net capital loss for the year of $70,000 would reduce its earnings and profits for the year by $70,000 even though its taxable income could not be reduced by that net capital loss.

D. A corporation that realizes a $200,000 gain on an installment sale, but which recognizes only $50,000 during the year of disposition pursuant to § 453, would increase its earnings and profits for the current year by $50,000.

71. Which of the following is false?

A. For earnings and profits purposes, organizational expenditure deductions under § 248 are taken ratably over five years.

B. The completed-contract method of accounting cannot be used in computing earnings and profits.

C. Five-year MACRS property is depreciated for earnings and profits purposes using the straight-line method.

D. The § 179 amount is deducted for earnings and profits purposes pro rata over five years.

72. In Year 3 accrual-method, calendar-year Elwyn, Inc. engaged in a like-kind exchange under § 1031 in which it realized a gain of $300,000 but recognized no gain. In addition, pursuant to an audit of its Year 1 tax return it paid $80,000 in tax and $32,000 in penalties. Finally, Elwyn sold property to its sole shareholder, realizing a loss of $125,000, all of which was disallowed under § 267. By how much should Elwyn adjust its Year 3 earnings and profits by virtue of the like-kind exchange? By virtue of the payments to the IRS? By virtue of the disallowed loss?

A. The like-kind exchange will increase Elwyn's earnings and profits by $300,000, while the payments to the IRS and the disallowed loss will decrease earnings and profits by $112,000 and $125,000, respectively.

B. The like-kind exchange and the payments to the IRS will have no impact on Elwyn's earnings and profits, but the disallowed loss will reduce its earnings and profits by $125,000.

C. The like-kind exchange will increase Elwyn's earnings and profits by $300,000, but the payments to the IRS and the disallowed loss will have no impact on its earnings and profits.

D. None of these events impact Elwyn's Year 3 earnings and profits.

BASIC FACTS FOR THE FOLLOWING FOUR QUESTIONS:

Concord, Ltd. incorporated on April 1, Year 1, having incurred $60,000 in organizational expenditures deductible under § 248. It properly deducted $3,000 of those expenditures on its return for Year 1. On January 1, Year 2, Concord acquired and placed in service an item of five-year MACRS personalty with a class life of eight years for which it paid $350,000. It was allowed and took a § 179 deduction of $250,000 that year with respect to that personalty. Its MACRS table follows:

| Year | MACRS Factor | Depreciation Deduction | Ending Adjusted Basis |
|------|------|------|------|
| 1 | .2000 | $20,000 | $80,000 |
| 2 | .3200 | 32,000 | $48,000 |
| 3 | .1920 | 19,200 | $28,800 |
| 4 | .1152 | 11,520 | $17,280 |
| 5 | .1152 | 11,520 | $5,760 |
| 6 | .0576 | 5,760 | $0 |
|   | 1.0000 | $100,000 | |

Concord sold the personalty in Year 4 for $325,000.

73.    For the personalty, determine the total depreciation deduction (MACRS and § 179) for Year 4 for earnings and profits purposes based solely on the above information.

ANSWER:

74.    Determine the deduction in Year 4 for earnings and profits purposes with respect to the § 248 expenditures.

ANSWER:

75.    Determine the recognized gain for tax purposes with respect to the disposition of the property in Year 4.

ANSWER:

76.    Determine recognized gain with respect to the disposition for earnings and profits purposes in Year 4.

ANSWER:

BASIC FACTS FOR THE FOLLOWING FOUR QUESTIONS:

Cash-method, calendar-year corporation Bresco Enterprises, Ltd. has the following tax items for Year 1:

| Item | Amount |
|------|------|
| Cash ordinary operating income | $1,000,000 |
| Long-term capital gain | $100,000 |
| Short-term capital loss | ($160,000) |
| Net operating loss carryforward from Year 0 | ($200,000) |
| Dividends from 10%-owned domestic corporation | $50,000 |
| Dividends-received deduction | ($35,000) |
| Loss disallowed under § 267 | ($60,000) |
| § 248 deduction | ($15,000) |
| Penalty paid to IRS re: audit of prior year's tax return | ($40,000) |

| Item | Amount |
|------|--------|
| Estimated taxes paid during Year 1 for Year 1 | ($110,000) |
| § 179 deduction | ($30,000) |
| MACRS deduction[fn] | ($10,000) |
| Life insurance premiums paid on key-person policies | ($25,000) |

[fn] *Bresco elected to use alternative depreciation system under § 168(g) for tax purposes*

Bresco has accumulated earnings and profits as of January 1, Year 1 of ($900,000); i.e., an accumulated deficit. It made no distributions during the year.

77.   Determine Bresco's taxable income for Year 1.

ANSWER:

78.   Determine Bresco's current earnings and profits for Year 1.

ANSWER:

79.   Determine Bresco's accumulated earnings and profits as of January 1, Year 2.

ANSWER:

80.   Determine Bresco's accumulated earnings and profits as of January 1, Year 2 assuming a distribution of $500,000 was made to the shareholders with respect to their stock during Year 1.

ANSWER:

81.   Which of the following is false?

A.   If there are § 301(a) distributions during the year on both preferred stock and common stock, earnings and profits are allocated to preferred stock first.

B.   If there are no earnings and profits, no distribution can be a dividend.

C.   If, during the same year, there are both redemption distributions (i.e., subject to § 302(a)) and non-redemption distributions (i.e., subject to § 301(a)), redemption distributions reduce earnings and profits before non-redemption distributions.

D.   Where positive accumulated earnings and profits and positive current earnings and profits exist at the time of a distribution, accumulated earnings and profits flow out only if current earnings and profits are insufficient to cover the full amount of the distribution.

82.   Which of the following is true?

A.  Where a corporation makes a series of nonliquidating distributions to its shareholders during a year that are not redemptions, each distribution carries out a pro rata amount of any positive accumulated earnings and profits in existence at the beginning of the year.

B.  The portion of the nonliquidating distributions during the year (other than redemptions) that are characterized as "dividends" cannot be determined until the end of the year.

C.  In a redemption distribution where positive earnings and profits exist, earnings and profits are always reduced by the amount of the distribution.

D.  Where beginning-of-year accumulated earnings and profits are positive but current earnings and profits are negative at the end of the year, the negative end-of-year current earnings and profits are netted against the positive accumulated earnings and profits; and if a positive balance results, that amount is allocated to the distributions during the year on a first-in-first-out (FIFO) basis.

*Tax law changes in the early 2000s have dramatically altered the stakes involved in characterizing a distribution from a corporation to a shareholder with respect to its stock. In the early 1980s a dividend (i.e., a distribution sourced from earnings and profits) could be taxed at a rate as high as 70%. In strong contrast, a long-term capital gain on the sale of stock back to the corporation (i.e., a redemption) could be taxed at a rate of no more than 28%. Given such an enormous difference in the tax consequences, shareholders went to extraordinary lengths to characterize the distributions to them from their corporations as redemptions rather than as dividends. If the status "redemption" could be secured, the effective tax rate was no more than 40% (28%/70%) of the rate imposed on distributions with the status "dividend." Under the current tax law both dividends and long-term capital gains are taxed at a default rate of 15%, significantly lowering shareholder preference for dividend treatment on the part of individuals. Note, however, that corporate shareholders tend to favor dividend characterization because of the availability of a 70%, 80% or even 100% dividends-received deduction, considered in Topic 4.*

*This topic explores the tax consequences of distributions of property (other than stock) to shareholders that are classified neither as redemptions nor as distributions in complete liquidation of the corporation.*

83.  Harmony Co., Inc. has beginning-of-year accumulated earnings and profits of $1,000,000 and current earnings and profits of $800,000. During the year Harmony distributes with respect to its stock a total of $3,000,000: $600,000 to 20% shareholder McGraw on March 1 and $2,400,000 to 80% shareholder O'Leary on November 1. Both shareholders had bases of $4,000,000 at the times of their respective distributions. How much of the distributions to McGraw and O'Leary are a dividend?

   A.  All of the distributions paid to McGraw and O'Leary are dividends if the board of directors directed that they be paid out of retained earnings.

   B.  None of the distribution to McGraw was a dividend for tax purposes; O'Leary received a dividend of $1,800,000 and treated $600,000 as a return of capital.

   C.  McGraw received $360,000 as a dividend; O'Leary received $1,440,000 as a dividend.

   D.  McGraw received $600,000 as a dividend; O'Leary received $1,200,000 as a dividend.

BASIC FACTS FOR THE FOLLOWING THREE QUESTIONS:

Serenity, Inc. (which has one class of stock) is owned 60% by individual Shep Book and 40% by the Alliance Corp. Shep's stock basis is $500,000; Alliance's is $600,000. Both shareholders have long-term holding periods. Serenity, which has current earnings and profits of $800,000 and no accumulated earnings and profits, distributes $2,000,000 (cash) to its shareholders pro rata.

84.  What are the tax consequences to Serenity?

ANSWER:

85. What are the tax consequences to Shep?

ANSWER:

86. What are the tax consequences to Alliance?

ANSWER:

BASIC FACTS FOR THE FOLLOWING TWO QUESTIONS:

Calendar-year corporation, Shangri-La, Ltd., has current earnings and profits of $1,000,000 and no accumulated earnings and profits. All of its preferred stock (cumulative, total par value $5,000,000, stated dividend rate 10%, no dividends in arrears) is owned by Oriental, Inc. All of its common stock is owned by Patty Herz. Oriental's stock basis is $4,000,000; Patty's is $3,000,000. Shangri-La distributes $600,000 on December 31 with respect to its stock, the only distribution during the year.

87. Which of the following is false?

  A. Shangri-La will recognize no gain or loss on the distribution.

  B. Patty will recognize dividend income of $100,000.

  C. Oriental will characterize none of the distribution to it as a dividend.

  D. If Shangri-La had also had negative accumulated earnings and profits (i.e., an accumulated deficit) of ($1,000,000), the amount of the distribution constituting a dividend would be unchanged.

88. Based on the above data, which of the following is false?

  A. Shangri-La will reduce its earnings and profits by $600,000.

  B. Patty's stock basis remains unchanged.

  C. Oriental's stock basis remains unchanged.

  D. If Shangri-La had had accumulated earnings and profits of $1,000,000 and negative current earnings and profits of ($1,000,000), the amount of the distribution constituting a dividend would be unchanged.

BASIC FACTS FOR THE FOLLOWING TWO QUESTIONS:

Accrual-method, calendar-year corporation, Medford, Ltd. has accumulated earnings and profits on January 1 of $3,200,000. It has negative current earnings and profits for the year of ($1,200,000). Medford, which has only one class of stock, has two unrelated shareholders: Carrie Eckhart and Ralph Ganon. Carrie owns 800 shares with a basis of $400,000 and a holding period of seven years. Ralph owns 200 shares with a basis of $100,000 and a holding period of two years. On December 31 Medford distributes $900,000 with respect to its stock pro rata. On the same day Medford redeems half of Ralph's stock for $600,000.

89. Which of the following is false?

    A. At the end of the year Medford's earnings and profits is $500,000.

    B. Carrie's stock basis remains unchanged.

    C. Ralph has a dividend of $180,000.

    D. Medford has no recognized gain or loss as a result of either distribution.

90. Based on the above data, which of the following is true?

    A. If the $900,000 distribution had occurred on January 1, the available earnings and profits would still have been measured at $2,000,000.

    B. If Carrie and Ralph had been married, the $600,000 paid to Ralph for his stock would have been characterized as a dividend.

    C. If the redemption of Ralph's stock had occurred on December 29, the amount of earnings and profits available to cover the $900,000 distribution would have been less.

    D. The amount of accumulated and current earnings and profits would, under all circumstances, be unchanged if Medford had used the cash method of accounting.

BASIC FACTS FOR THE FOLLOWING TWO QUESTIONS:

John Vinson is the sole shareholder of accrual-method calendar-year Birtchnell, Inc. His stock was acquired 11 years ago and has a basis of $700,000. On December 31, 20X5 Birtchnell, which has earnings and profits of $300,000 before taking into account the tax consequences of the distribution now described, made one distribution with respect to its stock during 20X5: it distributed to John a warehouse used in its business worth $2,500,000 (basis for taxable income purposes $2,000,000; basis for earnings and profits purposes $2,100,000; holding period four years). (Assume it is acceptable to not partition the warehouse between its land and improvements.) The warehouse is subject to a nonrecourse liability of $1,900,000. Birtchnell is in the 34% marginal tax bracket.

91. What are the tax consequences to John?

ANSWER:

92. How would the tax consequences to John change if the warehouse had a basis for taxable income purposes of $2,700,000 and for earnings and profits purposes of $2,800,000?

ANSWER:

93. Calendar-year Haverford, Inc. has three shareholders, Adams, Blunt and Crisp, who own the following respective proportions of the corporation's common stock (its only class): 60%, 30% and 10%. On January 1 the shareholders have the following respective bases in

their stock: $20,000, $250,000 and $25,000. On this date Haverford has accumulated earnings and profits of $310,000. During the year Haverford generates current earnings and profits of $120,000. Haverford also makes the following distributions to its shareholders: $300,000 to Adams on March 1, $150,000 to Blunt on June 15, and $50,000 to Crisp on December 31. How much gain does Crisp recognize as result of the distribution?

A.  $13,000.

B.  $25,000.

C.  $0.

D.  $30,000.

*Section 301, considered in the previous topic, is primarily directed at formally declared dividends. The context presumed is that the board of directors has declared a dividend, which made the corporation a debtor with respect to the dividend payable to the shareholders. That obligation was discharged when the dividend was actually distributed. But the essential nature of a dividend is a transfer of value from a corporation to a shareholder simply by virtue of the shareholder's status as such, with nothing of monetary value given back to the corporation by the shareholder in exchange.*

*There is no dividend when there is a contemporaneous exchange of value. A shareholder who is also an employee and who gets paid a reasonable salary for services provided to the corporation does not have a dividend when the corporation deposits that salary into the shareholder's bank account on payday. The money received by the shareholder-employee from the corporation is not due to the recipient's status as "shareholder," but rather with respect to the recipient's status as "employee." The same would be true for a shareholder-landlord, a shareholder-creditor, etc.*

*Sometimes, however, particularly in a closely held corporation, a controlling shareholder finds ways to force the corporation to distribute value in excess of any value given by the shareholder in return. Classic examples are excessive compensation paid to the shareholder or one of the shareholder's relatives, excessive rent paid for facilities leased by the corporation from the shareholder, unreasonably low interest rates on loans from the corporation to the shareholder, and unreasonably high purchase prices on property sales by the shareholder to the corporation. In all of these situations there is at least a purported contemporaneous exchange of value, but the two considerations are not equal — more value is flowing from the corporation to the shareholder than is flowing from the shareholder to the corporation.*

*These value differentials are properly called "constructive distributions." It is common to hear them called "constructive dividends," but that is technically incorrect because in the federal income tax domain a distribution is only a "dividend" if it is sourced from earnings and profits. Where the value distributed exceeds the corporation's earnings and profits, it is improper to call that excess a constructive "dividend."*

*This topic explores the tax consequences of constructive distributions (entitled "Constructive Dividends" here in acknowledgment of the widespread use of that term).*

94. The term "dividend" is used in both state law and federal tax law. Which of the following statements is true?

    A. If the board of directors directs a dividend to be distributed out of paid-in capital in excess of par, for federal income tax purposes the distribution will be treated as a return of capital to the shareholders.

B.   If the board of directors directs a dividend to be distributed out of earned surplus (in essence, cumulative undistributed earnings), for federal income tax purposes the distribution will be treated as a dividend.

C.   If the federal income tax law requires a particular distribution to be classified as a dividend, financial accounting rules will require that the distribution be shown as a distribution out of retained earnings.

D.   There is no necessary correlation between the classification of a particular distribution as a dividend for state law purposes and its classification as a dividend for federal income tax purposes.

95.   What is a "constructive dividend" as that term is used in the federal income tax law, and why is the word "dividend" as used in this phrase not technically correct?

ANSWER:

96.   Michael McWilliams is a minority shareholder in a family-owned corporation engaged in the slaughterhouse business. One of the byproducts is the blood from calves. The corporation has tried to market such blood for medical research but has given up that potential line of business as being insufficiently profitable given its desire to remain primarily invested in its core slaughterhouse business. To the corporation, then, the blood is a worthless byproduct. Michael believes he can make a viable business out of preparing such blood for medical research. With the full knowledge and consent of the board of directors, exercising bona fide business judgment unaffected by family relationships, Michael is allowed to remove and exploit the blood. Michael is successful. Has he received a constructive dividend with respect to the blood?

ANSWER:

97.   The sole shareholder and CEO of a corporation that produces pipe of various sizes has found his business increasingly undermined by overseas competition. She believes that personal relationships are the key to business survival. To facilitate such relationships, she causes the corporation to expend considerable sums turning her personal home into a horticultural showplace. She entertains customers and potential customers extensively at her home. Are the amounts paid by the corporation to create and maintain the horticultural showplace constructive dividends?

ANSWER:

98.   A corporate CEO and minority shareholder files fraudulent tax returns on behalf of the corporation. He secured no direct personal benefit from the tax savings. Upon audit the IRS detected the fraud and, among other things, imposed a $40,000 fine for tax fraud on the CEO. Because, in the opinion of the board of directors, the CEO's actions were for the benefit of the corporation, the board authorized a $40,000 payment to the IRS to pay the fine and characterized such payment as the equivalent of an indemnification. The CEO did not report the $40,000 as gross income. Is the $40,000 payment to the IRS a constructive dividend to the CEO?

ANSWER:

99.  A sole shareholder caused her cash-method corporation (which has a large amount of earnings and profits) to build homes for her children and to pay her children three times the value of their services to the corporation. The corporation deducted all such amounts under § 162. The IRS challenged the corporation's deductions and also opened audits of the sole shareholder and of the shareholder's children. Which of the following statements is true?

A.  The home-building expenses are not deductible to the corporation, but the compensation to the children for their services is deductible to the extent it does not exceed $1 million annually to each of them.

B.  The children will likely be entitled to tax refunds as a result of the audits.

C.  The amount of the home-building expenses and the excess compensation will be treated as constructive dividends to the children.

D.  The amount of the home-building expenses and the excess compensation to the children will be treated as constructive dividends to the shareholder and the shareholder will be required to reduce her basis in her stock by the sum of those amounts.

BASIC FACTS FOR THE FOLLOWING TWO QUESTIONS:

Hildegard (Hildi) Keogh is the sole shareholder of Tyrant, Inc. Hildi annually causes 20% of the corporation's revenues to be deposited directly into her personal bank account. Those amounts have not been reported either by her or by the corporation. She has also caused the corporation to sell a significant number of its land holdings to her at 60% of their actual values. Further, she has caused the corporation to pay her a salary that is five times the value of her services. Tyrant has a large amount of earnings and profits.

100.  How will the IRS characterize the facts above with respect to all open taxable years?

ANSWER:

101.  Hildi has sufficient resources only to repay the corporation for all of the revenues she misappropriated and half of the excess personal service compensation. Based solely on the above facts, if she makes those repayments, will she be allowed any deduction?

ANSWER:

*In a classic stock distribution (often called a "stock dividend"), all of the shareholders get additional shares of stock in proportion to the stock they already own. They all have more paper, but no one is any wealthier. After the stock distribution all of the shareholders are entitled to the same proportion of future distributions of corporate earnings to which they were entitled before the distribution. The same can be said of the shareholders' voting power and of their rights to asset distributions should the corporation liquidate. The tax law, acknowledging the substance, does not consider such a stock distribution to be a realization event (because there is no clearly realized accession to wealth). There being no realization event, no gain can be recognized.*

*But other versions of stock distributions can bring about changes in the shareholders' relative rights to future earnings, relative voting power, and relative rights to asset distributions upon a corporate liquidation. For example, if some of the common shareholders get preferred stock and other common shareholders get more common stock, there has been a shift in voting power. (The subset of common shareholders who got more common stock have increased their voting power vis-à-vis the subset that received preferred stock.) There has also been a shift in the rights to distributions of future earnings: the preferred shareholders have a priority claim on future distributions, but only to a limited extent (e.g., the preferred dividend may only be $4 per share regardless of the amount of corporate earnings; the common shareholders get the rest of any distributions). There has been a shift in the rights to assets upon corporate liquidation: preferred shareholders have a priority claim on those assets, but again only to a limited extent (e.g., the payout on a share of $100 par preferred stock might be limited to $104 per share, with the common shareholders receiving everything else). When a stock distribution causes such shifts in shareholder rights, the distribution is treated as a realization event and gain is recognized.*

*This topic considers the classic and the shareholder-rights-shifting versions of "stock dividends."*

BASIC FACTS FOR THE FOLLOWING FOUR QUESTIONS:

North Hollow, Ltd., a calendar-year corporation, has earnings and profits of $700,000. On August 26, it distributes one share of common stock (its only class) to every shareholder for each 10 shares already held. Fractional shares are permitted. Ten thousand shares are distributed having an aggregate fair market value of $100,000. North Hollow made no other distribution with respect to its stock during the taxable year.

102.  What are the tax consequences of the distribution to North Hollow?

ANSWER:

103.  What are the tax consequences to Michelle Harrington, who owns 20% of the North Hollow common stock? She acquired the stock three years ago and has a basis in her stock of $110,000.

ANSWER:

104.  How would the tax consequences to Michelle change if North Hollow had distributed stock rights in lieu of stock and if Michelle made no election with respect to the distribution?

ANSWER:


105.  If fractional shares were not permitted and North Hollow had distributed cash equal to the value of the fractional shares, could that change the tax consequences in to any shareholder?

ANSWER:


106.  Martin Katz owns 20% of the common stock and 50% of the preferred stock of Jersey Corp. During the year Jersey made only one distribution with respect to its stock. It distributed one share of preferred stock for each five shares of preferred stock already held. Fractional shares are permitted. Describe the tax consequences to Martin.

ANSWER:


107.  Which of the following is true?

A.  A corporation with only one class of outstanding stock allows all shareholders to receive either one share of stock for each share already held or to receive $80 (the value of one share). No shareholder elected to take the cash. All of the stock distributions are tax-free under § 305(a).

B.  A corporation with only one class of stock outstanding distributes one share of preferred stock for each share of outstanding common stock. The preferred stock is convertible into common stock. Based on all of the facts and circumstances, it is not unlikely that some of the shareholders will convert at least some of the preferred stock into common stock not long after the distribution. The distribution of the preferred stock is tax-free under § 305(a).

C.  The Supreme Court held in *Eisner v. Macomber*, 252 U.S. 189 (1920), that the receipt of a pro rata common stock dividend by the common shareholders was not a taxable event.

D.  The pro rata distribution of a common stock dividend to the common shareholders will be taxed under § 301 rather than being tax-free under § 305(a) if the stock distributed is treasury stock.

*In Topic 13, Redemptions, it will be necessary to perform tests based primarily on voting power to determine whether the redemption will be treated as a sale or exchange (potentially resulting in a long-term capital gain) or whether the redemption will be characterized as a disguised "dividend," taxed under a different set of rules (although under current law the tax consequences may not be meaningfully different).*

*Section 318 provides rules for determining who, in substance, owns the stock in question (and therefore is deemed to possess its voting power). The constructive ownership rules are not driven by form; e.g., the holder of legal title to the stock is not, per se, considered the "owner" of the stock. The substance is sought. For example, if a husband owns 50% of a corporation's stock and his wife owns the other 50%, would it not be fair to say that the husband (or the wife) owns 100% of the corporate stock for the purpose of deciding whether the husband (or the wife) can exert control over the corporation? If the sole shareholder of corporation X owns 50% of corporation Y's stock, and if corporation X itself owns the other 50% of the Y stock, would it not be fair to say that the stock in Y held by the shareholder and by X (the shareholder's controlled corporation) should be considered together in deciding whether the shareholder can exert control over Y?*

*This topic explores these constructive ownership rules.*

BASIC FACTS FOR THE FOLLOWING TWO QUESTIONS:

Son owns stock in High Tone, Inc., intends to redeem half of it, and wants to assert on his personal tax return that he is entitled to sale or exchange treatment with respect to the redemption under § 302(a). To determine his right to that treatment, the constructive ownership rules of § 318 have to be applied. Prior to the redemption by Son, the stock of High Tone is owned as follows:

| | | |
|---|---:|---|
| Father of Son | 36 | shares |
| Mother of Son | 40 | |
| Son | 2 | |
| Son's daughter | 3 | |
| Son's grandson | 5 | |
| Father's brother | 4 | |
| Father's father | 1 | |
| Mother's father | 6 | |
| Mother's nephew | 3 | |
| | 100 | shares |

108. Prior to the redemption, how many shares of High Tone stock is Son considered to own under § 318?

ANSWER:

109. Would the answer change if Son and Mother were irreconcilably estranged?

ANSWER:

110. Philip owns 6% of partnership P, 40% of corporation C, 70% of corporation D, and is a beneficiary of trust T (with an actuarial interest of 11%). Corporation E has 100 shares of stock outstanding, which are owned as follows:

| P owns | 36 | shares |
| C owns | 14 | |
| D owns | 43 | |
| T owns | 7 | |
| | 100 | shares |

Which of the following statements is true?

A. Philip is deemed to own 33.03 shares of corporation E; Philip's wife is deemed to own 33.03 shares of corporation E; Philip's mother-in-law is deemed to own none of corporation E.

B. Philip is deemed to own 38.63 shares of corporation E.

C. Philip is deemed to own 32.26 shares of corporation E.

D. C is deemed to own the stock actually and constructively owned by Philip.

BASIC FACTS FOR THE FOLLOWING TWO QUESTIONS:

Philip owns 6% of partnership P, 40% of corporation C, 70% of corporation D, and is a beneficiary of trust T (with an actuarial interest of 11%). Philip owns 65 shares of IBM stock and has an option on 100 additional shares.

111. How much IBM stock are P, C, D, and T deemed to own if they actually own no IBM stock?

ANSWER:

112. Sharon (unrelated to Philip) is also a partner in P, owning 57%. She owns no IBM stock personally. Based solely on the above facts, how many IBM shares is she deemed to own?

ANSWER:

113. Which of the following is true?

A. Stock owned by Gerald Rothstein's wife's father is not constructively owned by him.

B. Stock owned by Marla Peter's brother is constructively owned by her.

C. Stock owned by an adopted child is not constructively owned by the child's adopting parent.

D. Stock owned by Linnea Townsend is considered owned by her former husband.

BASIC FACTS FOR THE FOLLOWING TWO QUESTIONS:

Cori and Gwen, who are sisters, are equal partners in Pittsford Associates. Cori is also a 70% partner in Mendon Partners. Pittsford Associates owns stock in Alpha Corp. Cori owns stock in Gamma Corp.

114. Does Gwen constructively own any of Cori's Gamma stock?

ANSWER:

115. Does Mendon constructively own any of Pittsford's Alpha stock?

ANSWER:

116. Which of the following is true?

A. The constructive ownership rules automatically apply for all purposes under the Internal Revenue Code.

B. Stock subject to an option is constructively owned by the option holder.

C. The family member-to-family member attribution rules under § 318 can never be waived in the context of redemptions.

D. An individual constructively owns 50% of the stock actually owned by a corporation with respect to which the individual owns 50% of the total number of shares outstanding.

*As discussed previously, a redemption in substance is treated as a sale or exchange under the tax law, providing the possibility of long-term capital gain characterization. In the past individual shareholders have taken pains to have the distributions to them from their corporations characterized as redemptions rather than as dividends to avoid the previously-high dividend tax rate. Congress had to act to filter the distributions it believed warranted sale or exchange treatment from those it believed warranted standard dividend treatment.*

*This topic considers the tax consequences of a redemption and the tests used to determine whether the form (sale of stock by a shareholder back to the issuing corporation — technically a redemption under state law) corresponds to the substance (a disposition resulting in a third-party-sale-like reduction in the redeeming shareholder's rights to future earnings, voting power, and assets upon liquidation).*

117. Which of the following is true?

   A. The tax consequences to an individual of the redemption of stock held long-term at a gain are generally less favorable than those of a dividend.

   B. A redemption is accorded sale or exchange treatment if, in substance, it resembles a third-party sale more than it resembles a dividend.

   C. Qualification for sale or exchange treatment under § 301(b)(1)-(3) is tested by evaluating the effect of the redemption on the corporate distributor.

   D. A transaction qualifying as a redemption under state law results in a redemption qualifying for sale or exchange treatment under the federal income tax law.

BASIC FACTS FOR THE FOLLOWING FIVE QUESTIONS:

The Beverly Corporation is a C corporation with one class of stock. Beverly has earnings and profits of $600,000. It has the following three shareholders, all of whom have held their stock for at least six years: Husband (20 shares), Wife (50 shares) and an independent Third Party (30 shares). In the only distribution during the current taxable year, Beverly redeems all of Husband's stock for $800,000. This is not a partial liquidation of Beverly. Husband has a basis in his stock of $50,000.

118. What are the two alternative tax treatments with respect to any redemption?

ANSWER:


119. What is required for a distribution to a non-decedent shareholder to receive sale or exchange treatment?

ANSWER:

**120.** Do constructive ownership rules apply to the above facts?

ANSWER:

**121.** Will Husband's distribution receive sale or exchange treatment?

ANSWER:

**122.** What are the tax consequences of the redemption to Husband?

ANSWER:

**123.** Which of the following is true?

    A.  The fact that two shareholders are married would not impact the § 302(b)(1)-(3) tests for sale or exchange treatment.

    B.  The fact that the redeeming shareholder has a nephew who is also a shareholder would impact the § 302(b)(1)-(3) tests for sale or exchange treatment.

    C.  The fact that the redeeming shareholder holds options on additional shares of stock would not impact the § 302(b)(1)-(3) tests for sale or exchange treatment.

    D.  In testing whether a redemption is essentially equivalent to a dividend, the analysis focuses on the impact of the redemption on the redeeming shareholder's rights to participate in control, in earnings, and in assets upon liquidation.

**124.** Which of the following is false? Ignore § 303.

    A.  If a redemption satisfies any one of the tests under § 302(b), the redemption is characterized as a sale or exchange.

    B.  If a redemption is characterized as a sale or exchange, the corporation reduces its earnings and profits by the lesser of the amount it paid for the stock or the redeemed stock's proportionate share of such earnings and profits.

    C.  If a redemption fails to satisfy any of the tests under § 302(b), the basis of the redeemed stock disappears.

    D.  A redemption is not essentially equivalent to a dividend under § 302(b)(1) only if the redemption results in a meaningful reduction in the redeeming shareholder's rights to participate in control, in earnings and in assets upon liquidation. There has been no meaningful reduction in the control right unless the redeeming shareholder's post-redemption voting power is 50% or less.

**125.** Which of the following is false?

A. Ignoring § 303, if a redemption fails to satisfy any of the tests under § 302(b) the redemption is characterized as a § 301 distribution (i.e., dividend to the extent of earnings and profits, then reduction of stock basis, and finally capital gain).

B. If stock is redeemed and the shareholder receives from the corporation non-cash property, the shareholder takes a new holding period in the distributed asset under the express authority of § 1223.

C. If stock is redeemed and the shareholder receives from the corporation non-cash property, the shareholder takes a fair market value basis in the distributed asset.

D. If stock is redeemed and the shareholder receives from the corporation non-cash property, the corporation reduces its earnings and profits by the basis of the property (or by its fair market value if property is appreciated).

126. Which of the following is false?

A. If stock is redeemed and the shareholder receives from the corporation appreciated non-cash property, the corporation reduces its earnings and profits by the basis of the property.

B. If stock is redeemed and the shareholder receives from the corporation appreciated non-cash property, the corporation reduces its earnings and profits by any marginal federal income tax imposed as a result of the property's distribution.

C. It is possible to waive family attribution in a § 302(b)(3) redemption.

D. A redemption that fails the tests under § 302(b) may still qualify for sale or exchange treatment if the proceeds are used to pay the redeemed decedent shareholder's estate taxes.

127. Which of the following is false?

A. If a Subchapter C corporation distributes appreciated property in a redemption, its earnings and profits are increased by the gain (measured for earnings and profits purposes) on the distribution.

B. If a corporation has no earnings and profits, the tax consequences of a redemption by an individual are identical whether or not the redemption satisfies any of the § 302(b) tests.

C. If a Subchapter S corporation distributes appreciated property in a redemption, its earnings and profits is increased by the gain on the distribution.

D. If § 301 distributions occur in the same year as § 302(a) distributions, and if the total amount of the § 301 distributions exceeds the available earnings and profits, there will be no earnings and profits reduction associated with the § 302(a) distributions.

128. Which of the following could qualify for sale or exchange treatment under § 302(b)(1)?

A. The redemption reduces the shareholder's voting power from 60% to 55%.

B. The redemption reduces the shareholder's voting power from 90% to 55%.

C. The redemption reduces the controlling shareholder's preferred stock holdings from 80% of the preferred stock outstanding to 0%.

D. The redemption reduces the shareholder's directly owned common stock interest from 70% of the common stock outstanding to 5%. The shareholder's granddaughter owns the other outstanding common stock.

129. Which of the following would not qualify for sale or exchange treatment under § 302(b)(1)?

A. The common stock (only class) is owned as follows before the redemption: Sharon 28%, Leslie 24%, Karl 24%, and Hamid 24%. None of the shareholders are related. Sharon redeems 90% of her stock.

B. Tatiana owns .000001% of the outstanding common stock (only class) of a publicly traded corporation. She redeems 5% of her stock.

C. A sole shareholder redeems 99% of her stock.

D. A shareholder who owns only nonvoting, nonconvertible preferred stock redeems 0.8% of his stock.

BASIC FACTS FOR THE FOLLOWING THREE QUESTIONS:

Mother built a closely held family corporation into a business worth $30 million. She owns 85 of the 100 shares of outstanding common stock (only class). Son, Daughter and Granddaughter each own five shares. Mother redeems all of her stock.

130. Based solely on the above facts, which of the following is true?

A. Mother fails the test under § 302(b)(1) for sale or exchange treatment.

B. Mother fails the test under § 302(b)(2) for sale or exchange treatment.

C. Mother fails the test under § 302(b)(3) for sale or exchange treatment.

D. All of the above

131. Mother's tax advisor tells her that she can qualify under § 302(b)(3) through the waiver of family attribution under § 302(c)(2)(A). She satisfies all the requirements of that provision as of the date of the redemption: 1) she holds no interest in the corporation (including an interest as officer, director, or employee), other than an interest as a creditor; 2), she agrees to notify the IRS if she acquires stock or otherwise obtains an interest in the corporation during the next ten years; and 3) she agrees to certain recordkeeping requirements. Which of the following later actions or events will violate the family attribution waiver requirements?

A. Mother will act as a paid consultant to the corporation for three years following the redemption to ensure a smooth transition to Daughter taking over as CEO.

B. Two years after the redemption, Daughter dies and her stock becomes part of her estate. Daughter's will appoints Mother as executor. As executor, Mother voted the estate's stock until the probate proceedings ended.

C. Mother is the corporation's landlord with respect to its main production facility. That facility is leased on terms consistent with market conditions. Mother continues to be the corporation's landlord after the redemption.

D. Son dies four years after the redemption, leaving half of his stock to Mother.

132. Continuing with the above facts related to Mother's waiver of family attribution under § 302(c)(2)(A), which of the following is false?

A. Mother loaned the corporation $12,000,000 four years ago. Her remaining a corporate creditor does not cause the loss of the family attribution waiver.

B. Six years after the redemption, the corporation defaults on the $12,000,000 loan noted above. Mother exercises her creditor's rights and acquires the corporate assets that served as collateral for the loan. Her seizure of these assets does not cause the loss of the family attribution waiver.

C. To protect her rights as a material corporate creditor, Mother obtains the right, as part of the redemption transaction, to appoint one member of the board of directors. That right terminates if the $12,000,000 loan is fully repaid. Her right to appoint one member of the board does not cause the loss of the family attribution waiver.

D. Two years after the redemption Mother becomes CEO after Daughter, the prior CEO, suffers a stroke. Mother fails to notify the IRS of this fact. Eleven years later the IRS asserts a deficiency against Mother on the basis of her retroactive loss of the family attribution waiver. The statute of limitations for assessing a deficiency with respect to the redemption has not run.

133. Parent and Trust each own half of Corporation's outstanding common stock (only class). Trust's sole beneficiary is Parent's Child. Corporation redeems all of Trust's stock. This is the only distribution during the year by Corporation to its shareholders with respect to its stock. Which of the following is false?

A. If Trust does nothing, it is deemed to own 100% of the stock immediately after the redemption.

B. Trust can waive the stock attribution from Child and therefore qualify for sale or exchange treatment under § 302(b)(3).

C. Trust can waive the stock attribution from Child and therefore qualify for sale or exchange treatment under § 302(b)(2).

D. If the redemption is characterized as a § 301 distribution, Trust's stock basis transfers to Parent.

BASIC FACTS FOR THE FOLLOWING TWO QUESTIONS:

The outstanding stock (only class) of Ajax, Inc. is owned by the following three unrelated individuals as follows:

|        | Shares |
|--------|--------|
| Roy    | 70     |
| Bertha | 20     |
| Inez   | 10     |
|        | 100    |

Ajax does not permit fractional shares.

134. Which of the following is false?

   A. The minimum number of shares Roy must redeem to satisfy the test under § 302(b)(2)(B) is 40.

   B. The minimum number of shares Roy must redeem to satisfy the test under § 302(b)(2)(C) is 32.

   C. The minimum number of shares Roy must redeem to enjoy sale or exchange treatment under § 302(b)(2) is 41.

   D. None of the above.

135. Continue with the facts above, but now assume that Bertha is Roy's wife and that Inez is Roy's great-granddaughter. Which of the following is true?

   A. Roy is deemed to own Inez' stock.

   B. If Roy redeems 65 shares, the redemption will be accorded sale or exchange treatment under § 302(b)(2).

   C. If Inez redeems half of her shares as part of the same series of redemptions, Roy and Bertha (in some combination) must redeem 86 shares to enjoy sale or exchange treatment under § 302(b)(2).

   D. It is impossible for Roy to enjoy sale or exchange treatment under § 302(b)(3).

BASIC FACTS FOR THE FOLLOWING TWO QUESTIONS:

Linnea Clayton dies. Her gross estate is $40,000,000. Included in the gross estate is the stock of two corporations of which Linnea is the 90% shareholder: Townsend, Ltd. (her stock is worth $7,000,000) and Whidbey, Inc. (her stock is worth $5,000,000). The 10% shareholders in both corporations are unrelated to Linnea. Her estate tax liability is $10,500,000 and she has $500,000 of funeral and administrative expenses. Her total estate tax deductions under § 2053 are $10,000,000. Linnea's estate redeems all of the Townsend and Whidbey stock and uses the funds to pay the estate tax and funeral and administrative expenses. Evaluate both of the following statements.

136.  Since neither the Townsend nor the Whidbey stock individually exceeds 35% of the value of Linnea's gross estate less the § 2053 deductions, none of the stock is eligible for sale or exchange treatment under § 303.

ANSWER:

137. Even if the redemption does at least partially qualify for sale or exchange treatment under § 303, up to $1,000,000 of the amount received for the stock could be characterized as a dividend.

ANSWER:

138. Which of the following is false?

 A. The test for whether a partial liquidation has occurred focuses on whether the distribution is "not essentially equivalent to a dividend" determined at the corporate level, and not at the shareholder level.

 B. A partial liquidation entails a genuine contraction of corporate business activities combined with the distribution of no-longer-needed funds to the shareholders through a redemption.

 C. In a partial liquidation the assets of a discontinued business, or the proceeds therefrom, or any combination of the two may be distributed as part of the redemption.

 D. A corporation in the business of quarrying limestone has half of its limestone deposits taken by the state in a condemnation proceeding. The remaining deposits are sufficient for the corporation to maintain its present level of activity for 15 to 25 years. The corporation distributes the condemnation proceeds to its stockholders in a redemption. The redemption qualifies as a partial liquidation.

139. Which of the following is true?

 A. Where a line of business is discontinued, the assets which may be distributed in a redemption qualifying as a partial liquidation do not include the discontinued line of business' working capital.

 B. A corporation with multiple lines of business has one of its business lines destroyed in a fire. The distribution of the insurance proceeds via a redemption qualifies as a partial liquidation.

 C. A corporation with multiple lines of business abandons plans for expanding into a new line of business. It distributes the funds reserved for that purpose to its shareholders through a redemption. The redemption qualifies as a partial liquidation.

 D. A corporate shareholder may be eligible for sale or exchange treatment under § 302(b)(4).

140. An individual shareholder redeems stock that has been held for eight months at a gain. Identify the advantages and disadvantages of having the redemption characterized as a sale or exchange or as a dividend.

ANSWER:

141. How would a corporation assess the relative advantages and disadvantages of having its redemption of some of the minority-interest stock it owns in another corporation characterized as a dividend or as a sale or exchange? Assume the stock is redeemed at a gain.

ANSWER:

*Having just studied redemptions, it is understood that, if the redemption fails to satisfy one of the four tests under § 302(b) (or if it is not associated with the need to pay estate taxes and certain costs related to the shareholder's death per § 303), the redemption in form is treated as a dividend in substance.*

*A "bootstrap sale" is a two-part transaction intended to transfer all of the equity interests in a corporation to a new shareholder. The two parts (assuming, for the sake of simplicity, a single shareholder) are: 1) a sale by the shareholder of a portion of its stock to the buyer and 2) the redemption of the other portion of the shareholder's stock. The first part could precede the second, or vice versa. If the redemption goes first (or if the redemption is contractually compelled after the stock sale), can any of the tests under § 302(b)(1)-(3) be satisfied, or must that part of the transaction be characterized as a dividend? That question is addressed in this topic.*

142. Seller, a sole shareholder, wants to sell all of her stock (only one class outstanding). Buyer (who does not have the full purchase price) wants to use a substantial amount of the liquid assets inside the corporation (which has a large amount of earnings and profits) as consideration for the purchase. Buyer could borrow enough to buy the stock and then cause the corporation to distribute those liquid assets, which would enable the loan to be paid off; but that distribution would constitute a dividend and Buyer wants the transaction to be tax-free. So Seller agrees to a two-part transaction that will include: 1) Seller's redemption of 40% of the stock (40 shares) and 2) Buyer's purchase from Seller of 60% of the stock (60 shares). Which of the following is true?

   A. If the redemption precedes the stock purchase, the amount received for the stock in the redemption by Seller will be treated as a "dividend."

   B. If the stock purchase precedes the redemption, the amount received for the stock in the redemption by Seller will be treated as a "dividend."

   C. Assume, in the alternative, that there are not enough liquid assets in the corporation to, in conjunction with the funds Buyer has, allow Buyer to acquire 100% of the stock. Therefore, Seller agrees to have the corporation redeem 20% of the stock (20 shares) instead of 40%. Thus, Seller will be a minority shareholder after the transaction. If the redemption precedes the purchase by Buyer, the amount received for the stock in the redemption by Seller will be treated as a "dividend."

   D. None of the above.

*Shareholders seeking long-term capital gain treatment on distributions to them from their corporations came to realize that the § 302(b) tests posed real barriers to obtaining that outcome. One possible solution (instead of selling the stock back to the issuing corporation and becoming subject to the § 302(b) tests) was to sell the stock to another corporation — one controlled by the same shareholder. This topic considers § 304, Congress' attempt to thwart such strategies.*

BASIC FACTS FOR THE FOLLOWING THREE QUESTIONS:

Cori owns 96% of the stock (96 shares) of Marcus, Inc. and 2% of the stock (four shares) of Garibaldi Corp. Marcus owns 98% of the stock (196 shares) of Garibaldi. Garibaldi owns 4% of the stock (four shares) of Marcus.

143. Which of the following is true?

    A. If Cori redeems half of her Marcus stock, the distribution will be governed by § 301(a).

    B. If Marcus redeems half of its Garibaldi stock, Marcus' taxable income will likely change.

    C. Cori is not deemed to control Garibaldi for § 304 purposes.

    D. If Garibaldi buys half of Cori's Marcus stock, the transaction will be treated as a brother-sister acquisition under § 304(a)(1).

144. Which of the following is true?

    A. If Marcus buys all of Cori's Garibaldi stock, the transaction will be treated as a parent-subsidiary acquisition under § 304(a)(2).

    B. If Garibaldi buys all of Cori's Marcus stock, Cori's basis in her Marcus stock disappears.

    C. If Garibaldi buys half of Cori's Marcus stock, the determination of whether the sale qualifies for "sale or exchange" treatment under § 302(a) will be made by determining whether one of the tests under § 302(b) is satisfied with respect to Cori's ownership of Garibaldi stock.

    D. If Garibaldi buys half of Cori's Marcus stock, the earnings and profits of both Marcus and Garibaldi will be available in the determination of the amount of dividend Cori receives.

145. Which of the following is false?

    A. If Marcus buys all of Cori's Garibaldi stock using as consideration a parcel of appreciated law land, Marcus will recognize no gain or loss on the transfer of that land to Cori.

    B. If Marcus buys half of Cori's Garibaldi stock, Cori's basis in the Garibaldi stock sold is allocated to her remaining Garibaldi stock.

C.  If Marcus buys all of Cori's Garibaldi stock, Cori's basis in her Garibaldi stock disappears.

D.  If an unrelated third party buys all of Cori's Marcus stock, Cori will be able to qualify for "sale or exchange" treatment under § 302(b)(3) despite her ownership of Garibaldi stock.

BASIC FACTS FOR THE FOLLOWING FOUR QUESTIONS:

Parent Corp. has earnings and profits of $50,000 and its stock is held as follows (shares):

| | |
|---|---|
| Taxpayer | 15 |
| Daughter of Taxpayer | 36 |
| Independent third party | 49 |
| | 100 |

Subsidiary Corp. has earnings and profits of $10,000 and its stock is held as follows (shares):

| | |
|---|---|
| Taxpayer | 28 |
| Wife of Taxpayer | 15 |
| Mother-in-law of Taxpayer | 2 |
| Parent Corp. | 55 |
| | 100 |

Taxpayer sells all of his Parent stock to Subsidiary for $180,000. (Ignore for the purposes of this question the issue of control premiums and minority discounts.)

146.  Does Taxpayer control Parent?

ANSWER:

147.  Does Taxpayer control Subsidiary?

ANSWER:

148.  Does Parent control Subsidiary?

ANSWER:

149.  Which rules apply under § 304: the parent-subsidiary rules or the brother-sister rules?

ANSWER:

BASIC FACTS FOR THE FOLLOWING THREE QUESTIONS:

Taxpayer controls (for § 304 purposes) Issuing, Inc. and Acquiring, Inc. Neither corporation owns any stock in the other corporation. The value of all stock is proportional to its voting power. Taxpayer's basis in the Issuing stock is $100,000, with a holding period of six years. Taxpayer's basis in the Acquiring stock is $75,000, with a holding period of 11 years. Taxpayer sells all of his Issuing stock to Acquiring for $130,000. Assume all of the tests under § 302(b)(1)-(3) are failed with respect to Issuing's stock.

150.    Determine the tax consequences to Taxpayer.

ANSWER:

151.    Determine the tax consequences to Acquiring.

ANSWER:

152.    Determine the tax consequences to Issuing.

ANSWER:

BASIC FACTS FOR THE FOLLOWING THREE QUESTIONS:

Taxpayer controls (for § 304 purposes) Issuing, Inc. and Acquiring, Inc. Issuing also controls Acquiring. The value of all stock is proportional to its voting power. Taxpayer's basis in the Issuing stock is $100,000, with a holding period of six years. Taxpayer's basis in the Acquiring stock is $75,000, with a holding period of 11 years. Taxpayer sells all of his Issuing stock to Acquiring for $130,000. Assume all of the tests under § 302(b)(1)-(3) are failed with respect to Issuing's stock.

153.    Determine the tax consequences to Taxpayer.

ANSWER:

154.    Determine the tax consequences to Acquiring.

ANSWER:

155.    Determine the tax consequences to Issuing.

ANSWER:

*Frustrated in their inability to have distributions to them from their corporations characterized as long-term capital gains, shareholders tried another tactic (for the sake of simplicity, assume that presently only one class of stock is outstanding): 1) have the corporation distribute preferred stock to the common shareholders (which will be tax-free so long as the stock is distributed pro rata), followed by 2) sell the preferred stock. If it works, the preferred stock sale generates a long-term capital gain (while ensuring that the controlling shareholders remain in control through the common stock they still hold undiminished). Does this work? That is the issue in this topic.*

156. With regard to the application of § 306, which of the following is true?

   A. Stock received in a distribution not taxable under § 305(a) is § 306 stock.

   B. Whether the distributing corporation has earnings and profits at the time stock is distributed in a § 305(a) transaction is irrelevant in determining whether the distributed stock is § 306 stock.

   C. Section 306 is inapplicable to the distribution of stock rights.

   D. Only preferred stock can be § 306 stock.

157. The tax consequences of which of the following dispositions of § 306 stock is governed by § 306(a)?

   A. Section 306 stock in X Corp. was sold in the same transaction in which all other X Corp. stock held by the shareholder was sold.

   B. Preferred stock received in a § 305(a) distribution on common stock is sold.

   C. The shareholder holding the § 306 stock had sold the common stock with respect to which the § 306 stock had been distributed three taxable years before the year in which the shareholder disposed of the § 306 stock.

   D. The shareholder disposing the § 306 stock received in a § 305(a) distribution on common stock at all times owns .000001% of the distributing publicly traded corporation's common stock.

BASIC FACTS FOR THE FOLLOWING FOUR QUESTIONS:

In Year 1 Natalie Keith purchased 10,000 shares of common stock (only class) in Melbourne, Ltd. for $160,000. During Year 3 Melbourne made its only distribution to its shareholders with respect to its stock when it distributed one share of preferred stock for each outstanding share of common stock. On the date of the distribution there were 1,000,000 shares of common stock outstanding, Melbourne had earnings and profits of $8,000,000, the preferred stock was worth $10 per share, and the common stock was worth $30 per share.

During Year 5 Natalie sold her preferred stock for $13 per share. Melbourne made no distributions to its shareholders with respect to its stock during Year 5. Its earnings and profits at the end of Year 5 was $3,000,000.

158. Which of the following is false?

    A.  Natalie recognized no gain or loss on the receipt of the preferred stock.

    B.  Natalie's basis in the 10,000 shares of preferred stock is $40,000.

    C.  Melbourne decreased its earnings and profits in Year 3 when the preferred stock was distributed.

    D.  The preferred stock is § 306 stock.

159. Which of the following is true?

    A.  Melbourne reduces its earnings and profits when Natalie sells her preferred stock.

    B.  Natalie has $80,000 of ordinary income, but this is taxed as though it was a dividend.

    C.  Natalie has $30,000 of ordinary income, but this is taxed as though it was a dividend.

    D.  Natalie has a long-term capital gain of zero.

160. Which of the following is true?

    A.  If Natalie had sold the preferred stock for $8.50 per share she would have had a long-term capital loss of $35,000.

    B.  If Natalie had sold the preferred stock for $8.50 per share her common stock basis would have been $155,000.

    C.  The holding period in the preferred stock began in Year 3.

    D.  Section 306(a) would have applied if Natalie had sold all of both her preferred and common stock.

161. Continue with the above facts, except now assume that in Year 5 Natalie redeemed her stock for $12 per share instead of selling it for $13 per share. This was Melbourne's only distribution to shareholders with respect to its stock in Year 5. Which of the following is false?

    A.  Natalie's common stock basis is $160,000.

    B.  Melbourne's earnings and profits at the end of Year 5 is no less than $2,880,000.

    C.  The redemption is treated as a § 301 distribution even if it satisfies one of the tests under § 302(b)(1)-(3).

    D.  Section 302(b)(3) would not have applied if Natalie had sold all of her common stock in Year 3.

*Return to a time in the early 1980s when individuals faced a maximum tax rate of 70% and corporations faced a maximum tax rate of 46%. (Presently the situation has almost inverted, with corporations and (at least at the time of this writing) individuals both having a maximum 35% tax rate.) In that environment it could make enormous financial sense to allow earnings to accumulate inside the corporation for reinvestment rather than to distribute them and have the shareholders reinvest the post-double-taxation proceeds. For example, at that time if a corporation generated $10,000,000 in income, it would pay (approximately) $4,600,000 in tax and have $5,400,000 to reinvest. But if the corporation distributed that $5,400,000 as a dividend to individual shareholders, the shareholders might have to pay as much as $3,780,000 in tax, leaving only $1,620,000 to reinvest. The choice was to have the corporation reinvest $5,400,000 or to have the individual shareholders reinvest $1,620,000. It is true that, when the corporation ultimately liquidated in order to get the accumulated invested funds into the hands of the individual shareholders, there would be a round of taxation; but the tax rate would be 28% on the long-term capital gain recognized many years in the future rather than the 70% that would have been paid annually on the dividend distributions. Mathematically, the choice was obvious.*

*Thus, the corporate retention of earnings was strongly incentivized, undermining the double-taxation regime (earnings retained and eventually taxed at the low long-term capital gain rate are not economically equivalent to earnings taxed "continuously" at the high dividend tax rate). Congress had to act. The result was the accumulated earnings tax, sometimes called a "forced dividend" because of the pressure it put on corporations to distribute presently those earnings for which they could not demonstrate a plausible business need requiring funding in the near future. The accumulated earnings tax is the subject of this topic.*

162. Which of the following is false with respect to the accumulated earnings tax (AET)?

    A.  The purpose of the AET is to deter corporations from failing to distribute their earnings and profits so as to defeat the corporate double-taxation regime.

    B.  The AET is imposed on a corporation at the same rate as a dividend would typically be taxed to one of its shareholders.

    C.  Most corporations are allowed to accumulate $250,000 of earnings and profits without justification.

    D.  A corporation can be subject to the AET and the personal holding company tax in the same taxable year.

163. Which of the following is false with respect to the AET?

A. Accumulating earnings and profits to provide a reserve against the disruption of business should Iceland invade the U.S. would be considered an accumulation to meet the reasonable needs of the corporation's business.

B. If the IRS can demonstrate that a corporation has retained earnings and profits beyond the reasonable needs of its business, the corporation is presumed to be subject to the AET.

C. When adjusting taxable income in order to determine the AET base, the dividends-received deduction is disallowed.

D. Earnings and profits retained to pay reasonably estimated federal income taxes are generally not subject to the AET.

164. Which of the following is true with respect to the AET?

A. A corporation with no earnings and profits can still be subject to the AET.

B. The amount of a corporation's current charitable contribution that reduces its AET base is the same as the deduction allowed for income tax purposes.

C. A calendar-year corporation paid out dividends of $1 million during Year 1. It also paid dividends of $80,000 on February 19 of Year 2. Its shareholders agreed to a $300,000 consent dividend on December 29 of Year 1. The corporation's dividends paid deduction for AET purposes for Year 1 is $1,300,000.

D. In determining the accumulated earnings credit for a taxable year, the corporation's beginning earnings and profits are reduced by dividends paid during the first 2½ months of that taxable year.

*This topic covers the tax consequences of complete liquidations. As a general rule complete liquidations are fully taxable at both the corporate and shareholder levels. A major exception exists if a parent corporation owns at least 80% of a subsidiary corporation. Then the subsidiary's complete liquidation is tax-free at both the parent and subsidiary levels (subject to a caveat regarding distributions to minority shareholders).*

BASIC FACTS FOR THE FOLLOWING THREE QUESTIONS:

Individual shareholders Q and R have bases in their stock in calendar-year corporation C of $10,700,000 and $12,000,000, respectively. Q has 40% of the stock (40 shares, acquired 16 years ago); R has 60% (60 shares, acquired 14 years ago). C's balance sheet on January 1 is below. C ceased all business operations on the day before, December 31. It has no liabilities, having satisfied them all in anticipation of completely liquidating on January 1.

| Asset | Value | Basis | Original Cost | Holding Period |
|---|---|---|---|---|
| Cash | $5,700,000 | N/A | N/A | N/A |
| Receivables | $2,400,000 | $3,100,000[fn] | N/A | < 1 year |
| Inventory | $3,100,000 | $3,400,000[fn] | $3,400,000 | < 1 year |
| Equipment | $4,000,000 | $8,200,000 | $10,500,000 | 22 months |
| Factory-Building | $27,200,000 | $10,700,000 | $12,000,000 | 4 years |
| Factory-Land | $2,000,000 | $2,000,000 | $2,000,000 | 5 years |

[fn]: *Resulting from bulk sale discount*

On January 1, C distributes all of its assets proportionately to its shareholders in exchange for all of their stock in a liquidating distribution. The shareholders will each take an undivided interest in each asset (other than cash). C is in the 35% tax bracket. (Remember: corporate taxes must be paid before the cash can be distributed.) Assume that all assets were acquired by C by purchase. Ignore any depreciation for the year of liquidation.

165.  Determine the tax consequences to C.

ANSWER:

166.  Determine the tax consequences to both shareholders.

ANSWER:

167.  Assume instead that the Equipment was acquired from Q in a § 351 transaction 19 months before the complete liquidation. At the time of its contribution it had a basis of $10,500,000 and a value of $8,000,000. How do the tax consequences to C change with respect to the Equipment?

ANSWER:

168. Which of the following is false with respect to a § 332 liquidating distribution involving a wholly owned subsidiary?

    A. The parent corporation succeeds to the subsidiary's earnings and profits, capital loss carryovers and other tax attributes.

    B. If the subsidiary holds a note of the parent, the distribution of that note does not result in income from the discharge of indebtedness to the parent.

    C. If the subsidiary is indebted to the parent, the parent generally does not recognize a gain or loss on the receipt of assets as part of the liquidating distribution in satisfaction of such debt.

    D. The subsidiary's only liability is a loan from its parent $1,000,000. The subsidiary has only one asset, raw land worth $600,000 and with a basis of $400,000, which it distributes to the parent. The parent has a basis in its subsidiary stock of $1,300,000. The parent takes a basis in the raw land of $400,000.

BASIC FACTS FOR THE FOLLOWING TWO QUESTIONS:

The stock of calendar-year Subsidiary, Inc., which has earnings and profits of $700,000, is owned as follows: Parent, Inc. 90% (90 shares; basis $450,000; holding period seven years); Unrelated Individual 10% (10 shares; basis $250,000; holding period 11 years). Subsidiary will completely liquidate on January 1, on which date it has the following partial balance sheet:

| Asset | Value | Basis | Holding Period |
|---|---|---|---|
| Cash | $842,000 | N/A | N/A |
| Raw Land Parcel 1 | $2,300,000 | $1,000,000 | 18 years |
| Raw Land Parcel 2 | $1,000,000 | $500,000 | 21 years |

Both parcels of raw land were acquired by purchase from unrelated persons. Assume that Subsidiary has no taxable income during the year of liquidation except for any taxable income that might result from the liquidating distribution itself. Subsidiary will distribute Raw Land Parcel 1, subject to a $2,200,000 mortgage, to Unrelated Individual. It will distribute Raw Land Parcel 2 and any remaining cash to Parent.

169. Which of the following is false?

    A. Parent will succeed to all of Subsidiary's earnings and profits.

    B. Subsidiary will recognize no gain with respect to its distribution of Raw Land Parcel 2.

    C. Parent will take a basis in Raw Land Parcel 2 of $500,000.

    D. Parent will take a holding period in Raw Land Parcel 2 of 21 years.

170. Which of the following is true?

    A. Parent will receive $842,000 in cash.

B. Unrelated Individual will recognize no gain or loss as a result of the liquidating distribution.

C. Unrelated Individual will take a holding period in Raw Land Parcel 1 of 18 years.

D. Subsidiary will have a federal income tax liability with respect to the liquidating distribution of $442,000.

# TOPIC 19: PARTNERSHIPS

*The rules governing partnerships are among the most difficult in the tax law. Entirely unlike C corporations and substantially different from S corporations, a partnership can allocate its tax items (i.e., its individual items of gross income, deduction, etc.) among its partners any way it wishes so long as those tax allocations adequately correspond to economic reality as measured by the Code and Regulations. Economic reality is evaluated by looking at the manner in which the economic benefits and burdens of the partnership's tax items are actually enjoyed or borne by the partners, with due regard for the time value of money.*

*The latitude intentionally provided by Subchapter K for partnerships to craft unique and even complex economic arrangements among their partners is directly responsible for the challenges faced by taxpayers and practitioners who have to cope with the partnership tax rules.*

*In a C corporation the stockholders' shares of distributed corporate income (i.e., dividends) are determined on a per-share basis as measured on a single day — the day preceding the ex-dividend date. The only differences that can arise in how this corporate income is allocated have to do with dividend preferences (e.g., preferred stockholders receive a dividend before common stockholders). In an S corporation it is more complicated. All of the corporation's tax items are allocated to each day of the taxable year, and then each day's allocations are assigned pro rata to each share outstanding on that day (the "per-day, per-share" rule). In both types of corporation the stockholders are all assigned same amount per share (C corporation dividend or S corporation tax items).*

*While a partnership can be designed to achieve the same economic outcome as could be achieved through the use of a corporation, it is also possible for a partnership to make allocations like: all capital gains are allocated to Partner 3, all § 179 deductions are allocated to Partner 6, all tax credits are allocated to Partner 8, the first $100,000 of operating cash flow is allocated to Partner 11, etc. The price of this flexibility is a sometimes bewildering, occasionally incomprehensible, and almost always more complicated (as compared to either C or S corporations) set of tax rules.*

*This topic considers Subchapter K.*

171. Which of the following is true?

   A. Under the "check-the-box" rules of § 7701(a)(3), any unincorporated business entity with at least two members is taxed as a partnership unless the entity elects "association" status and is thus taxed as a corporation. An association can elect to be taxed as a Subchapter S corporation.

   B. The definition of partnership for federal income tax purposes is the same as that for state law purposes. (Ignore the "check-the-box" rules.)

C. The rules of partnership taxation were deliberately designed by Congress to enable the partners to mechanically generate favorable tax results by strict adherence to the literal language of the Code.

D. If a business entity which would be taxed as a partnership if it did not elect association status makes no such election, Subchapter K applies under all circumstances.

172. On December 31, Year 1 individual X contributes a machine (value $80,000; cost $100,000; adjusted basis $60,000) to a new partnership, Z, in exchange for a 1/6 partnership interest. (The other partner, Q, receives a 5/6 partnership interest.) Assume that it is proper to take no depreciation in Year 1 and that the machine will be depreciated straight-line over Year 2 and Year 3. On January 1, Year 3, Z sells the machine for $90,000. Assume it is proper to take no depreciation in Year 3 and that the "ceiling rule" applies. How much ordinary income from depreciation recapture under § 1245 will X have?

ANSWER:

173. Which of the following is false?

A. A partner would receive $300,000 if the partnership sold all of its assets at their fair market value, paid all of its liabilities and distributed all of the remaining cash in complete liquidation. This amount is received with respect to the partner's capital interest.

B. The receipt of a profits interest in exchange for future services is not a taxable event.

C. A partner has a basis in its partnership interest of $90,000. The partnership distributes $110,000 (cash) to the partner at the end of its taxable year. The partner generally has a capital gain of $20,000.

D. A new calendar-year partnership, which began business on November 1, Year 1, spent $52,000 for organizational costs. The electing partnership's deduction for organizational costs in Year 1 is $578 ($52,000/180 months).

174. Which of the following is false?

A. The basis of a partnership interest acquired by purchase from an existing partner (with the unanimous consent of the other partners) is its cost.

B. A partnership distributes to a partner $50,000 (cash) and a capital asset with a basis to the partnership of $30,000 (value $65,000). The partner's basis in its partnership interest immediately before the distribution is $100,000. The partner recognizes no gain or loss on the distribution and takes a basis of $30,000 in the capital asset. The partner's basis in his partnership interest after the distribution is $0.

C. An important difference between a partner's basis in his partnership interest and a partner's capital account is that the latter does not include the partner's share of partnership liabilities.

D. Upon the admission of a new partner, a partnership could elect to adjust all of its assets and liabilities to their fair market values, allocating the changes among the partners' capital accounts in accordance with the partnership agreement as though they were recognized gains and losses.

175. Which of the following is false?

A. An increase (decrease) in a partner's share of partnership liabilities increases (decreases) the partner's basis in its interest.

B. Partnership recourse liabilities are allocated among the partners in proportion to the "economic risk of loss" they bear with respect to such liabilities.

C. A new partner contributes, in exchange for a 50% partnership interest, a parcel of raw land worth $1,000,000 (basis $200,000; mortgage $550,000). The partnership assumes the liability. Assume that the partner bears the economic risk of loss for one half of the liability. The partner will recognize a gain of $350,000 on the contribution.

D. For liability allocation purposes, a partnership is generally deemed to have assumed a nonrecourse liability that encumbers a contributed asset.

BASIC FACTS FOR THE FOLLOWING FOUR QUESTIONS:

On January 1, calendar-year, accrual-method partnership XYZ was formed (and began business) with the following partner contributions:

| Individual | Item Contributed | Amount/ Value | Adjusted Basis | Nonrecourse Encumbrance | Interest in Partnership |
|---|---|---|---|---|---|
| X | Cash | $100,000 | N/A | N/A | 20% |
| Y | Cash | 350,000 | N/A | N/A | 70% |
| Z | Raw Land | 250,000 | $230,000 | $200,000[fn] | 10% |
| | | $700,000 | | | 100% |

[fn] *XYZ takes Raw Land subject to encumbrance; principal due in eight years; bears market rate of interest payable each December 31*

During the year XYZ purchased Equipment (a single item) for $1,000,000, paying $200,000 in cash and borrowing $800,000 on a recourse note (principal due in three years; bears market rate of interest payable each December 31).

On December 31, XYZ's balance sheet is:

|  |  |  | Book Value | Adjusted Basis |
|---|---|---|---|---|
| Assets: | Cash |  | $80,000 | N/A |
|  | Accounts Receivable |  | 200,000 | $200,000 |
|  | Inventory |  | 100,000 | $100,000 |
|  | Equipment |  | 800,000 | $800,000 |
|  | Raw Land |  | 250,000 | $230,000 |
|  |  |  | $1,430,000 |  |
| Liabilities: | Accounts Payable$^{(fn)}$ | $400,000 |  |  |
|  | Recourse note-Equipment | 800,000 |  |  |
|  | Nonrecourse note-Raw Land | 200,000 | $1,400,000 |  |
| Capital Accounts: | X | $6,000 |  |  |
|  | Y | 21,000 |  |  |
|  | Z | 3,000 | 30,000 |  |
|  |  |  | $1,430,000 |  |

$^{fn}$ *Relates to deductible business expenses and Inventory*

Exclusive of the allocations of the recourse and nonrecourse liabilities, the partners' bases in their interests on December 31 are:

| Partner | Adjusted Basis in Partnership Interest |
|---|---|
| X | $6,000 |
| Y | $21,000 |
| Z | $183,000 |

If a partner has a deficit balance in its capital account at the time the partnership liquidates, state law requires the partner to make a sufficient capital contribution to bring the deficit to zero.

The partnership agreement specifies that Tier III allocations of nonrecourse liabilities are made using the following procedure: first, any remaining post-Tier II § 704(c) gain potential is allocated to the contributing partner and, second, any remaining liability is allocated among the partners in proportion to their profit-sharing ratios.

**176.** How is the nonrecourse liability allocated among the partners on December 31?

ANSWER:

**177.** How are the recourse liabilities allocated among the partners on December 31?

ANSWER:

**178.** What are the partners' bases in their partnership interests on December 31?

ANSWER:

179. How would the allocation of recourse liabilities change if Z had guaranteed the accounts payable?

ANSWER:

180. How would the allocation of recourse liabilities change if Z had agreed to indemnify X and Y with respect to the accounts payable?

ANSWER:

181. How would the allocation of the nonrecourse liability (Raw Land) change if X guaranteed that liability?

ANSWER:

182. Which of the following is false?

   A. A partnership is not a taxable entity. The partners, in the aggregate, take into account at their level all of the partnership's tax items.

   B. If a partnership has a long-term capital gain, the partners to whom that gain is allocated also have a long-term capital gain.

   C. A partnership is not required to compute its taxable income.

   D. With a few exceptions, a partnership makes its own tax elections.

183. Which of the following is false?

   A. A partnership is not entitled to a deduction for charitable contributions.

   B. Partners are informed of their share of a partnership's tax items through a Schedule K-1.

   C. The Code and Regulations, combined, set forth an exhaustive list of all of the partnership tax items that require separate statement.

   D. A partner (with a fiscal year-end of March 31) of a partnership with an October 31 fiscal year-end would take its distributive share of the partnership's tax items for the partnership's taxable year ending October 31, Year 1, into account in the partner's taxable year ending March 31, Year 2 (the following calendar year).

184. Which of the following is true?

   A. A partnership as 24 equal partners. Two partners have taxable years that end on January 31, two have taxable years that end on February 28, etc. In other words, on the last day of each month of the year two partners have a taxable year-end. This partnership must adopt the calendar year. (Ignore the possibility of short years and 52-53 week years.)

B. The tax return for a calendar-year partnership is due on March 15 of the following year (assuming no extensions).

C. The "substantial economic effect" rules come into play when the partnership agreement is silent on the allocation of a particular partnership tax item.

D. The general rule is that a partner's distributive share of a partnership tax item is determined in accordance with the partnership agreement.

185. Which of the following is false?

A. For the economic effect of an allocation of a partnership tax item under the partnership agreement to be substantial, there must be a realistic possibility that the allocation will substantially affect the dollar amounts to be received by the partners from the partnership, taking into account the tax consequences associated with the allocation.

B. The allocation of a partnership tax item under the partnership agreement is valid if it satisfies one of the following tests: 1) the allocation has substantial economic effect, 2) the allocation is in accordance with the partners' interests, or 3) the allocation is deemed to be in accordance with the partners' interests.

C. For an allocation of a partnership tax item under the partnership agreement to have economic effect, the partnership must maintain the partners' capital accounts as required by the Regulations.

D. For an allocation of a partnership tax item under the partnership agreement to have economic effect, the economic benefits (and burdens) related to the partnership tax item being allocated must be enjoyed (or borne) by the partner to whom the item is allocated.

186. Which of the following is false?

A. Partnership agreement allocations of tax credits can have substantial economic effect.

B. If an asset with a tax basis to the partnership of $10,000 (value $100,000) generates tax depreciation over three years of $5,000, $3,000 and $2,000, the book depreciation for those three years will be $50,000, $30,000 and $20,000.

C. A partnership acquires an item of depreciable property for $100,000, the only consideration given being a $100,000 nonrecourse note. The property generates depreciation during its first year of $20,000, all of which is allocated to Partner 6 under the partnership agreement. This allocation cannot have substantial economic effect because no person bears the economic risk of loss with respect to the $100,000 nonrecourse debt that created the depreciable basis. Therefore, the $20,000 of depreciation must be allocated in accordance with the partners' interests.

D. In determining the partners' interests in the partnership, the following factors are among those considered: 1) the partners' relative contributions to partnership capital, 2) the partners' interests in the operating cash flow, and 3) the rights of the partners to liquidating distributions.

187. Which of the following is true?

    A. When a 10% partner sells its entire interest in the partnership, the partnership must determine the tax items allocable to the selling partner using the "interim-closing-of-the-books" method.

    B. Parent joined with Child (a minor) in forming the PC partnership. Parent contributed $100,000 to fund the venture. Child's 50% interest in the partnership was a gift from Parent. In PC's first year of operation it had ordinary revenues of $300,000 and business-related expenses of $100,000, exclusive of any compensation for personal services rendered by either Parent or Child. Child rendered PC no services; Parent rendered services worth $80,000 but received no compensation. PC's taxable income of $200,000 ($300,000 - $100,000) was allocated $100,000 each to Parent and Child. The IRS has no basis for objecting to this allocation.

    C. At the beginning of the calendar-year partnership's taxable year, Kevin has a basis in his partnership interest of $50,000. He is allocated the following amounts from the partnership for the taxable year: interest income $90,000, long-term capital loss $30,000, and short-term capital loss $20,000. Kevin received a cash distribution from the partnership of $125,000 on the last day of the taxable year. As a result, Kevin has a $125,000 capital gain with respect to the distribution. He will take $90,000 of interest income onto his personal tax return. He will include both of the capital losses in the determination on his personal tax return of his gain or loss from capital asset transactions during the year.

    D. Janice is a 40% partner in New Age Housewares. During the current taxable year New Age has $110,000 of operating income, a long-term capital gain of $20,000, a short-term capital loss of $10,000, and $40,000 of § 212 investment expenses. Janice's Schedule K-1 will show ordinary income of $44,000, a long-term capital gain of $8,000, a short-term capital loss of $4,000, and $16,000 of § 212 expenses.

188. Which of the following is true?

    A. A 10% partner dies and his interest is immediately liquidated by the partnership. The taxable year of the partnership closes for all partners.

    B. A 15% partner sells her entire interest in the partnership. The taxable year of the partnership closes, but only with respect to her.

    C. A 60% partner sells his entire interest in the partnership. The taxable year of the partnership closes, but only with respect to him.

    D. A 60% partner sells one fifth of his interest in the partnership. The taxable year of the partnership closes, but only with respect to him.

189. Which of the following is true?

    A. The partnership does not terminate when a partner who owns 99% of the capital interests and 49% of profits interests sells his entire equity in the partnership.

B. Roy is a 15% partner in a partnership that sells and installs carpets. Roy is also a certified public accountant who prepares the tax return and manages the accounting records for the partnership, for which he receives an hourly rate. The money he receives from the partnership for these services is an allocation of partnership income.

C. Jim is a 30% partner in a partnership that provides catering services. He receives a fixed amount of $60,000 per year for his services to the partnership as general manager. Before considering Jim's compensation, the partnership has only one tax item: ordinary operating income of $200,000. Jim's allocation of partnership tax items is $42,000 ($140,000 x 30%).

D. Les is a 30% partner in a partnership that provides catering services. He receives the first $60,000 of net operating income each year for his services to the partnership as general manager. Les is receiving a guaranteed payment.

190. Which of the following is false?

A. Frances owns a dozen fully developed building lots acquired from an unrelated failed real estate developer. She holds the lots as an investment and has a basis in them of $480,000. She sells the lots to a partnership in which she has an 80% profits interest for their current value, $700,000. The partnership will include the lots with the rest of the realty it holds for sale in its real estate business. Frances has ordinary income of $220,000.

B. Terry is a 40% partner in Organic Works, which manufactures and distributes organic cosmetics. She personally owns a specialized machine for processing organic compounds worth $700,000 (basis $210,000) that she contributes to the partnership. Within three days the partnership distributes $420,000 to her. The IRS concludes that this is a disguised sale governed by § 707(a). As a result, Terry will recognize a gain of $294,000; her basis in her partnership interest will increase by $84,000.

C. Elaine owns 70% of the capital and profits interests of a partnership. The partnership needs land to build a new warehouse; Elaine agrees to sell a parcel she owns to the partnership for its value, $800,000. The parcel's basis to Elaine is $1,100,000. A few months later the partnership is forced to abandon its warehouse plans and sells the parcel for $850,000. Elaine will not be allowed to recognize the $300,000 loss ($800,000 - $1,100,000) and the partnership will not recognize the $50,000 gain ($850,000 - $800,000).

D. Guy is a 20% partner in a coffee shop. He receives a guaranteed payment of $40,000 for his services as manager. Before considering his guaranteed payment the partnership has only one tax item, $30,000 of ordinary operating income. Guy's total allocation of partnership tax items is $40,000.

191. Which of the following is false?

A. A partnership never recognizes gain or loss on the distribution of non-cash property to its partners.

B. When determining whether a partner recognizes gain with respect to a partnership distribution, marketable securities can sometimes be deemed the equivalent of cash.

C. Throughout the entire year of a calendar-year partnership a partner's basis in its interest is $10,000 (without considering the next sentence). On August 15, the partner takes a draw of $50,000, which she repays on December 13. The partner never recognizes a gain with respect to that draw.

D. A partner holding a one-third partnership interest has a basis in that interest of $10,000. He receives a distribution from the partnership of a crane worth $200,000 (basis to the partnership $100,000; subject to a recourse liability $120,000 which the partner will assume). The partner's basis in the crane is $100,000.

192. Which of the following is false?

A. Partner 1 contributes an item of depreciable personalty worth $30,000 (basis $20,000; original cost $35,000). After three years, due to depreciation, the book value of the asset is $21,000 and the basis is $14,000. Partner 1's original $20,000 basis in the property has not changed because: 1) the partnership has generated no pre-depreciation expense taxable income and no other tax items other than depreciation during these three years, and 2) under the traditional method all of the depreciation deductions on the contributed property were allocated to other partners. The partnership distributes raw land worth $30,000 (basis also $30,000) to Partner 1. Partner 1 will recognize no gain or loss on the distribution.

B. Change the facts in "A": instead of the raw land being distributed to Partner 1, the depreciable property was distributed to Partner 7. Partner 1 will recognize a gain of $7,000.

C. Theresa has a basis in her 30% partnership interest of $70,000. The partnership has been a failure as a business enterprise and will distribute its remaining asset, $50,000, to its partners in complete liquidation. Theresa will have a capital loss of $55,000.

D. A partnership with no cash, no marketable securities, no receivables, no inventory, no asset with potential § 1245 claim, and no liabilities makes an in-kind distribution of all of its remaining assets to its partners in complete liquidation. No partner will recognize gain or loss on the distribution.

193. Which of the following is false?

A. Section 737(a) does not apply when the property distributed by the partnership to the partner is the same property as the partner contributed to the partnership.

B. A cash-method partnership pays a key employee $30,000 per month, payable at the end of each month. On November 21, Dan sells his 25% partnership interest to new partner Margie. Dan will be allocated none of the key employee's compensation cost for November.

C. As a general rule, when a partner receives non-cash property from a partnership, the partner's holding period in the distributed asset includes the holding period of the partnership.

D. Kelly sells specialized high-technology equipment through her sole proprietorship. In her inventory is a machine is worth $800,000. (Its cost to Kelly was $600,000.) Kelly decides to establish a partnership with an unrelated person to enter a business for which such a machine is critical. She contributes the machine to the partnership. Three years later the machine is sold by the partnership for $700,000. (The machine's adjusted basis at the date of sale is $230,000.) The partnership disposes of no other § 1231 property during the year. All $470,000 ($700,000 - $230,000) of the gain is ordinary.

194. Keith has a one third interest (basis $100,000) in a calendar-year, cash-method consulting partnership that leases its business premises and all of its equipment. The assets of the partnership (it has no liabilities) as of December 31, Year 1 are:

| Asset | Value |
|---|---|
| Cash | $90,000 |
| Receivables[fn1] | 170,000 |
| Raw land[fn2] | 320,000 |
| | $580,000 |

[fn1] All due from consulting clients [fn2] Acquired in anticipation of building a business premises; construction plans on hold

An appraisal prepared for the purpose of Keith's upcoming retirement values the partnership at $960,000.

It is agreed that the partnership will pay Keith $80,000 per year each December 31 in Year 2, Year 3, Year 4 and Year 5. The partners elect to treat goodwill as partnership property. Determine the tax consequences to Keith for each of the four years.

ANSWER:

195. X, Y and Z, all individuals, are equal partners of the XYZ partnership, which has no liabilities. The partnership's balance sheet, accompanied by basis accounts, follows:

| | | Book Value | Adjusted Basis |
|---|---|---|---|
| Assets: | Inventory | $120 | $60 |
| | Land | 240 | 180 |
| | | $360 | $240 |
| | | | |
| Capital: | X | $120 | $80 |
| | Y | 120 | 80 |
| | Z | 120 | 80 |
| | | $360 | $240 |

XYZ distributes to X Inventory worth $60. Determine the tax consequences to XYZ and all of its partners with respect to this distribution.

ANSWER:

196. Which of the following is true?

A. Emily's partnership interest is being completely liquidated. Assume § 751(b) does not apply because she is receiving a pro rata amount of each partnership asset. The basis in her partnership interest is $100. Emily will receive the following assets:

| Asset | Basis to Partnership | Value |
|---|---|---|
| Cash | $10 | $10 |
| Unrealized Receivables | 0 | 30 |
| Inventory Items | 20 | 35 |
| Capital Asset 1 | 70 | 50 |
| Capital Asset 2 | 25 | 20 |
| Capital Asset 3 | 17 | 40 |
| | $142 | $185 |

Emily's basis in Capital Asset 3 will be $17.

B. If Emily (in A, above) sells the unrealized receivables and inventory items received, any gain or loss recognized will always be ordinary.

C. A partnership, which has no liabilities, has the following assets:

| Asset | Value | Basis |
|---|---|---|
| Cash | $200,000 | $200,000 |
| Receivables | $300,000 | $300,000 |
| Equipment | $800,000 | $100,000 |
| Raw Land 1[fn] | $1,000,000 | $950,000 |
| Raw Land 2[fn] | $1,300,000 | $500,000 |

[fn] Capital assets held for investment

Partner Q has a basis in her interest of $900,000 and a capital account of $1,400,000. In a complete liquidation of her interest, the partnership distributes to her $100,000 and Raw Land 2. After incorporating the tax consequences of these events, the partnership has a basis in Raw Land 1 of $950,000.

D. P is a calendar-year, accrual-method partnership with an election in effect under § 754. Its balance sheet follows:

| | | | Value | | Basis | |
|---|---|---|---|---|---|---|
| Assets: | Cash | | $15,000 | | $15,000 | |
| | Receivables | | 30,000 | | 30,000 | |
| | Inventory | | 63,000 | | 60,000 | |
| | Capital Asset | | 120,000 | | 60,000 | |
| | | | $228,000 | | $165,000 | |
| Liabilities | | | $30,000 | | $30,000 | |
| Capital: | X | $66,000 | | $45,000 | | |
| | Y | 66,000 | | 45,000 | | |
| | Z | 66,000 | 198,000 | 45,000 | 135,000 | |
| | | | $228,000 | | $165,000 | |

X sells his partnership interest to W for its value, $66,000. The total § 743 basis adjustment will be $21,000. Of that, $1,000 will be allocated to the Inventory and $20,000 will be allocated to the Capital Asset.

197. Which of the following is true?

    A. Immediately before the liquidating distribution described below, the general partners of partnership QRL have the following capital accounts: Q $300,000; R ($40,000) — i.e., a deficit; L $100,000; total $360,000. The partnership distributes its remaining asset, $360,000, equally to the three general partners. This liquidating distribution raises no issues with respect to whether the partnership's allocations of partnership tax items have (or had) economic effect.

    B. An equal general partnership consisting of two partners expects to have only two partnership tax items during the forthcoming taxable year: ordinary income of $30,000 and § 103 interest of $20,000. All of the § 103 interest and $5,000 of the ordinary income is allocated to Partner #1. Partner #2 is allocated $25,000 of ordinary income. These facts will never raise an issue as to whether the economic effect of these allocations is substantial.

    C. Four years later the general partnership described in B estimates that it will have $100,000 of ordinary income in the next taxable year and $103,000 of long-term capital gain in the taxable year after that. The partnership allocates all of the future $100,000 of ordinary income to Partner #2 and all of the future $103,000 of long-term capital gain to Partner #1. These facts will never raise an issue as to whether the economic effect of these allocations is substantial. Assume that an appropriate discount rate would be 3 percent.

    D. On April 15 of Year 7 a calendar-year general partnership retroactively alters its partnership agreement for Year 6, reallocating various partnership tax items in a manner that poses no problems with respect to substantial economic effect or with respect to the varying interest rules of § 706. It then timely files its Year 6 tax return. Based solely on these facts, the IRS will not disregard the retroactive allocations.

198. Which of the following is true?

    A. Partner Fran (who has a 25% interest) originally contributed raw land with a built in loss of $400,000 to the partnership. Several years later, when the partnership still holds the raw land, Fran sells her partnership interest to new partner Ned. A year later the partnership sells the raw land at a loss of $500,000. Ned will be allocated $425,000 of that loss.

    B. Guy, a 40% partner in a general partnership, has a basis in his interest of $60,000 immediately before the following distribution, which is in complete liquidation of the partnership. The partnership has only one asset at the time of liquidation: cash. Guy receives $20,000, the balance in his capital account. Guy has a capital loss of $40,000.

    C. Keith is a 30% partner in a cash-method general partnership, Q. Q completely liquidates, distributing its remaining assets proportionately to the partners. There are two such assets: cash and accounts receivable arising from the sale of services. When Keith collects his share of the accounts receivable he might have a capital gain.

D. If a partner realizes a gain or loss upon its sale of its interest in a partnership that has no § 751 assets, the recognized gain or loss can be all capital, all ordinary, or a combination of both.

199. Which of the following is false?

A. Dale is a general partner who acquired his interest by purchase from one of the original partners. Dale has a positive § 743 adjustment with respect to Asset #4 of $40,000. The partnership later sells Asset #4 and allocates $100,000 of the resulting gain to Dale. Dale will report on his personal tax return a gain of $60,000.

B. Cunningham is a general partner in partnership Washington Associates (which has no § 754 election in effect). When Cunningham has a basis in his interest of $1,000,000, Washington distributes to him in complete liquidation of his interest a parcel of raw land with a basis to the partnership of $600,000. Washington has a negative basis adjustment of $400,000 that it must allocate under § 755.

C. Section 755 allocates § 734 adjustments arising from distributions in which neither gain nor loss is recognized by first dividing all partnership property into two classes: 1) capital assets and 2) all other assets.

D. The purpose of a § 743 adjustment is to allow a partner who acquires its interest from a prior partner (by sale, exchange, or as the successor to a decedent partner) to avoid recognizing (presently or in the future) any of the gains and losses built into the partnership's assets at the time of acquisition.

*Subchapters C and K are generally studied prior to Subchapter S because the latter is a hybrid of the two. Subchapter C sets forth rules grounded on the concept of a separate taxable entity, the C corporation. Subchapter K sets forth rules grounded on the concept of a pure passthrough entity, the partnership (also applicable to limited liability companies (LLCs) that have not elected "association" status). Subchapter S is Congress' attempt to create a tax structure with features of both. The primary goals in enacting Subchapter S were: 1) to permit the investors to enjoy limited liability, and 2) to avoid the worst consequences of having a separate taxable entity (i.e., losses trapped at the entity level, income subject to double taxation, and the character of the tax items realized at the entity level lost).*

*The default is that Subchapter C governs Subchapter S except to the extent the latter expressly overrides the former (or to the extent employing the rules of Subchapter C would be inconsistent with the congressional intent in creating Subchapter S).*

*This topic considers Subchapter S corporations.*

200. The calendar-year Fedor Corporation is a Subchapter S corporation. Its shareholders, all of whom are U.S. citizens or residents or domestic entities, are:

Mike

Sue (wife of Mike)

Michelle (daughter of Mike and Sue)

Art (friend of Mike)

The Polly Trust, a Qualified Subchapter S Trust (QSST) (the sole beneficiary of which is Polly, Art's wife)

The Fisher Trust, an Electing Small Business Trust (ESBT) (the sole beneficiary of which is Pittsford College)

New York University

Claude and Mildred (both unrelated to all other shareholders), who hold their shares as tenants-in-common

Chris, as custodian for Gwendolyn under the Uniform Gift to Minors Act, both unrelated to all other shareholders

Which of the following is false?

A. Fedor has seven shareholders.

B. The income tax rate applicable to that portion of Fedor's income allocated to the Fisher Trust will not be less than the rate applicable to such income allocated to the Polly Trust.

C. All of the shareholders of Fedor at the time of its S election had to consent to that election.

D. If Fedor came into existence and began business on January 1 but its application for Subchapter S status was not filed until March 30 due to the personal illness of the corporation's CPA, the corporation could not have become an S corporation prior to January 1 of the following year.

201. Marilyn's grantor trust is the sole shareholder of Butler, Inc. She loaned Butler $300,000 on a 20-year term note at market interest, which note was subordinated to all other creditors. Based on the facts that: 1) Butler's total capitalization (debt and equity) is only $350,000, 2) the note has a fairly long maturity, and 3) the loan was made on the same day Butler was created and capitalized, the IRS successfully recharacterized the loan as equity for general tax purposes. From time to time Marilyn also informally loans Butler up to $8,000 for working capital, which is always repaid within 60 days. Butler has two classes of common stock outstanding; they both have the same distribution rights, but one class is nonvoting. Which of the following is false with respect to Butler's eligibility to elect Subchapter S status?

A. The periodic advances of up to $8,000 do not preclude Butler from being a Subchapter S corporation.

B. The 20-year term loan precludes Butler from being a Subchapter S corporation.

C. The fact that the stock is owned by a grantor trust does not preclude Butler from being a Subchapter S corporation.

D. The fact that two classes of common stock are outstanding does not preclude Butler from being a Subchapter S corporation.

202. Which of the following events cause an S corporation to cease being a "small business corporation"?

A. One of its shareholders residing in a community property state marries a nonresident alien and then purchases an additional share from their joint bank account.

B. One of its shareholders goes bankrupt, all of her property, including the stock, becoming part of the bankruptcy estate.

C. One of its shareholders dies and his will transfers his stock to a testamentary trust.

D. Two of its shareholders who are married get divorced, each keeping their own stock. The corporation had 99 shareholders prior to the divorce.

203. Which of the following is false?

A. An S corporation that distributes appreciated property to its shareholders with respect to their stock must recognize gain under § 311(b)(1).

B. A new corporation which immediately elects Subchapter S status must carefully track its earnings and profits.

C. As a general rule an S corporation makes its own tax elections.

D. An S corporation is generally not subject to the corporate income tax.

204. Which of the following is true?

A. Subchapter S corporations are allowed deductions for charitable contributions.

B. A distribution by an S corporation to one of its shareholders can never reduce that shareholder's stock basis.

C. A distribution of cash by an S corporation to one of its shareholders cannot result in a recognized gain to such shareholder.

D. An S corporation separates the components of its taxable income into two categories. The first category is any item of gross income or deduction that could possibly affect different shareholders differently. The second category is the net amount of all remaining items of gross income and deduction, which will be ordinary in character.

205. Which of the following is true?

A. An S corporation's § 179 deduction and its exempt income must be separately stated.

B. When taken together, the Code and the Regulations provide a comprehensive listing of all separately stated items under § 1366(a)(1)(A).

C. S corporations are not entitled to deductions for organizational expenditures under § 248.

D. An S corporation shareholder is informed of its share of the S corporation's separately stated items and nonseparately computed income or loss on Schedule K.

BASIC FACTS FOR THE FOLLOWING TWO QUESTIONS:

On January 1, Gwen joined with Londo, Sheridan, Kosh and Ivanova to form the new calendar-year, cash-method Babylon, Inc., which immediately elected Subchapter S status. Also on that date Gwen received 20% of the Babylon stock in exchange for raw land worth $9,000,000 (basis $300,000; holding period five years) in a transaction qualifying for § 351 treatment. On that date she also loaned Babylon $35,000 on a three-year term note at the market rate of interest.

For the year, Babylon had the following tax items:

| | |
|---|---|
| Sales | $10,000,000 |
| Cost of sales | $6,000,000 |
| Marketing expense | $1,000,000 |
| Administration expense | $500,000 |
| § 179 amount | $100,000 |
| Short-term capital loss | $120,000 |
| § 1231 gain | $80,000 |
| Exempt interest income | $10,000 |
| Penalties paid for safety violations | $5,000 |
| Personal injury lawsuit damages paid | $2,250,000 |

After the § 351 transaction, no further stock was issued, nor were there any redemptions or stock distributions. Babylon distributed $1,800,000 to its shareholders pro rata on December 31.

206.    Determine the tax consequences to Gwen for the taxable year.

ANSWER:

207.    Determine the tax consequences to Gwen for the following taxable year assuming Babylon's only tax item is nonseparately computed income of $200,000.

ANSWER:

208.    Which of the following is true?

   A.    When a shareholder guarantees a loan between the S corporation (debtor) and a third party (creditor), the shareholder is permitted to treat the guaranteed loan as though it had been made by the shareholder to the corporation for the purposes of providing basis against which deductions may be taken.

   B.    During Year 1 an S corporation shareholder loaned the S corporation $10,000. That year it reduced the loan basis by $8,000 to permit deductions to be taken. During Year 2 the shareholder loaned the corporation another $6,000. That year deductions in excess of the shareholder's stock basis were $2,000. In Year 3 the shareholder was allocated $5,000 of ordinary income (the corporation's only tax item that year). The shareholder's basis in the second loan at the end of Year 3 is $5,250.

   C.    An S corporation shareholder has suspended losses of $11,000 due to a lack of stock and loan basis. The shareholder sells half of her stock to an unrelated person. The buyer succeeds to $5,500 of the seller's suspended losses.

   D.    If an individual who is an S corporation shareholder has sufficient stock or loan basis to take into account a corporate long-term capital loss allocated to the shareholder of $10,000, the individual will have a deduction of that amount on his or her personal income tax return for the same year.

209.    Which of the following is false?

   A.    If an S corporation and all of its shareholders elect, the interim-closing-of-the-books method can be used to allocate the corporation's tax items among the shareholders should any of the following occur during the taxable year: 1) a shareholder redeems an amount of stock representing at least 20% of the outstanding stock within any 30-day period in a transaction entitled to § 302(a) treatment; 2) a shareholder disposes (other than by a redemption described in 1), above) an amount of stock representing at least 20% of the outstanding stock within any 30-day period; or 3) the corporation issues stock to new shareholders in an amount exceeding 25% of the previously outstanding stock within any 30-day period.

B. An individual was the owner of ten shares of the stock of a calendar-year S corporation on March 1 and 11 shares on March 2. The individual owned no stock on any other days that year. On March 1 there were 1,000 shares outstanding; on March 2 there were 2,000 shares outstanding. The year had 365 days. The S corporation's only tax item for the year was ordinary income of $365,000. The shareholder will report $15.50 of ordinary income from the S corporation for taxable year.

C. Lauren owns 26% of the stock of an S corporation that operates a high-security storage facility. Lauren is also the facility manager and is required by the S corporation to live on the facility premises because of the sensitive and risky nature of the items stored. Lauren and her family reside on the premises at no cost. The lodging provided to her and her family is excluded from her gross income under § 119.

D. An S corporation shareholder sold all of her stock to a person not presently a shareholder. Both the seller and the buyer agreed to use the interim-closing-of-the-books method to allocate between them the income for the year of sale associated with the sold shares. The S corporation, with respect to these shareholders only, used its accounting system to determine the exact amount of income earned with respect to the sold shares through the day of sale and allocated that amount to the seller. The remaining portion of the income earned during the year with respect to the sold shares was allocated to the buyer. This procedure was correct.

210. Which of the following is false?

A. The stock of an S corporation is owned 50% by Father and 50% by Daughter, a minor. The corporation's taxable income was $70,000, all ordinary, half of which was reported on each of the shareholders' personal tax returns. Compensation of $10,000 was paid by the corporation to Father for services rendered that year; no compensation was paid to Daughter, who rendered no services. Reasonable compensation for the services rendered by Father would have been $30,000. The IRS can allocate an additional $20,000 of the $70,000 of taxable income to Father as compensation. This would result, among other things, in daughter's income from the corporation being reduced to $25,000.

B. An S corporation has a taxable year ending April 30. One of the corporation's shareholders is an individual. Her allocation of the S corporation's tax items for the S corporation's taxable year ending April 30, Year 1, will appear on her personal tax return for that calendar year, the filing of which will be due in April of the following year (Year 2).

C. A redemption of S corporation stock that is eligible for sale or exchange treatment under § 302(a) which is made by an S corporation that was previously a C corporation and that has an accumulated adjustments account (AAA) reduces the AAA by the lesser of the amount of the redemption distribution or the redeemed stock's pro rata share of the AAA.

D. To eliminate the need for an AAA, a newly electing S corporation that was formerly a C corporation could elect, with the consent of all of its shareholders, to make a constructive dividend distribution that eliminates all of its earnings and profits. Since nothing is actually distributed, the constructive dividend distribution is offset by a constructive contribution to capital.

211. Ignoring short taxable years and 52-53 week taxable years, an S corporation has four choices for its taxable year. Identify them.

ANSWER:

212. Which of the following is false with respect to a Subchapter S corporation that was previously a Subchapter C corporation?

    A.  If the C corporation used the last-in-first-out (LIFO) method of inventory, it must in its last year of existence as a C corporation recognize as ordinary income the difference between its inventory measured under first-in-first-out (FIFO) and its inventory measured under last-in-first-out.

    B.  No distribution to shareholders with respect to their stock by the S corporation will ever be characterized as a dividend to such shareholders.

    C.  Except with respect to the built-in gains tax, the S corporation cannot use any of the net operating loss carryforwards arising during its Subchapter C years.

    D.  The S corporation's accumulated adjustments account is adjusted for the corporation's tax items and distributions in a manner similar to, but not exactly the same as, the way those tax items and distributions adjust the shareholders' stock bases.

213. On January 1, Year 1, calendar-year C corporation Picard, Inc. becomes an S corporation. It has one shareholder, Warf. On this day Picard has earnings and profits of $200,000. The following are relevant to Years 1-3:

| Year | S Corporation Tax Items & Distributions | Amount |
|------|------------------------------------------|--------|
| 1 | Ordinary income | $250,000 |
|   | Ordinary deductions | $100,000 |
|   | Distributions to shareholder | $120,000 |
| 2 | Ordinary income | $300,000 |
|   | Short-term capital loss | $700,000 |
|   | Distributions to shareholder | $100,000 |
| 3 | Ordinary income | $100,000 |
|   | Long-term capital loss | $400,000 |
|   | Distributions to shareholder | $150,000 |

Determine the amount of the distributions in each of the three taxable years that will be characterized as dividends.

ANSWER:

214. Which of the following is false with respect to the built-in gains tax?

A. The purpose of the built-in gains tax is to stop C corporations with highly appreciated assets from converting to S status shortly before liquidation to avoid the corporate level of taxation on its assets' net built-in gain.

B. Immediately before its S election takes effect, a cash-method C corporation has three assets: Factory (value $500,000; basis $900,000), Receivables (value $300,000, basis zero), and Inventory (value $350,000; basis $100,000). The corporation's Accounts Payable (all representing deductible business expenses) is $100,000. The corporation's net unrealized built-in gain is $150,000.

C. If an asset held by a C corporation on the date of conversion to S status had a built-in loss of $80,000 on such date, but was sold after conversion to S status at a gain of $130,000, that $130,000 would not be classified as a recognized built-in gain and, therefore, could not cause or increase the imposition of the built-in gains tax.

D. On the date of its conversion to S status an accrual-method C corporation was under an obligation to pay out $3,000,000 in tort damages within the next 60 days. This loss will not be deductible for tax purposes until paid because of the economic performance requirement. The net unrealized built-in gain for the corporation would be reduced by the $3,000,000.

215. Which of the following is false with respect to the built-in gains tax?

A. A C corporation has a net unrealized built-in gain of $70,000 on the date of conversion to S status. That gain relates to a parcel of raw land worth $400,000 (basis $330,000). The corporation had no other assets and had no liabilities on the date of conversion. The corporation's taxable income for its final year as a C corporation was $0. It sells the land shortly after becoming an S corporation for $400,000. All other things equal, the corporation would have been better off selling the asset before its conversion to S status.

B. For any taxable year, the amount upon which the built-in gains tax is imposed cannot exceed the corporation's taxable income.

C. The built-in gains tax computed for any year is reduced by any business credit carryforwards from the Subchapter C years of the corporation.

D. An S corporation sells an asset and recognizes a long-term capital gain of $100,000, which is subject to the built-in gains tax and which results in a marginal tax liability of $35,000. The S corporation's sole shareholder is allocated only a $100,000 long-term capital gain with respect to this asset disposition.

216. Which of the following is true with respect to passive investment income in the context of an S corporation?

A. Passive investment income can lead both to the imposition of a tax at the corporate level and the termination of the corporation's S status.

B. When measuring gross receipts for the purpose of the tax on excess passive investment income under § 1375, the proceeds from the sale of inventory and from the sale of § 1231 asset are reduced by the bases of such assets.

C. Royalties and rents are always included in passive investment income.

D. An S corporation with earnings and profits of $2,000,000 has gross receipts for the purpose of the tax under § 1375 of $3,821,000. It has two sources of passive investment income: rental income (gross receipts $350,000; related expenses $25,000) and interest on a bond investment (gross receipts $665,000; related expenses $15,000). The tax under § 1375 is $20,088. The sole shareholder will report rental income on her personal tax return of $318,073.

217. Which of the following is false with respect to the termination of S corporation status?

A. Termination can result from three events: 1) the corporation terminates its election with the consent of shareholders holding the majority of its stock; 2) the corporation ceases to be a "small business corporation," or 3) the corporation has earnings and profits and for three consecutive years has passive investment income in excess of 25% of its gross receipts.

B. In taxable Year 11 an S corporation revokes its S election effective the beginning of taxable Year 12. It can re-elect S status effective the beginning of taxable Year 17.

C. An S corporation shareholder dies and her stock passes by operation of law to a nonresident alien. The S election involuntarily terminates. The corporation immediately redeems the nonresident alien's stock and asks the IRS to waive the involuntary termination. It is likely that the IRS will grant the waiver.

D. If a calendar-year corporation's S election terminates on January 1 of the following taxable year, that following taxable year is called an "S termination year" and special accounting rules apply.

BASIC FACTS FOR THE FOLLOWING SEVEN QUESTIONS:

On August 13, Year 6 (a leap year) Galactica, Inc., a calendar-year S corporation, was determined by the IRS to have a second class of stock which had different distribution rights, resulting in the termination of its S status. Galactica took no steps to waive the termination. Galactica's only taxable income for that year was ordinary income of $1,098,000. Galactica will file both its S and C short-year tax returns on March 15 of Year 7. (It will not seek any extensions.) On the date of S status termination, Galactica had earnings and profits of $700,000 and a balance in its accumulated adjustments account of $150,000. Galactica makes no elections with respect to its accounting methods.

On August 13, Year 6, Galactica had two equal (50 shares each) shareholders: Cori ($0 stock basis; $300,000 suspended ordinary loss) and Gwen ($100,000 stock basis).

On August 14, Year 6, Gwen sold her stock to Starbuck for $450,000.

On August 11, Year 7, both Cori and Starbuck transferred $500,000 to Galactica in exchange for additional stock.

On August 13, Year 7, Galactica made its only distribution during the year: $600,000 ($300,000 to each shareholder).

Galactica had a taxable income of $0 for Year 7. (An unexpected injunction, which is expected to be lifted in due course, prohibited Galactica from conducting its business during Year 7.) Its shareholders made no contributions to capital and received no distributions during Year 7 except for those identified above.

218. When did Galactica's S status terminate?

ANSWER:

219.  How is Galactica's Year 6 ordinary income allocated between the S corporation and the C corporation?

ANSWER:

220.  What is Galactica's tax liability for the C short year?

ANSWER:

221.  When are the tax returns for the S short year and the C short year due?

ANSWER:

222.  When does the post-termination transition period begin and end?

ANSWER:

223.  What are the tax consequences to Cori of her contribution of $500,000 on August 11, Year 7?

ANSWER:

224.  What are the tax consequences to Cori and Starbuck of the $600,000 distribution on August 13, Year 7?

ANSWER:

*This topic seeks to highlight the differences in the basic tax rules governing C corporations, S corporations, partnerships and limited liability companies (both those that have elected "association" status and those that have not). The issues covered include status eligibility, latitude in choosing a taxable year, the tax consequences of capital contributions and distributions, fringe benefits, and specialized internal accounting (e.g., the need to maintain an accumulated adjustments account).*

225. Which of the following is false with respect to a limited liability company (LLC)?

    A. If an LLC with two or more members makes no election to be an "association," it will be taxed as a partnership.

    B. For an LLC that makes no election to be an "association," all LLC liabilities will be analyzed as nonrecourse, unless a member provides a guarantee.

    C. If an LLC makes an election to be an "association," it can allocate any of its tax items to any member so long as such allocation has substantial economic effect.

    D. If an LLC makes an election to be an "association," it can also elect to be taxed under Subchapter S.

226. Giving consideration to C corporations, S corporations and general partnerships (which include for these purposes limited liability companies that do not elect to be taxed as an association), which of the following is true?

    A. The only entity subject to the alternative minimum tax is the C corporation.

    B. All of these entities are subject to the at-risk rules of § 465.

    C. All of these entities could have their taxable years terminated simply because an equity holder dies and the decedent's equity interest passes by operation of law to another person.

    D. The equity holders of all of these entities can increase their opportunity to take entity-level losses by making loans to the entity.

227. Which of the following is true?

    A. If a person not presently an equity holder transfers (in conjunction with no other transferor) appreciated property to a partnership (or an LLC that is taxed like a partnership) in exchange for a 10% equity interest, the exchange will be taxable to the property transferor.

B.  No distribution made by a partnership (or an LLC that is taxed like a partnership) to a partner (or member) ever results in a recognized gain or loss at the entity level.

C.  As compared to what is true for a partner (or a member of an LLC that is taxed like a partnership), the guarantee by an S corporation shareholder of a corporate obligation provides the same opportunity to deduct additional entity-level losses.

D.  An LLC that does not elect to be an association is always taxed like a partnership.

228.  Giving consideration to C corporations, S corporations and general partnerships (which include for these purposes limited liability companies that do not elect to be taxed as an association), which of the following is true?

A.  All of these entities must compute their taxable income and generally must file a tax return.

B.  All of these entities are subject to double taxation.

C.  Only corporations have the opportunity to take deductions for organizational expenditures.

D.  All of these entities are able to provide nontaxable meals and lodging under § 119 to their equity holders who render services to the entity.

229.  Giving consideration to C corporations, S corporations and general partnerships (which include for these purposes limited liability companies that do not elect to be taxed as an association), which of the following is true?

A.  All of these entities are subject to rules that can disallow the recognition of loss on the sale or exchange of property between the entity and an equity holder with more than 50% of the equity interests in the entity.

B.  There is a high risk to equity holders in all of these entities that the sale or exchange of their equity interest could cause them to recognize ordinary income.

C.  For all of these entities it is possible that a distribution of property could cause the bases of the entity's retained assets to change.

D.  All of these entities confront serious problems when they have as an equity holder a nonresident alien, but only S corporations have to be concerned about the kinds of trusts that hold stock.

230.  Giving consideration to C corporations, S corporations and general partnerships (which includes for these purposes limited liability companies that do not elect to be taxed as an association), which of the following is true?

A.  All of these entities are allowed to take deductions for charitable contributions.

B.  Only C corporations prohibit entity-level losses from being potentially deductible by equity holders.

C.  All of these entities have an accumulated adjustments account.

D. All of these entities allocate the gain recognized with respect to contributed property to the contributing equity holder to the extent of the property's pre-contribution built-in gain (as adjusted over time for factors such as depreciation).

231. Which of the following is false?

    A. An LLC receives tax-exempt state bond interest. Whether one or more of its members' tax returns also show tax-exempt income as a result depends on whether the LLC elected to be an association.

    B. A partnership (and an LLC which has not elected to be an association) can, in general, allocate its tax items to its partners (members) any way it chooses so long as the allocation has substantial economic effect.

    C. The transfer within a taxable year of 90% of a C corporation's stock to new shareholders never closes of the taxable year of the corporation.

    D. Regardless of the form of business entity selected, the bases of the owners in their equity interests change as the entity recognizes gross income and deductions.

232. Which of the following is true?

    A. The receipt of stock, without restriction, from a corporation in exchange for personal services rendered by an individual is always a taxable event to the recipient.

    B. The receipt of a profits interest in a partnership (or in an LLC that has not elected to be an association) is always a taxable event to the recipient.

    C. A partnership that elects to be an association and then elects to be taxed under Subchapter S avoids the double-taxation regime and obtains corporation-like limited liability.

    D. A C corporation is generally the best form of business entity when the equity holders intend the entity to hold rapidly appreciating assets.

233. Giving consideration to C corporations, S corporations, general partnerships and limited liability companies, which of the following is false?

    A. It is possible for any of these entities to have an earnings and profits account.

    B. If the objectives of the organizers of a closely held business entity are limited liability, no double taxation, maximum flexibility in allocating entity-level tax items among equity holders, and a high degree of robustness against having the personal matters of the equity holders impact the entity, limited liability companies are likely the entity of choice.

    C. The issues confronting entities taxed under Subchapter K tend to be substantially more complex than those confronting either C or S corporations.

    D. C corporations have the least discretion in the selection of a taxable year.

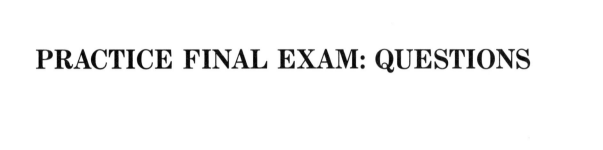

# PRACTICE FINAL EXAM: QUESTIONS

# PRACTICE FINAL EXAM

1. The Fayette Co., Inc., has taxable income (all ordinary) of $2,000,000. It also has the following capital gains and losses:

| | |
|---|---|
| Long-term capital gain | $700,000 |
| Short-term capital gain | $900,000 |
| Long-term capital loss | $1,100,000 |
| Short-term capital loss | $800,000 |

There are no capital loss carryovers. In addition, this year Fayette has its first § 1231 loss of $50,000. Fayette's taxable income is:

A. $1,950,000.

B. $1,650,000.

C. $1,700,000.

D. $2,000,000.

2. Which of the following is true?

A. Section 351 provides for the permanent nonrecognition of gain or loss with respect to assets contributed to a corporation in exchange for stock.

B. The control requirement for § 351 treatment focuses exclusively on voting stock.

C. All of the stock received by a person who, as part of a single transaction, transfers property in exchange for 100 shares of stock, and who renders professional services to the corporation in exchange for five additional shares of stock, counts in measuring control.

D. The rules for determining whether a corporation has assumed, for tax purposes, a liability that encumbers property contributed to it by a person in exchange for stock are the same for both recourse and nonrecourse liabilities.

3. Which of the following is true?

A. In a complete liquidation of a subsidiary under § 332, the parent corporation's basis in the stock of the subsidiary disappears.

B. A wholly owned subsidiary begins to make a series of distribution to its parent in complete liquidation in Year 1. The last distribution in the series occurs in Year 6. The subsidiary will recognize no gain or loss on any liquidating distribution under § 337(a).

C. Lori is the sole shareholder of the Wagoner Corporation. When Wagoner liquidated, Lori recognized a $1,000,000 long-term capital gain under § 331(a). Three years later Wagoner was held responsible for damages of $900,000 in a product liability lawsuit. Wagoner having been dissolved, Lori was required to pay the damages under state law as the distributee of the corporation's assets. The payment is properly characterized as an ordinary loss on her personal tax return.

D. Rupert, the sole shareholder of calendar-year Earnest, Inc., has a stock basis of $60,000. Earnest made two distributions in its complete liquidation. Late in December of Year 1 Earnest distributed $50,000. Early in January of Year 2 Earnest made its second and final distribution of $80,000, for a total of $130,000. In the aggregate Rupert will have a capital gain of $70,000 [($50,000 + $80,000) - $60,000]. On his Year 1 tax return Rupert must report a capital gain of $26,923 [$70,000 total gain x ($50,000 distribution during Year 1 ÷ $130,000 total distribution)].

4. Which of the following is false?

A. As a general rule, for an allocation of a partnership tax item under the partnership agreement to have economic effect, liquidating distributions by the partnership to the partners must be in accordance with the partners' positive capital account balances. Partners with negative capital account balances must be unconditionally obligated to make capital contributions sufficient to bring those balances to zero. (Ignore qualified income offsets.)

B. Present value concepts are not employed in evaluating whether the economic effect of an allocation of a partnership tax item under the partnership agreement is substantial.

C. Two equal partners realized that it was highly likely that the partnership would have both capital losses and ordinary losses during the current taxable year. Partner 1 expects personally to have significant capital gains this year; Partner 2 expects personally to have no capital gains this year but to have significant ordinary income this year. The partnership agreement is amended so that the year's capital losses are allocated to Partner 1 and a corresponding amount of ordinary losses is allocated to Partner 2. All other partnership tax items are allocated equally. The economic effect of this partnership allocation is not substantial.

D. Two equal partners realized that it was highly likely that their partnership would have a large capital loss during the current year and a large ordinary loss the following year. The partnership agreement is amended to allocate the first $100,000 of capital losses to Partner 1 in the first year and to allocate the first $100,000 of ordinary losses the following year to Partner 2. All other partnership tax items (including capital losses in excess of $100,000 in the first year and ordinary losses in excess of $100,000 in the second year) will be allocated equally in both years. Partner 1 expects to personally have over $100,000 of capital gain this year and none next year; Partner 2 expects personally to have little income this year but a great deal of ordinary income next year. The economic effect of this partnership allocation is not substantial.

5. Robert Brown owns a sole proprietorship. One of the proprietorship's assets is an item of equipment that cost $600,000, is worth $500,000, and has a basis of $0. Robert wanted to sell the equipment to the Heavy Construction Co., a general partnership of which Robert is a 70% partner.

Robert's CPA advised him that, if such a sale took place, the full $500,000 gain on the equipment would be ordinary income under §§ 1245 and 1239. Therefore, the following plan was implemented.

Robert created the Patrick Corp. and capitalized it solely with the equipment in a § 351 transaction. The next day he sold the Patrick stock to Heavy Construction. Robert reported the stock sale as a long-term capital gain.

Upon audit the IRS argues that, under the step-transaction doctrine, Robert's § 351 transaction and stock sale should be disregarded and that the events should be recast as a sale of the equipment to Heavy Construction, thereby converting Robert's long-term capital gain into ordinary income under §§ 1245 and 1239. Will the IRS' position be upheld if litigated?

ANSWER:

6. Which of the following is false?

   A. Transfers of shares within the control group shortly after an attempted § 351 transaction pose no problem with respect to satisfying the control test.

   B. A corporation never recognizes gain or loss when it gives its stock in exchange for property, whether or not § 351 applies.

   C. If an attempted § 351 transaction fails, the normal gain and loss recognition rules of § 1001(c) apply.

   D. Where a person transfers multiple non-cash properties to a corporation in exchange for stock in a qualifying § 351 transaction and boot is received, the amount of gain recognized is the lesser of the amount of the boot or the net gain on all of the assets transferred (i.e., the sum of the realized gains and losses on the individual assets).

7. Goliad, Inc. has owned the same shares in the Lipscomb Corp. for eight years. Goliad receives a $100,000 dividend from Lipscomb. Ignore § 246(b). By how much will Goliad's taxable income increase by virtue of the dividend if Goliad owns 8% of the Lipscomb stock? If it owns 25% (both voting power and value)? If it owns 98% (both voting power and value)?

ANSWER:

8. Which of the following is false?

   A. The tax consequences to a corporate shareholder of the redemption of stock held long-term are generally more favorable than those of a dividend.

   B. The tests for whether a redemption receives sale or exchange treatment under § 302(b)(1)-(3) all attempt to determine whether the economic impact of the redemption on the redeeming shareholder is essentially equivalent to a dividend.

C.  Whether the redemption has sufficient impact on the redeeming shareholder's control is the primary requirement for sale or exchange treatment under § 302(b)(1)-(3).

D.  If a series of redemptions is planned, the test for whether any single redemption that is part of such series (which may include the redemption of multiple shareholders' stock) qualifies as a substantially disproportionate redemption under § 302(b)(2) generally cannot be determined until the last redemption in the series has been completed.

BASIC FACTS FOR THE FOLLOWING FOUR QUESTIONS:

New, calendar-year, cash-method partnership P comes into existence on January 1, Year 1. The partners (all individuals) capitalize P as follows:

| Individual | Contribution | Value | Adjusted Basis | Holding Period | Partnership Interest |
|---|---|---|---|---|---|
| B | Cash | $200,000 | N/A | N/A | 12.5% |
| C | Raw Land | 1,000,000 | $50,000 | 24 years | 62.5% |
| D | Equipment | 400,000 | $30,000 | 4 years[fn] | 25.0% |
| | | $1,600,000 | | | 100.0% |

[fn] *Only one year remaining in recovery period*

9A.  Determine the tax consequences to P.

ANSWER:

9B.  Determine the tax consequences to C.

ANSWER:

9C.  How will the remaining year of depreciation on the Equipment be allocated among the partners under the "ceiling rule" using the traditional method?

ANSWER:

9D.  If the Equipment is sold on January 1, Year 2 for $300,000, how would the gain be allocated?

ANSWER:

10.  The tax consequences of which of the following dispositions of § 306 stock (or stock that might be § 306 stock) is governed by § 306(a)?

A.  Actual § 306 stock is redeemed as part of the complete liquidation of the issuing corporation.

B.  Actual § 306 stock is redeemed in a partial liquidation qualifying under § 302(b)(4).

C.  Stock is sold that was distributed tax-free under § 305(a) when the corporation had no earnings and profits.

D.  Actual § 306 stock is redeemed in a transaction that would generally qualify for sale or exchange treatment under § 302(b)(1).

11.  Kilwilly, Inc. has retained earnings of $3,000,000, additional paid-in capital (i.e., contributed equity capital in excess of the par value of the stock issued) of $4,000,000, and earnings and profits of $2,800,000. The Kilwilly board of directors declares a $2,000,000 cash dividend, which the corporation pays. The board directed that the dividend be sourced from additional paid-in capital, not from retained earnings (i.e. it declared a liquidating dividend — a return of investment). Angus Highlander owns 55% of the Kilwilly stock, with a basis of $1,300,000 and a long-term holding period. Because of the board's decision to source the dividend from additional paid-in capital, Angus reduced his stock basis to $200,000 ($1,300,000 - 55% x $2,000,000) and reported neither a dividend nor a capital gain on his personal tax return. Upon audit of that return, what will the IRS's position be with respect to the distribution?

ANSWER:

12.  Barbara Wilson is the sole shareholder and CEO of calendar-year Essex, Ltd. She travels extensively furthering Essex' business. The corporate policy is that employees submit expense reimbursement claims for costs incurred on the corporation's behalf. On December 31 Barbara returns from a business trip to the Far East. Her total travel and business-related costs are $13,000. Instead of submitting a reimbursement claim she simply decides to deduct these costs on her personal tax return as business expenses. Is Barbara's treatment of the $13,000 appropriate?

ANSWER:

BASIC FACTS FOR THE FOLLOWING FIVE QUESTIONS:

On January 1, individuals Q and R create the new calendar-year partnership T. Q contributes $100,000 (cash). R contributes a machine worth $1,000,000 (adjusted basis $50,000; nonrecourse lien $600,000). The principal of the lien is due in five years; interest payments are made each December 31. Q receives a 20% partnership interest; R receives an 80% interest. The machine has a remaining recovery period of two years and is being depreciated under the straight-line method for both book and tax purposes. All allocations are made using the traditional method. The partnership agreement specifies that Tier III allocations of nonrecourse liabilities are made first by taking § 704(c) into account, with any remaining liability allocated in proportion to the partners' profit-sharing ratios (20:80).

During the first year the partnership's pre-depreciation expense taxable income (all cash, all ordinary) is $300,000. Other than depreciation, it had no other tax items.

13A.  How will the nonrecourse lien be allocated on January 1?

ANSWER:

13B.  Determine the partners' adjusted bases in their partnership interests on January 1.

ANSWER:

13C. How will the nonrecourse lien be allocated on December 31, Year 1?

ANSWER:

13D. Determine the partners' adjusted bases in their partnership interests on December 31.

ANSWER:

13E. Determine the partners' capital accounts on December 31.

ANSWER:

14. Ashland Corp., which is wholly owned by Georgia (one class of stock) and which has a large amount of earnings and profits, has a successful line of business. It also holds a variety of investment assets that are both irrelevant to the business and doing poorly. Medford, Inc., wants to acquire Ashland's business line and prefers to acquire the Ashland stock rather than simply to acquire the assets of the business in order to safeguard the business' going concern value.

Medford, Ashland and Georgia agree that Ashland will first redeem 27% of Georgia's stock, which leads to the distribution of the unwanted investment assets to her. Then Georgia will sell Medford the remaining 73% of the Ashland stock (which represents the business portion of Ashland's assets). Will the redemption of Georgia's stock be entitled to "sale or exchange" treatment under § 302(a)?

ANSWER:

15. Which of the following is true?

A. Stock received for services is never considered received for property and never counts for control purposes.

B. Section 351 is not directly relevant to persons who receive stock solely in consideration for cash.

C. A transferor can always avoid gain recognition when the aggregate basis of property contributed to the corporation is less than the aggregate liabilities encumbering such properties by contributing a personal note with a sufficient amount of principal. Assume § 357(b) does not apply.

D. Where a contributing shareholder gets multiple classes of stock, the shareholder's stock basis is allocated among the classes in proportion to the number of shares received.

16. Calendar-year Bainbridge Corp., currently a Subchapter C corporation, is considering an election under Subchapter S to be effective next January 1. Bainbridge has 143 shareholders, of whom 116 are members of the Roy family: Great-grandfather Roy and his children,

grandchildren, great-grandchildren and their spouses. The other 27 shareholders are unrelated corporate employees, all but one of whom are U.S. citizens or residents. One shareholder-employee is Bainbridge's representative in China and is a Chinese citizen.

All of the shareholders have outstanding loans to Bainbridge in amounts proportionate to their equity holdings. The IRS has successfully characterized these loans as equity and has disallowed interest deductions with respect to them.

Bainbridge had previously elected to be a Subchapter S corporation, effective on January 1, 1995, but that status ended in 2002 when Bainbridge revoked its S election effective January 1, 2002.

Bainbridge cannot make a Subchapter S election because:

A.  It has more than 100 shareholders.

B.  It has a nonresident alien shareholder.

C.  It has a second class of stock.

D.  It too recently in the past had a Subchapter S election in place.

17.

A.  Does Chan have a realized gain? If so, how much.

B.  Determine the tax consequences to Chan if X is a general partnership.

C.  Determine the tax consequences to Chan if X is a C corporation with only one class of stock.

D.  Redetermine the tax consequences to Chan in "C" assuming Chan received an 85% interest in X, which is a C corporation.

BASIC FACTS FOR THE FOLLOWING FOUR QUESTIONS:

Business entity X has three current owners. A fourth, Chan, is to be admitted as a new 20% equity holder. He will transfer a parcel of raw land worth $70,000 (basis $10,000) to X in exchange for the 20% interest. Chan acquired the raw land four years ago.

17A.  Does Chan have a realized gain? If so, how much.

ANSWER:


17B.  Determine the tax consequences to Chan if X is a general partnership.

ANSWER:


17C.  Determine the tax consequences to Chan if X is a C corporation with only one class of stock.

ANSWER:

**17D** Determine the tax consequences to Chan if X is a C corporation with only one class of stock and Chan receives an 85% interest in X.

ANSWER:

BASIC FACTS FOR THE FOLLOWING THREE QUESTIONS:

The 100 shares of outstanding common stock (only class) of Nesnong, Ltd. is owned by the following two unrelated individuals: Louise 80 shares and Dick 20 shares. Louise redeems half of her stock.

**18A.** Why does Louise not satisfy, in the opinion of the IRS (not necessarily the courts), the test for sale or exchange treatment under § 302(b)(1)?

ANSWER:

**18B.** Why does Louise not satisfy the test for sale or exchange treatment under § 302(b)(2)?

ANSWER:

**18C.** Why does Louise not satisfy the test for sale or exchange treatment under § 302(b)(3)?

ANSWER:

19.     Which of the following is false?

    A.  Dan Clements, a 40% (by value) shareholder of Ryan Corp., constructively owns 40% of any stock actually owned by Ryan.

    B.  Mike Hinder, a 40% partner in Auburn Partners, constructively owns 40% of any stock actually owned by Auburn.

    C.  All of the stock actually owned by Lewis Messer, who has a 70% actuarial interest in the Bainbridge Trust, is constructively owned by Bainbridge.

    D.  Stock constructively owned by a person under § 318 is considered actually owned by that person.

20.     Which of the following is false?

    A.  A Subchapter S shareholder must treat the corporation's tax items allocated to it on the Schedule K-1 consistently with the treatment accorded such items by the corporation.

    B.  A distribution by an S corporation which has never been a C corporation (and which has never been involved in a merger that included a C corporation) to one of its shareholders might be characterized as a dividend under § 301(c)(1).

C. A sole shareholder who creates a new corporation, causes the corporation to elect Subchapter S status, and then transfers her sole proprietorship assets to the corporation will determine the tax consequences of her capital contributions under § 351.

D. An S corporation shareholder would increase its stock basis by its share of the corporation's exempt income and reduce its stock basis by its share of the corporation's nondeductible meals.

21. Potsdam Enterprises, Inc. distributes cash to its shareholders with respect to their stock. Which of the following is false?

A. Potsdam will recognize no gain or loss on the distribution.

B. The individual shareholders of Potsdam will recognize dividend income to the extent their distributions are sourced from earnings and profits.

C. Potsdam's earnings and profits can be reduced below zero by the distribution.

D. A distribution by Potsdam to one of its corporate shareholders will likely increase that shareholder's taxable income by less than the amount of the distribution.

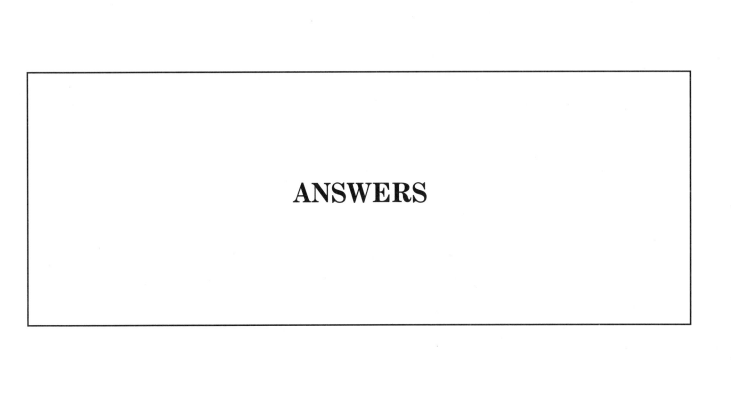

# ANSWERS

1.     **The best answer is "A."** Cori's realized loss is:

| | | |
|---|---|---|
| Amount realized | $1,000,000 | § 1001(b) |
| Adjusted basis | (1,300,000) | § 1011(a); § 1012(a) |
| Realized loss | ($300,000) | § 1001(a) |

However, she will recognize no loss because Cori and Corporation are related persons. § 267(a)(1), (b)(2). Three years later, Corporation's realized gain is:

| | |
|---|---|
| Amount realized | $1,400,000 |
| Adjusted basis | (1,000,000) |
| Realized gain | $400,000 |

But Corporation's recognized gain will be reduced by Cori's unrecognized loss. § 267(d). Corporation will therefore recognize a gain of $100,000 ($400,000 - $300,000).

**Answer "D" is correct, but it is not the best answer** because it only addresses Cori and Corporation's realized gains and losses, not the recognized gains and losses that will result.

**Answer "B" is incorrect** because it ignores the impact of § 267 on both transactions. **Answer "C" is incorrect** because it applies the rules of § 267(a)(1) and (b)(2) to the first transaction when Cori sells the property to Corporation, but fails to apply § 267(d) when Corporation sells the property to an independent party three years later.

2.     **The best answer is "A."** Gwen's recognized gain is:

| | | |
|---|---|---|
| Amount realized | $300,000 | § 1001(b) |
| Adjusted basis | (0) | § 1011(a); § 1012(a); § 1016(a)(2) |
| Realized gain | $300,000 | § 1001(a) |
| All recognized | | § 1001(c) |

Because Gwen and Marcus are related, all of this gain is ordinary. The first $250,000 of gain is ordinary under § 1245; the remaining gain is also ordinary. § 1239(a)-(b)(1), (c)(1)(A). The purpose of § 1239 is to preclude related parties from selling a depreciable asset under circumstances where the seller enjoys a long-term capital gain or a § 1231 gain while stepping up the asset's basis to the related party for depreciation purposes (which will yield ordinary deductions).

**Answer "B" is incorrect.** Had Gwen and Marcus not been related, this would have been the correct answer. To the extent that the gain on personalty is simply the recapture of depreciation deductions previously taken, the gain is ordinary under § 1245. The ordinary gain offsets the ordinary character of the depreciation deductions. The remaining gain is

§ 1231 gain since the personalty was used in Gwen's business.

**Answer "C" is incorrect** because it fails to take § 1239 into account. Even if § 1231 governed, the § 1245 ordinary gain was ignored.

**Answer "D" is incorrect** because it fails to take § 1239 into account. The § 1245 ordinary gain was ignored. Further, the property is not a capital asset. § 1221(a)(2). Thus there could not have been a long-term capital gain. § 1222(3).

3.   **The best answer is "C."** Uncompensated worthlessness sustained during the taxable year is sufficient to support a loss deduction. § 165(a). The stock was a capital asset. § 1221(a). To have a capital loss there must be a sale or exchange. § 1222(2), (4). However, worthlessness is not a sale or exchange, so there can be no *capital* loss. As a result, the loss would be ordinary but for the fact that § 165(g) creates a constructive sale or exchange. § 165(g)(1)-(2)(A). Thus, William has a capital loss, which is long-term because the constructive sale or exchange is deemed to occur on the last day of the loss year. § 165(g)(1).

**Answer "A" is incorrect** because it ignores the constructive sale or exchange created by § 165(g). *Id.* **Answer "B" is incorrect** because an actual disposition is not required to take a loss deduction under § 165(a). **Answer "D" is also incorrect.** The capital loss is long-term because of the end-of-year timing of the deemed constructive sale or exchange. § 165(g)(1).

4.   **The best answer is "B."** Section 1244 converts up to $50,000 ($100,000 on a joint return) of capital loss into ordinary loss. § 1244(a), (b). But even if all of the statutory requirements are met (discussed in conjunction with answer "C" below), those seeking to enjoy the benefits of § 1244 must come within the congressional purpose for enacting the provision. That purpose was to encourage investment in small business — to give it the ability to carry on business; it was not intended to provide ordinary loss deductions for those bailing out insolvent corporations that had ceased doing business.

Helping her daughter by bailing out the defunct corporation was Maria's objective. Therefore, § 1244 relief will be disallowed and Maria will have a $225,000 short-term capital loss. *Hill*, 51 T.C. 621 (1969). Note: the IRS might assert that, in substance, the $225,000 was really a gift, not a stock purchase, and disallow the loss altogether.

**Answer "A" is a correct statement and, therefore, not the right answer.** Because Elizabeth's stock is § 1244 stock, she will be able to convert $50,000 of her $200,000 long-term capital loss into ordinary loss.

**Answer "C" is a correct statement and, therefore, not the right answer.** To be § 1244 stock the statute requires that: 1) the corporation be domestic; 2) the stock be issued for money or property; 3) during its most recent five years (or the corporation's period of existence if less than five years), at least 50% of the corporation's gross receipts are non-passive (e.g., not royalties, rents, dividends); 4) at the time the stock was issued the corporation's total capitalization did not exceed $1,000,000 (measured using the corporate assets' bases, not values); and 5) the shareholder claiming the loss was the shareholder to whom the stock was originally issued. § 1244(a), (c)(1)–(2)(A)(i), (c)(3)(A). The stock issued to Elizabeth and Maria satisfies all of these conditions. As explained above, Maria cannot take advantage of § 1244 because she does not come within the class of persons intended to benefit from the provision, despite the fact that she meets all of the literal requirements.

**Answer "D" is a correct statement and, therefore, not the right answer.** Section 1244 applies equally to Subchapter C and Subchapter S corporations. § 1371(a).

5.  In *Moline Properties, Inc. v. Comm'r*, 319 U.S. 436 (1943), an individual organized a corporation to be used as a security device in connection with real estate owned by him. After transferring the real estate to the corporation, the individual transferred all of the stock to a voting trustee. The stock was held as security for a loan to pay back taxes on the realty. The corporation maintained no books or checking accounts but sold and leased several parcels of the real estate. The individual reported all of the income with respect to the property on his personal tax return, asserting that the corporation should be disregarded as the taxpayer. The Supreme Court said, "The doctrine of corporate entity fills a useful purpose in business life. [S]o long as that purpose is the equivalent of business activity or is followed by the carrying on of business by the corporation, the corporation remains a separate taxable entity. . . . The choice of the advantages of incorporation to do business . . . required the acceptance of the tax disadvantages." Referencing the corporation's property dispositions and leasing, the Court held: "The facts . . . compel the conclusion that the [corporation] had a tax identity distinct from its stockholder" and is therefore the taxpayer with respect to the income from the realty.

Determining the quantum of activity that precludes a corporation from being disregarded as a taxpayer was the issue in *Paymer v. Comm'r*, 150 F.2d 332 (2d Cir. 1945). There an individual used two corporations, Raymep and Westrich, in an attempt to put several parcels of realty beyond his creditors' reach. Neither corporation maintained records, opened a bank account, or adhered to corporate formalities other than for the initial organizational meeting. All income was collected and all expenses were paid by the individual. Westrich engaged in no activity other than holding title. The same was true of Raymep except that it obtained a loan secured by its realty. The Second Circuit held, under *Moline Properties* principles, that Westrich should be disregarded as a taxpayer, but that Raymep had engaged in sufficient business activity to preclude its being disregarded.

Since Corinth engaged in no business activity other than holding title, it will be disregarded as a taxpayer. However, since Sylvar obtained a loan secured by the property, it will not be disregarded as a taxpayer.

6.  **The best answer is "C."** Eastmark is Kristin's agent and is therefore not the taxpayer with respect to the net rentals relayed to Kristin. The Supreme Court held in *National Carbide Corp. v. Comm'r*, 336 U.S. 422 (1949), that a corporation could be the agent for its controlling shareholder. It set forth six factors required to find such agency: "1) Whether the corporation operates in the name and for the account of the principal, 2) binds the principal by its actions, 3) transmits money received to the principal, . . . 4) whether receipt of income is attributable to the services of employees of the principal and to assets belonging to the principal[,] 5) [the corporation's agency] relations with its principal must not be dependent upon the fact that it is owned by the principal, [and] 6) [i]ts business purpose

must be the carrying on of the normal duties of an agent."

The ambiguous fifth factor was considered in *Comm'r v. Bollinger*, 485 U.S. 340 (1988), in which the Supreme Court held that a corporation satisfies this factor if: "the fact that the corporation is acting as agent for its shareholders with respect to a particular asset is set forth in a written agreement at the time the asset is acquired, the corporation functions as agent and not principal with respect to the asset for all purposes, and the corporation is held out as the agent and not principal in all dealings with third parties relating to the asset." This condition is satisfied here.

Since all six *National Carbide* factors are satisfied, Eastmark is Kristin's agent with respect to the realty. Eastmark cannot be disregarded as the taxpayer, however, with respect to its management fee. Under *Moline Properties, Inc. v. Comm'r*, 319 U.S. 436 (1943), a corporation cannot be disregarded as the taxpayer if it engages in business activity. Serving as Kristin's agent constitutes such business activity. Thus, **answer "A" is incorrect.**

**Answer "B" is incorrect.** Since Eastmark satisfies all of the *National Carbide* factors and is therefore considered Kristin's agent, Eastmark is not the taxpayer with respect to the net rentals remitted to Kristin.

**Answer "D" is incorrect.** A distribution from a corporation to a shareholder can be a dividend for tax purposes only if the distribution is made with respect to the shareholder's stock. § 301(a), (c)(1); § 1.301-1(c). Here the distribution is made to Kristin in her capacity as principal, not in her capacity as shareholder.

7. **The best answer is "D."** Any business entity that is not a "corporation" can elect "association" status. § 301.7701-3(a). "Corporation" includes any foreign business entity the legal characteristics of which are, in substance, equivalent to a U.S. corporation. § 301.7701-2(b)(8)(i). All other foreign business entities, however, are eligible to elect "association" status.

   **Answer "A" is a correct statement and, therefore, not the right answer.** In *Morrissey v. Comm'r*, 296 U.S. 344 (1935), the Supreme Court defined an "association" as "a body of persons organized, for the prosecution of some purpose, without a charter, but having the general form and mode of procedure of a corporation."

   **Answer "B" is a correct statement and, therefore, not the right answer.** Section 7701(a)(3) defines "corporation" to include "association." Therefore, associations are taxed like corporations.

   **Answer "C" is a correct statement and, therefore, not the right answer.** As noted above, an association is taxed like a corporation. Corporations may (if they meet the requirements) elect to be taxed under Subchapter S. § 1362(a)(1). Subchapter S corporations are pass-through entities. § 1363(a).

8. **The best answer is "C."** Associations are taxed like corporations. § 7701(a)(3). Assuming a corporation does not elect under Subchapter S, an employer-employee relationship can exist between it and some or all of its shareholders, thereby making available a variety of tax-free fringe benefits.

   **Answer "A" is incorrect.** LLCs are not treated as associations unless they elect that status. § 301.7701-3(b)(1).

   **Answer "B" is incorrect.** A single-member LLC is, by default, "[d]isregarded as an entity separate from its owner." § 301.7701-3(b)(1)(ii). In such a situation, the LLC's tax items would be reported as a sole proprietorship on Schedule C if its owner is an individual.

   **Answer "D" is incorrect.** The general rule is that a business entity may not re-elect association status for five years after surrendering that status. The IRS can waive that requirement if more than 50% of the ownership interests become held by new members. § 301.7701-3(c)(1)(iv).

9. **The best answer is "A."** If an unincorporated business entity with two or more equity holders fails to elect "association" status, the entity is treated as a partnership, not as a disregarded entity. § 301.7701-3(b)(1)(i).

   **Answer "B" is a correct statement and, therefore, not the right answer.** A domestic corporation (a.k.a., a "per se" corporation) is not an eligible entity and therefore cannot elect "association" status. § 301.7701-3(a).

**Answer "C" is a correct statement and, therefore, not the right answer** because § 301.7701-2(b)(8)(i) contains such a list.

**Answer "D" is a correct statement and, therefore, not the right answer.** The filing of a Subchapter S election results in a deemed election to be an association. § 301.7701-3(c)(1)(v)(C).

10. The marginal tax rate is the percentage of the next dollar of taxable income that will be owed in tax. The average tax rate is the percentage of the taxpayer's taxable income that is owed in tax.

11. The average tax rate is computed as follows: Tax liability ÷ Taxable income. For Nottoway this is: 32.3% = $80,750 ÷ Taxable income. Algebraically, Nottoway's taxable income is $250,000 ($80,750 ÷ 32.3%).

12. **The best answer is "C."** Section 11(b)(1) contains the corporate income tax rate structure. The tax consists of two components. First, there is a tax determined using the four rates in subparagraphs (A) through (D) (i.e., 15%, 25%, 34% and 35%). Second, there are two surtaxes contained in the flush language. A 5% surtax is imposed on taxable income between $100,000 and $335,000. A 3% surtax is imposed on taxable income between $15,000,000 and $18,333,333. The 5% surtax recaptures the benefits of the sub-34% tax rate once taxable income reaches $100,000. The total benefit of the sub-34% rate is $11,700. The 3% surtax recaptures the tax benefits of the sub-35% tax rate once taxable income reaches $15,000,000. The total benefit of the sub-34% tax rate (after the prior application of the 5% surcharge) is $100,000. The computation for Gregg is:

| | | | |
|---|---|---|---|
| 50,000 x 15% | | $7,500 | |
| 25,000 x 25% | | 6,250 | |
| (300,000 - 75,000) x 34% | | 76,500 | $90,250 |
| LESSER: | 11,750, or | | |
| (5% surtax) | (300,000 - 100,000) x 5% | | 10,000 |
| | | | $100,250 |

**Answer "A" is incorrect** because it does not include the $10,000 surtax.

**Answer "B" is incorrect.** This answer comes from multiplying the $300,000 taxable income by the 34% marginal tax rate.

**Answer "D" is incorrect** because the determination of federal taxable income already takes state income taxes into account.

13. Bedford's net long-term capital gain is $1,000,000 - $600,000 = $400,000. § 1222(7). Its net short-term capital loss is $100,000 - $150,000 - $75,000 = ($125,000). § 1222(6). Therefore Bedford has a net capital gain of $400,000 - $125,000 = $275,000. § 1222(11).

14. Bedford has a taxable income of $5,000,000 + $275,000 = $5,275,000.

15. Corporations do not receive a preferential tax rate on net capital gains. Section 1201 merely precludes a tax rate on corporate net capital gains in excess of 35%, which is the current

maximum corporate tax rate under § 11(b). The two corporate surtaxes of 5% (on taxable income between $100,000 and $335,000) and 3% (on taxable income between $15,000,000 and $18,333,333) are not considered for these purposes even though they result in effective marginal tax rates of 39% (34% + 5%) and 38% (35% + 3%) on the income within those ranges. § 1201(a).

16.    An income tax is imposed on corporate taxable income by § 11(a). Section 11(b) taxes corporate income at rates up to 35%. When the corporation distributes its income as a dividend, the receiving shareholders have gross income in the amount of the dividend. § 61(a)(7). Thus, corporate income is taxed both at the corporate level and at the shareholder level. This is the double-taxation regime.

17.    Corporate shareholders generally enjoy a 70%, 80% or 100% dividends-received deduction under § 243. Thus, only 30%, 20% or 0%, respectively, of the dividends distributed to them are taxed. Note, however, that when the income of the corporate shareholder (which includes the dividends received) is later distributed, its shareholders will have gross income, bringing about the possibility of triple-taxation (or worse depending on the number of corporations in the distribution chain, albeit similarly mitigated by their own dividends-received deduction).

18.    **The best answer is "C."** The bribes are disallowed under § 162(c)(2), as are half of the meals and entertainment under § 274(n)(1).

       **Answer "A" is incorrect** because the bribes and all of the meals and entertainment were deducted.

       **Answer "B" is incorrect** because, while the bribes were properly not deducted, all of the meals and entertainment were deducted.

       **Answer "D" is incorrect** because, while the bribes were properly not deducted, none of the meals and entertainment were deducted.

19.    **The best answer is "B."** Penalties are disallowed as deductions. § 162(f). Only a half-year of depreciation, $28,800 ($57,600 ÷ 2), is allowed in the year disposition. § 168(d)(4)(A). Therefore, Cooke's taxable income is $421,200 ($450,000 - $28,800).

       **Answer "A" is incorrect** because the penalty and all of the depreciation were both taken as deductions.

       **Answer "C" is incorrect** because all of the depreciation was improperly deducted.

       **Answer "D" is incorrect** because no depreciation was deducted.

20.    **The best answer is "C."** A corporation can deduct charitable contributions made during a taxable year up to 10% of its taxable income before the charitable contribution (and other items not relevant here). § 170(a)(1), (b)(2)(A), (b)(2)(C). If its current charitable contribution is less than this maximum it can use its charitable contribution carryforwards to fill the shortfall. § 170(d)(2)(A). If the board of directors of an accrual-method corporation authorizes a contribution during the taxable year, payments made through the 15th day of the third month following the close of the taxable year are treated as though made during the taxable year. § 170(a)(2).

       Craig's maximum charitable contribution is $100,000 (10% x $1,000,000). The $20,000 contribution made on March 1 of the following year is treated as paid during the current taxable year. Consequently the current charitable contribution is $50,000 ($30,000 + $20,000). Since this is less than the $100,000 maximum deduction, the $45,000 charitable contribution carryforward may be used. Therefore the current year's deduction is $95,000 ($50,000 + $45,000).

**Answer "A" is incorrect.** It improperly includes the $60,000 paid on May 2 of the following year. It also improperly exceeds the $100,000 maximum charitable deduction allowable.

**Answer "B" is incorrect.** It treats the maximum charitable contribution as the deduction without regard to the timing of the actual payments or the availability of the carryforward.

**Answer "D" is incorrect** because it ignores the $20,000 payment made on March 1 of the following year.

21. **The best answer is "A."** A corporation can deduct charitable contributions made during a taxable year up to 10% of its taxable income. § 170(a)(1), (b)(2)(A). For these purposes taxable income is defined as taxable income without, among other things, the charitable contribution itself or any net operating loss carryback. § 170(b)(2)(C). Here this amount is $700,000 ($1,000,000 - $300,000). Thus, York's maximum deduction is $70,000 (10% x ($1,000,000 - $300,000)), which is less than its current charitable contribution of $200,000. York's taxable income is:

| | |
|---|---|
| Gross income | $1,000,000 |
| Business expenses | (300,000) |
| Charitable deduction | (70,000) |
| Net operating loss carryback | (400,000) |
| | $230,000 |

**Answer "B" is incorrect.** It fails to exclude the net operating loss carryback in the computation of taxable income for purposes of determining the charitable contribution. It computed the maximum charitable contribution as: 10% x ($1,000,000 - $300,000 - $400,000) = $30,000 (versus the correct $70,000). For this reason its calculation of taxable income is $40,000 too high.

**Answer "C" is incorrect** because it fails to recognize that the charitable contribution is limited. It computed taxable income as:

| | |
|---|---|
| Gross income | $1,000,000 |
| Business expenses | (300,000) |
| Charitable deduction (entire amount) | (200,000) |
| Net operating loss carryback | (400,000) |
| | $100,000 |

**Answer "D" is incorrect** because it ignores the net operating loss carryback. Thus its taxable income computation is $400,000 too high.

22. **The best answer is "B."** Organizational expenditures are those which are: 1) incident to the creation of the corporation, 2) chargeable to capital, and 3) would be amortizable if the corporation had a limited life. § 248(b). Section 1.248-1(b)(2) provides examples of costs that are organizational expenditures; § 1.248-1(b)(3) provides examples of costs that are not organizational expenditures. The first six items in the table are listed in the former, the last

two are listed in the latter. Therefore, the total amount eligible for deduction under § 248 is $17,100 ($21,000 - $1,500 - $2,400).

**Answer "A" is incorrect** because it includes the last two items.

**Answer "C" is incorrect** because it fails to exclude the stock issuance costs.

**Answer "D" is incorrect.** It improperly includes the last two items and also improperly excludes the accounting fees.

23.  **The best answer is "D."** Organizational expenditures are deductible at the election of the corporation. § 248(a). The "bonus" deduction in the first year is $5,000 - ($53,300 - $50,000) = $1,700. § 248(a)(1). The remaining $51,600 ($53,300 - $1,700) is amortized over 180 months, for a (rounded) monthly amount of $287 ($51,600 ÷ 180). Expensing begins in the month during which business began (August). Therefore, Bandera has a total § 248 deduction of $1,700 (bonus amount) +(5 x $287) (monthly amount) = $3,135.

**Answer "A" is incorrect** because it expenses only the bonus amount.

**Answer "B" is incorrect.** This is a "red herring" answer in that it treats none of these costs as deductible, completely ignoring the existence of § 248.

**Answer "C" is incorrect** because it expenses the entire amount.

24.  **The best answer is "C."** Dividends received by a domestic corporation from a "qualified 10-percent owned foreign corporation" are eligible for a dividends-received deduction using the 70% and 80% rates found in § 243(a). § 245(a)(1). A qualified 10-percent owned foreign corporation is one in which the domestic corporation owns at least 10% of the stock (by vote and value). § 245(a)(2). This condition is satisfied here.

The dividends-received deduction is limited to the U.S.-source portion of the dividend. This is, in essence, the portion of the dividend that was subject to U.S. taxation. § 245(a)(3)-(5). Therefore $75,000 (75% x $100,000) of the dividend is eligible for a dividends-received deduction. Since Titus owns 60% of Hood, the deduction rate is 80%. § 243(a)(1), (c). Titus' dividends-received deduction is $60,000 (80% x $75,000).

**Answer "A" is incorrect.** It correctly uses the 80% dividends-received deduction rate, but applied it to all of the dividend.

**Answer "B" is incorrect.** It incorrectly uses the 70% dividends-received deduction rate and applied it to all of the dividend.

**Answer "D" is incorrect.** It allows Titus no dividends-received deduction, presumably because of its foreign status.

25.  A corporation gets no dividends-received deduction with respect to stock held less than 46 days during the 91-day period beginning on the date 45 days before the stock goes ex-dividend. § 246(c)(1)(A). The day of disposition, but not the day of acquisition, is included in the holding period. § 246(c)(3)(A).

Given an ex-dividend date of Monday, October 31, the above rules give a 91-day period that runs from Friday, September 16 to Thursday, December 15. Carson excludes the date of acquisition (September 20) but includes the day of disposition (November 3). Carson's holding period was therefore 44 days (ten days in September, 31 days in October, three days in November), which is less than the minimum holding period required of 46 days. Therefore

Carson gets no dividends-received deduction with respect to the Salem dividend.

26. **The best answer is "D."** In the case of debt-financed portfolio stock the dividends-received deduction is reduced by the average indebtedness percentage. § 246A(a). All stock is portfolio stock unless the taxpayer owns at least 50% (by vote and value) or unless five or fewer corporate shareholders each own at least 20% (by vote and value). § 246A(c)(2). Neither of these conditions apply, so this is portfolio stock.

Portfolio stock is debt-financed if the taxpayer incurred any indebtedness directly attributable to its investment in such stock. § 246A(d)(3)(A). Therefore this is debt-financed portfolio stock. § 246A(c)(1).

The average indebtedness percentage is 80%. As a result Cameron's dividends-received deduction is reduced by 80% (i.e., Cameron gets only 20% of the regular dividends-received deduction). Cameron's dividends-received deduction would ordinarily be $25,600 (80% x $32,000). § 243(a)(1), (c). With the reduction, the tentative dividends-received deduction is $5,120 ($25,600 x 20%). The reduction in the dividends-received deduction cannot exceed the interest expense allocable to the debt used to find the portfolio stock. § 246A(e). The reduction is $20,480 ($25,600 + $5,120), which is less than the interest of $60,480 ($630,000 x 80% x 12%). Therefore, the dividends-received deduction is $5,120.

**Answer "A" is incorrect** because the 80% deduction rate was applied to the full dividend.

**Answer "B" is incorrect** because the 70% deduction rate was improperly applied to the full dividend.

**Answer "C" is incorrect.** Although the dividends-received deduction was reduced by 80%, the 70% deduction rate was improperly used.

27. **The best answer is "B."** An extraordinary dividend occurs when a corporation receives a dividend in excess of 10% of the amount it paid for the stock. § 1059(c)(1),(2). Page received a $150,000 dividend, which is over 13% of the cost of the Johnson stock. Therefore, this is an extraordinary dividend. Because Page received an extraordinary dividend and did not hold the Johnson stock at least two years prior to the dividend announcement, it must reduce its basis in the Johnson stock by its dividends-received deduction. § 1059(a), (b).

Page's dividends-received deduction is $105,000 (70% x $150,000). § 243(a)(1). Therefore Page's basis in the Johnson stock is $1,045,000 ($1,150,000 - $105,000).

Upon the disposition of the Johnson stock, Page has a short-term capital loss of $45,000 ($1,000,000 - $1,045,000). § 1222(2). Its net short-term capital gain is $155,000 ($200,000 - $45,000). § 1222(6). Page's taxable income is $450,000 ($250,000 (ordinary income) + $150,000 (dividend) - $105,000 (dividends-received deduction) + $155,000 (net short-term capital gain)).

Had Page not purchased the Johnson stock, its taxable income would also have been $450,000 ($250,000 (ordinary income) +$200,000 (short-term capital gain)). Thus, the purchase of the Johnson stock failed to reduce Page's taxable income and **answer "A" is incorrect.**

**Answer "C" is incorrect.** Page's net short-term capital gain is $155,000 because the extraordinary dividend provision reduces the basis in the Johnson stock.

**Answer "D" is incorrect.** Page held the stock for at least 50 days, which exceeds the 46-day minimum provided by § 246(c)(1)(A). Therefore Page's transitory holding period does not disallow a dividends-received deduction.

28.     **The best answer is "B."** One of the principal justifications for imposing the alternative minimum tax was to require the present taxation of persons with substantial economic income who, through various tax preferences, reported little taxable income. The adjusted current earnings adjustment used to be based on the difference between reported financial accounting income and taxable income. It has been replaced with a measure related to earnings and profits, which is also a proxy for economic income. § 56(g).

**Answer "A" is incorrect.** The minimum tax credit arises when there are temporary differences between the regular tax and the alternative minimum tax, such as differences associated with the timing of depreciation deductions. Although regular tax and alternative minimum tax depreciation deductions can differ during any given taxable year, in the long run, the total depreciation deductions under both tax systems will be the same. No credit will arise from the example given because it is not a timing difference but rather a permanent difference that will never reverse.

**Answer "C" is incorrect.** The gross receipts test is based on a maximum average of $7,500,000 ($5,000,000 during a corporation's first three years of existence). § 55(e)(1).

**Answer "D" is incorrect.** The exemption amount is phased out once the corporation's alternative minimum taxable income exceeds $150,000. § 55(d)(2), (3)(A). Therefore, not all corporations get a $40,000 exemption amount.

29.     **The best answer is "D."** Section 56(a)(1)(A)(ii) limits depreciation on tangible property to 150% declining balance as defined in § 168(b)(2).

**Answer "A" is incorrect.** The corporate alternative minimum tax rate is 20%. § 55(b)(1)(B)(i).

**Answer "B" is incorrect.** Alternative minimum tax preferences are always positive adjustments, increasing the alternative minimum tax base.

**Answer "C" is incorrect.** S corporations are not subject to any of the taxes in Chapter 1 of Subtitle A of the Internal Revenue Code, which includes the alternative minimum tax. § 1363(a).

30.    **The best answer is "D."** The taxable year specified on the first filed return establishes the taxable year (unless found to be in contravention of a specialized rule affecting taxable year selection). § 1.441-1(c)(1).

**Answer "A" is incorrect.** Section 441(d) defines a calendar year as a 12-month period ending on December 31. Section 441(e) defines a fiscal year as a 12-month period ending on the last day of any other month. The taxpayer has a calendar year in this example.

**Answer "B" is incorrect.** A taxpayer must obtain the IRS' consent before it can change its taxable year. § 442.

**Answer "C" is incorrect.** The taxpayer has an annual accounting period (§ 441(c)), but that annual accounting period does not qualify as a taxable year because it is neither a fiscal year nor a calendar year. § 441(b)(1). In such cases the taxpayer is required to use the calendar year. § 441(g)(3).

31.    **The best answer is "B."** A taxpayer must always secure the IRS' consent before changing its method of accounting. § 446(e). In certain situations, such as a change from straight-line to units-of-production depreciation, the IRS may consent in advance. Rev. Proc. 2008-52, 2008-36 I.R.B. 587.

**Answer "A" is a correct statement and, therefore, not the right answer.** A taxpayer for whom the sale of inventory is an income-producing factor must generally use the accrual method of accounting (at least through the determination of gross profit). § 1.446-1(a)(4)(i). A limited exception, which allows the taxpayer to use the cash method of accounting, is available for taxpayers (other than tax shelters) with average annual gross receipts of no more than $1 million. Such taxpayers can account for inventory as though it were incidental supplies under § 1.162-3. Rev. Proc. 2001-10, 2001-1 C.B. 272.

**Answer "C" is a correct statement and, therefore, not the right answer.** The cash and accrual methods of accounting are the principal methods used for tax purposes. § 446(c)(1), (2). They are called the "overall" methods. § 1.446-1(a)(1).

**Answer "D" is a correct statement and, therefore, not the right answer.** Taxpayers with more than one business may use different methods of accounting for each. § 446(d). However, a complete and separate set of books and records must be maintained for each business. § 1.446-1(d)(2).

32.    **The best answer is "B."** No method of accounting may be used if it does not clearly reflect the taxpayer's income. § 446(b). If the IRS determines that the taxpayer's method fails this test, it may impose any method of accounting it believes does clearly reflect the taxpayer's income.

**Answer "A" is incorrect.** The general rule is that no Subchapter C corporation may use the cash method of accounting. § 448(a)(1). There is one principal exception: the cash method may be used if the corporation's gross receipts for all prior years (based on a three-year moving average) are $5,000,000 or less. § 448(b)(3), (c)(1).

**Answer "C" is incorrect.** The term method of accounting includes both the overall methods (e.g., cash and accrual) and the specific accounting treatments required for any item. Such specific treatments include depreciation, the installment method, research and development expensing and net operating losses. § 1.446-1(a)(1).

**Answer "D" is incorrect.** A taxpayer who discovers that an item of gross income should have been included in a prior taxable year is required, if the statute of limitations for the correct taxable year has not yet run, to amend the return for the correct year to include the omitted gross income. § 1.451-1(a). As a general rule the statute of limitations runs three years after the return is filed. § 6501(a). Since Year 3 is within this period with respect to Year 1, an amended return must be filed.

33. Under the cash method of accounting gross income is recognized when received in cash (or cash equivalent, or through the receipt of property or services with a cash value). § 451(a); § 1.451-1(a). Expenses are recognized when paid in cash (or in property with a cash value). § 1.461-1(a)(1). However, costs must be capitalized rather than expensed if they benefit more than the current taxable year. § 1.441-1(a)(4)(ii). For example, the cost of a delivery truck must be capitalized as an asset, its cost allocated across the taxable years benefited (presumed to be the truck's recovery period) through annual depreciation deductions. This rule also applies to accrual-method taxpayers.

Hartley's taxable income under the cash method is:

| Income: | Current year's cash sales | $3,000,000 | |
|---|---|---|---|
| | Collections on current year's credit sales | 3,300,000 | |
| | Collections on prior year's credit sales | 800,000 | $7,100,000 |
| Expenses: | Current year's cash expenses | $200,000 | |
| | Payments on current year's expenses on credit | 4,100,000 | |
| | Payments on prior year's expenses on credit | 400,000 | (4,700,000) |
| | | | $2,400,000 |

34. Under the accrual method of accounting an item of gross income is recognized when all of the events have occurred that fix the right to receive the income and the amount is reasonably estimable. § 1.451-1(a). The all-events test is deemed to be satisfied at the earliest of the time: 1) the income is earned, 2) the income is received, or 3) the payment of the income is due. Rev. Rul. 74-607, 1974-2 C.B. 149. There are limited exceptions for pre-paid income for services and goods. See § 1.451-5 and Rev. Proc. 71-21.

An item of expense is recognized when all of the events have occurred that establish the fact that a liability has been incurred with respect to the expense, the amount is reasonably estimable, and economic performance has occurred. § 1.461-1(a)(2)(i). The facts state that the economic performance test is satisfied for all of the expenses given.

Hartley's taxable income under the accrual method is:

| | | | |
|---|---|---|---|
| Gross income: | Current cash sales | $3,000,000 | |
| | Current credit sales | 4,000,000 | $7,000,000 |
| | | | |
| Expenses: | Current cash expenses | 200,000 | |
| | Current expenses on credit | $4,700,000 | (4,900,000) |
| | | | $2,100,000 |

35. **The best answer is "C."** The IRS may grant an extension of the due date for filing a return for up to six months. § 6081(a). The grant of a six-month extension is automatic. § 1.6081-3(a). However, extending the due date of the return does not automatically extend the due date for payment. § 1.6081-3(b).

**Answer "A" is a correct statement and, therefore, not the right answer.** The due date for a corporate tax return is the 15th day of the third month following the close of the taxable year. § 6072(b). If the due date falls on a weekend or holiday, it is extended to the next business day. § 7503.

**Answer "B" is a correct statement and, therefore, not the right answer.** An extension of the time for making a tax payment requires a showing of undue financial hardship. Such hardship means more than mere inconvenience. The taxpayer must demonstrate that a substantial financial loss will result if timely tax payment is made; for example, if timely payment would require the sale of property at a sacrifice price. § 1.6161-1(b).

**Answer "D" is a correct statement and, therefore, not the right answer.** As noted above, a six-month extension is automatic. To receive the extension, the request must be filed by the due date of the return and the corporation must include a good-faith estimated payment of any tax due. § 1.6081-3(a).

36. **The best answer is "D."** Section 6511(a) allows a refund claim to be filed within three years of filing the return or, if later, within two years after making a tax payment. The two-year situation could arise, for example, if an additional tax deficiency is assessed and paid pursuant to an audit.

**Answer "A" is incorrect.** The statute of limitations on assessment is generally three years from the date the return was filed. § 6501(a).

**Answer "B" is incorrect.** The three-year rule above applies to late-filed nonfraudulent returns as well.

**Answer "C" is incorrect.** If a fraudulent return is filed, the statute of limitations never starts to run. § 6501(c)(1). An amended return does not have the legal status "tax return." There is no statutory provision for amended returns; the IRS has established the amended return program on its own initiative to facilitate the administration the tax laws. Since amended returns are not "tax returns," a nonfraudulent amended return does not remove the fraudulent taint of the original. Therefore, the statute of limitations never starts to run. *Badaracco v. Comm'r*, 464 U.S. 386 (1984).

37. **The best answer is "C."** A corporation is not subject to the estimated tax penalty if the tax shown on its return is less than $500. § 6655(f).

**Answer "A" is a correct statement and, therefore, not the right answer.** A corporation must make its estimated tax payments on the 15th day of the fourth, sixth, ninth and twelfth months of its taxable year. § 6655(c)(2), (i)(1).

**Answer "B" is a correct statement and, therefore, not the right answer.** As a general rule a corporation must make an estimated tax payment on each of the four installment dates of 25% of the required annual payment. § 6655(d)(1). Although the required annual payment is generally the lesser of 100% of the tax shown on the current year's return or 100% of the tax shown on the prior year's return (§ 6655(d)(1)(B)), the option to use the prior year's return is not available to large corporations. § 6655(d)(2)(A). A large corporation is one whose taxable income exceeded $1,000,000 in any of its three preceding taxable years. § 6655(g)(2)(A), (B)(i).

**Answer "D" is a correct statement and, therefore, not the right answer.** The estimated tax penalty is, in substance, an interest charge. It is determined by multiplying the following three quantities: 1) the underpayment interest rate under § 6621, 2) the amount of the underpayment, and 3) the period of the underpayment. § 6655(a).

38.   Smith was advised of the different tax consequences of "loan" and "capital contribution" characterization, and she selected the form of "loan." Briscoe booked the money as a "shareholder loan." All parties treated the $1,300,000 as repayment as "principal" not as a return of equity. Smith controls Briscoe and no independent third party is involved, which makes it hard to assert that her characterization satisfies the arm's-length standard.

39.   No formal loan documentation was created; the maturity and interest rate were unspecified.

40.   Mary will be unsuccessful disavowing the form. Taxpayers are generally "bound by the 'form' of their transaction and may not argue that the 'substance'. . . triggers different tax consequences." *Estate of Leavitt v. Comm'r*, 875 F.2d 420 (1989). The form of the transaction is "loan" as is the substance. *Estate of Hoffman v. Comm'r*, 8 Fed Appx 262 (4th Cir. 2001).

41.   The business purpose doctrine stands for the proposition that, where a transaction has no substantial business purpose but is simply a device to achieve tax avoidance, the tax law will disregard the transaction. *Gregory v. Helvering*, 293 U.S. 465 (1935). John's capital gain was achieved through the sale or exchange treatment afforded by § 331. Congress enacted § 331 to provide relief where a corporation ceases the conduct of business and distributes its assets which are no longer required for business activities. This was not John's purpose in undertaking the described transaction. Rather, the complete liquidation was simply a device through which John disguised a dividend distribution from Devonchire, simultaneously taking advantage of the circumstances to produce results in which no party had any taxable income from the disguised distribution. *Davant v. Comm'r*, 366 F.2d 874 (5th Cir. 1966).

42.   In the liquidation/reincorporation area, courts look at the beginning and ending points of the series of events and apply the substance-over-form doctrine. Jones is/was in control of both corporations, Boutique has continued Flowers' historical business uninterrupted, and the only difference is that Jones came into possession of $200,000 of liquid assets under circumstances that would normally give rise to dividend characterization. Therefore, in substance, there was no liquidation/reincorporation. The $200,000 in Patricia's hands will be characterized as a dividend.

43.   The binding-commitment test is the most rigorous and is applicable only where a substantial amount of time passes between the various transactional steps being undertaken in prime usually at least one year). Under it, steps separated by a significant amount of time are combined only if there is a legal duty to take each consecutive step.

      The end result test combines the individual steps taken when it appears that they are merely components of a plan in existence at the outset to achieve a particular final result. It emphasizes the taxpayer's subjective intent: did the taxpayer undertake all of the steps solely to achieve a specific ultimate objective.

The interdependence test focuses on whether "the steps are so interdependent that the legal relations created by one transaction would have been fruitless without a completion of the series." It is an objective test, asking whether each step had independent economic significance apart from facilitating the eventual achievement of a tax result. *Andantech, L.L.C. v. Comm'r*, 83 T.C.M. (CCH) 1476 (2002).

44.    The binding-commitment test does not apply because the entire transaction was completed within three months.

Under the end result test, the transaction was not a merger. The Mason shareholders made clear their desire for a cash transaction. Throckmorton intentionally facilitated this desire by offering stock that could be cashed out within three months. Both parties intended for substantially all of the Mason shareholders to terminate their equity interests from the outset.

The transaction was also not a merger under the interdependence test. The objective question is whether the merger step would have taken place without there being arrangements in place for the next step — the quick sale of the Throckmorton stock received by the Mason shareholders. The answer is likely no. *McDonald's Restaurants of Illinois, Inc. v. Comm'r*, 688 F.2d 520 (7th Cir. 1982).

45.    Under § 7701(o) a transaction has economic substance only if it: 1) meaningfully changes the taxpayer's economic position (apart from federal income tax effects), and 2) has a substantial business purpose (apart from federal income tax effects).

Measured at the beginning and the end of the two-day period during which the same $20,000,000 made two round trips between the corporations, there was no change in the economic position of either corporation except for the tax benefits to Hansford. No business purpose could plausibly be found for issuing and redeeming a class of stock on a single day. Therefore, the IRS' economic substance argument will prevail. *Intertan, Inc. v. Comm'r*, 87 T.C. M. (CCH) 767 (2004).

46.   Section 351 provides for full or partial nonrecognition of gain or loss when a person contributes property to a corporation in exchange for stock. Loss is never recognized. § 351(b)(2). If no boot is received, gain is generally not recognized. § 351(a). If boot is received the realized gain is recognized, but not in excess of the amount of boot received. § 351(b)(1). To be eligible for § 351, the contributor (or group of contributors — the "control group") must have control immediately after the contributions. Control is defined as stock possessing at least 80% of the voting power, as well as stock comprising at least 80% of the nonvoting shares. § 368(c). Neither the contribution of services, indebtedness of the corporation (unless evidenced by a security), nor interest thereon constitutes "property." § 351(d).

    Section 1001(c) states: "Except as otherwise provided . . . , the entire amount of the [realized] gain or loss . . . shall be recognized." Section 351(a) is one of those exceptions. § 1.1002-1(c).

47.   Deferral nonrecognition transactions like § 351 operate under a common, fundamental theory: "[Although] at the time of the exchange . . . differences exist between the property parted with and the property acquired, . . . such differences are [deemed] more formal than substantial. [T]he Code provides that such differences shall not be . . . controlling, and that gain or loss shall not be recognized at the time of the exchange. *The underlying assumption of these exceptions is that the new property is substantially a continuation of the old investment still unliquidated* [.]" § 1.1002-1(c) [emphasis added].

    The nonrecognized gain or loss is preserved through the basis mechanism. The basis in the stock received is determined first by including the bases in the assets contributed. Then any gain recognized increases the stock basis so that, when the stock is sold, that gain is not recognized a second time. Finally, that total amount of basis is allocated between any boot received (allocated its fair market value) and the stock received. §§ 358(a), 351(f). The result is a stock basis that, were the stock sold for its fair market value immediately after the § 351 transaction, the resulting recognized gain or loss would be exactly equal to the deferred gain or loss on the § 351 transaction.

48.   **The best answer is "B."** A corporation recognizes gain on the distribution of appreciated property with respect to its stock as part of a § 351 transaction. § 311(b)(1). The parcel is appreciated property since its value is $300,000 and its basis is $100,000.

    **Answer "A" is incorrect.** A corporation never recognizes gain or loss on the receipt of property in exchange for its stock. § 1032(a).

    **Answer "C" is incorrect.** This transaction qualifies for partial nonrecognition treatment because Zahlen owns 90% of the stock (i.e., he has control) immediately after the contribution. § 368(c). Nonrecognition is partial because Zahlen received boot ($200,000 in cash and land worth $300,000). § 351(a)-, (b)(1). Because § 351 applies, the corporation takes a basis in the contributed property equal to the transferor's basis plus any gain recognized by the transferor with respect to that property. § 362(a)(1). Where a person receives property in an exchange and that person's basis in the property is determined by reference to the basis of the transferor, such person's holding period in the property includes the transferor's holding period. § 1223(2). Therefore, Hillman's holding period in the tug is three years.

**Answer "D" is incorrect.** Assuming that the transaction reflects good faith, arms-length bargaining, the stock is worth $750,000 — the value of the tug ($1,250,000) less the value of the boot received ($200,000 in cash and land worth $300,000). In addition, a block of 90% of the stock would almost certainly carry a control premium reflecting the added value associated with being able to control virtually all corporate decisions, both routine operating decisions which require only a simple majority and certain decisions which impact the corporation's well-being and generally require a supramajority, such as mergers, amending the articles of incorporation, or selling substantially all of the business' assets.

49.   **The best answer is "C."** Although § 351(a) does not apply because Zahlen did not receive "solely" stock, § 351(b)(1) does apply, making this a partial nonrecognition transaction.

**Answer "A" is a correct statement and, therefore, not the right answer.** The definition of capital asset excludes real property used in business. § 1221(a)(2). Section 1231 governs such assets if they have a holding period in excess of one year. § 1231(b)(1). The land is used in Hillman's business and has a holding period of eight years. Therefore, it is a § 1231 asset.

**Answer "B" is a correct statement and, therefore, not the right answer.** Zahlen's realized gain is:

| Amount realized: | Stock | $750,000[fn] | |
|---|---|---|---|
| | Cash | 200,000 | |
| | Land | 300,000 | $1,250,000 |
| Adjusted basis | | | (650,000) |
| Realized gain | | | $600,000 |

[fn] *value of tug less value of boot received*

Under § 351(b)(1) the recognized gain is $500,000, the lesser of the realized gain ($600,000) or the value of the boot received ($500,000 — cash $200,000 and land $300,000). A taxpayer should never have to recognize more gain than there is (i.e., the realized gain). Further, a taxpayer should not have to recognize more gain than the amount of boot received (i.e., the portion of the contributed asset that no longer maintains continuity of investment — the portion that was liquidated).

**Answer "D" is a correct statement and, therefore, not the right answer.** The recognized gain of $500,000 must be characterized. Since, as noted above, the tug is a § 1231 asset, the gain could ultimately be a long-term capital gain. However, the tug is also a § 1245 asset (tangible, depreciable personalty). Therefore the gain is recharacterized from § 1231 to ordinary to the extent of the cumulative depreciation taken on the asset, here $200,000 ($850,000 cost - $650,000 adjusted basis). Therefore, $200,000 of the gain is ordinary and $300,000 of the gain is § 1231.

50.   **The best answer is "C."** Boot is assigned a basis equal to its fair market value, $300,000. § 358(a)(2).

**Answer "A" is incorrect.** Zahlen's adjusted basis in the stock is determined under § 358(a)(1) as follows: Adjusted basis in property/properties transferred - Value of boot received + Gain recognized. Therefore, Zahlen's adjusted basis in the stock is: $650,000 - ($200,000 + $300,000) + $500,000 = $650,000.

The gain potential in the tug was $600,000 ($1,250,000 value - $650,000 adjusted basis). Of that gain potential, $500,000 was recognized. The remaining gain potential of $100,000 is associated with the stock received. The stock has a basis of $650,000 and, as noted above, is worth $750,000. Therefore, if the stock is sold immediately after the § 351 transaction at its fair market value, a $100,000 gain would be recognized, thereby proving that the correct amount of gain potential was preserved.

**Answer "B" is incorrect.** In a successful § 351 transaction the shareholder's basis in the stock is determined by reference to the shareholder's basis in the asset contributed. § 358(a)(1). If the asset is a capital asset or a § 1231 asset, the holding period in the stock includes the holding period in the asset contributed. § 1223(1). The tug is a § 1231 asset (used in Zahlen's business, holding period of three years). Therefore, the holding period in the stock is also three years.

**Answer "D" is incorrect.** The basis in the land is its fair market value. § 358(a)(2). The holding period in a newly acquired asset is other than zero only if one of the provisions of § 1223 applies. Only §§ 1223(1) and (2) are relevant to § 351 transactions. Since Zahlen's basis in the land is not determined by reference to his basis in the tug, neither provision applies. Therefore, his holding period in the land is zero.

51. **The best answer is "D."** Stock rights are not "stock" under § 351. § 1.351-1(a)(1). Therefore, § 351 would not apply and the transaction would be treated as part-sale (with respect to the cash boot received) and part-exchange (with respect to the land and stock rights received). The entire transaction would be fully taxable. § 1001(a), (c). As noted above, the realized gain was $600,000, all of which would be recognized.

**Answer "A" is incorrect.** Cash boot paid in the form of liability assumption never offsets cash boot actually received.

**Answer "B" is incorrect.** Control is defined for the purposes of § 351 as holding at least 80% of the voting power and at least 80% of the nonvoting shares. § 368(c). Zahlen's 400 shares of common stock (the only class) would have constituted 80% [400/(100 + 400)] of the voting power, entitling him to § 351 treatment.

**Answer "C" is incorrect.** Recognition of shareholder losses is not allowed in § 351 transactions. § 351(b)(2).

52. None of the shareholders will receive § 351 treatment because, as a control group, they will not be deemed to have control immediately after the property transfers as required by § 351(a). Control means the ownership of stock possessing at least 80% of the voting power, as well as the ownership of at least 80% of the shares of nonvoting stock. § 368(c). There is no nonvoting stock here.

At the end of the first day after the capitalization transaction, the three members of the control group actually own only the following amount of stock:

| | Shares Originally Owned | % | Shares Disposed Day Following | Shares Owned End of Day Following | % |
|---|---|---|---|---|---|
| Dolf | 120 | 33.33% | 80 | 40 | 11.11% |
| Elaine | 120 | 33.33% | 120 | 0 | 0.00% |
| Fasul | 120 | 33.33% | 90 | 30 | 8.33% |
| | 360 | 100.00% | 290 | 70 | 19.44% |

Whether the "immediately after" requirement is satisfied is determined under the "freedom of action" test of *Intermountain Lumber Co.*, 65 T.C. 1025 (1976), in which the Tax Court said: "A determination of 'ownership,' as that term is used in section 368(c) . . . , depends upon the . . . freedom of action of the transferee with respect to the stock when he acquired it from the corporation. . . . If the transferee . . . has irrevocably foregone . . . at that time the legal right to determine whether to keep the shares, ownership . . . is lacking for purposes of section 351. By contrast, if there are no restrictions upon freedom of action at the time he acquired the shares, it is immaterial how soon thereafter the transferee elects to dispose of his stock or whether such disposition is in accord with a preconceived plan not amounting to a binding obligation."

Dolf had no plans to dispose of any stock on the date of the capitalization transaction. Therefore, he is deemed to own 33.33% of the stock "immediately after." Elaine had promised to make a gift of all of her stock prior to the capitalization transaction; but gifts are not binding and, therefore, she possessed the freedom of action not to go forward with the gift. She is thus deemed to own 33.33% of the stock "immediately after." However, Fasul entered a binding contract before the capitalization transaction to sell 75% of the stock to be received by him. Therefore, he is deemed to own only 8.33% of the stock "immediately after." In the aggregate, the control group owned the following number of shares "immediately after" the capitalization transaction:

| | Shares Owned "Immediately After" | % |
|---|---|---|
| Dolf | 120 | 33.33% |
| Elaine | 120 | 33.33% |
| Fasul | 30 | 8.33% |
| | | 75.00% |
| 3rd party | 90 | |
| | 360 | |

Since the control group owned less than 80% of the stock immediately after the capitalization transaction, no member of the group is entitled to § 351 treatment.

53.   As a general rule the client's understanding is correct. § 357(a). There are two exceptions.

First, if the shareholder transfers assets the aggregate basis of which is less than the amount of the shareholder's liabilities assumed by the corporation, there will be a forced gain to the shareholder. The only alternative is to allow the shareholder to take a negative basis in the stock. Liability relief is treated as constructive cash received. § 358(d)(1). If, for example, the aggregate basis of the assets transferred by the shareholder is $1,000,000 (the aggregate value of the assets is $5,000,000) and the corporation assumes $3,000,000 of the shareholder's liabilities, the basis in the stock under the normal rules would be: $1,000,000 (the aggregate basis of the assets transferred) - $3,000,000 (constructive cash received by virtue of the liability assumption) + 0 (gain recognized on transfer) = ($2,000,000), a negative amount. Except in one situation involving consolidated returns, the tax law does not permit negative basis. The solution here is to force the shareholder to recognize a $2,000,000 gain. § 357(c)(1)(A). Including the $2,000,000 gain in the basis formula, the stock basis is: $1,000,000 - $3,000,000 + $2,000,000 (forced gain) = $0.

Second, if the shareholder's principal purpose in having the corporation assume a shareholder liability is to avoid tax or if the principal purpose of the assumption is not a *bona fide* business purpose, then all of the shareholder's liabilities assumed by the corporation are treated as cash boot. § 357(b)(1). Even if only one liability fails this principal-purpose test, all of the assumed liabilities are tainted. § 1.357-1(c). The cash boot will trigger at least partial gain recognition under § 351(b)(1).

54.  **The best answer is "D."** Section 351 only applies when property is transferred to a corporation in exchange for stock. § 351(a). Services do not constitute "property." § 351(d)(1). Therefore, § 351 does not apply to a contribution of services in exchange for stock. Instead, § 83 applies.

**Answer "A" is incorrect.** As noted above, § 351 only applies if property is transferred to a corporation in exchange for stock. Stock rights are not considered "stock," so § 351 does not apply. § 1.351-1(a)(1).

**Answer "B" is incorrect.** Stock acquired from an underwriter is deemed acquired directly from the corporation as long as the underwriter is acting as the issuing corporation's agent (i.e., a best-efforts underwriting) or the underwriter's ownership of the stock is transitory (i.e., a firm-commitment underwriting). § 1.351-1(a)(3)(i). The underwriter's ownership would be transitory if it acquired the stock from the issuing corporation with a view to its immediate sale to the public (versus with a view to holding the stock for its own account).

**Answer "C" is incorrect.** If a corporation's own liability is transferred to it in an attempted § 351 transaction, such liability qualifies as "property" and is eligible for § 351 treatment only if the liability is evidenced by a security. § 351(d)(2). A claim for past wages would not be so evidenced and would therefore be ineligible for § 351 treatment.

55.  **The best answer is "C."** Section 362(e)(2) prohibits loss-doubling in § 351 transactions. If the aggregate basis of all properties contributed by a shareholder exceeds the aggregate value of such properties, the corporation has to reduce the basis of the properties with built-in loss to the extent necessary to bring such excess to zero. Basis is reduced in proportion to each loss asset's built-in loss.

Assume a shareholder transfers the following assets in a § 351 transaction:

| Asset | Value | Basis | Built-in Gain or Loss |
|---|---|---|---|
| #1 | $100,000 | $250,000 | ($150,000) |
| #2 | 200,000 | 450,000 | (250,000) |
| #3 | 300,000 | 100,000 | 200,000 |
|  | $600,000 | $800,000 | ($200,000) |

Since the aggregate basis, $800,000, exceeds the aggregate value, $600,000, § 362(e)(2) applies. The $200,000 overall built-in loss is allocated to reduce the bases of Assets #1 and #2 in proportion to their respective built-in losses. The basis reduction is as follows:

| Asset | Built-in Loss | % | Allocation of Aggregate Built-in Loss | Original Adjusted Basis | Revised Adjusted Basis |
|-------|-------|-------|-------|-------|-------|
| #1 | ($150,000) | 37.5% | ($75,000) | $250,000 | $175,000 |
| #2 | (250,000) | 62.5% | (125,000) | 450,000 | 325,000 |
|  | ($400,000) | 100.0% | ($200,000) | $700,000 | $500,000 |

This reduces the aggregate built-in loss to zero, as follows:

| Asset | Value | Basis | Built-in Gain or Loss |
|-------|-------|-------|-------|
| #1 | $100,000 | $175,000 | ($75,000) |
| #2 | 200,000 | 325,000 | (125,000) |
| #3 | 300,000 | 100,000 | 200,000 |
|  | $600,000 | $600,000 | 0 |

**Answer "A" is a correct statement and, therefore, not the right answer.** "Property" includes indebtedness of the transferee corporation only if evidenced by a security. § 351(d)(2). A bond is so evidenced and its contribution to the corporation could therefore qualify for § 351 relief.

**Answer "B" is a correct statement and, therefore, not the right answer.** Simultaneous transfers to the corporation by all members of the control group are not required. It is sufficient if the capitalization "proceeds with an expedition consistent with orderly procedure." § 1.351-1(a)(1).

**Answer "D" is a correct statement and, therefore, not the right answer.** The recognition of loss is prohibited under § 351. § 351(b)(2).

56.    **The best answer is "B."** Where an asset with a built-in gain is transferred to a corporation in a § 351 transaction, the original gain potential in the asset doubles. As a general rule the shareholder takes the same basis in the stock received as the shareholder had in the asset transferred. § 358(a)(1). Therefore, the gain that would have been recognized by the shareholder had the asset been sold will be recognized when the stock is disposed. The corporation takes the same basis in the asset that the shareholder had. § 362(a)(1). Therefore, the corporation has the same gain potential in the asset that the shareholder had (and that the shareholder now has in the stock). Thus, the original gain potential in the pre-contribution asset now resides in both the asset in the corporation's hands and in the stock in the shareholder's hands.

**Answer "A" is incorrect.** In addition to possessing stock holding at least 80% of the voting power, control requires that the control group possess stock representing at least 80% of the number of nonvoting shares, not the value of the nonvoting shares. § 368(c); Rev. Rul. 59-259, 1959-2 C.B. 115.

**Answer "C" is incorrect.** Even if a shareholder receives no boot, gain will be recognized if either: 1) the aggregate basis in the properties transferred is less than the amount of the shareholder's liabilities assumed by the corporation under § 357(c)(1)(A) or 2) the liabilities were assumed by the corporation either in furtherance of a tax avoidance purpose or in furtherance of other than a *bona fide* business purpose under § 357(b)(1).

**Answer "D" is incorrect.** Congress enacted § 351 to promote the incorporation of unincorporated businesses. Treating the transfer of accounts receivable as an assignment of income would frustrate this legislative purpose. Rev. Rul. 80-198, 1980-2 C.B. 113, discussing *Hempt Bros., Inc. v. U.S.*, 490 F.2d 1172 (3d Cir. 1974). Therefore, when a going concern is incorporated, the transfer of accounts receivable is not treated as an assignment of income.

57.   **The best answer is "C."** A corporation may not, under § 362(a)(1), increase the basis of property received in a § 351 transaction by gain recognized as a result of § 357(b)(1) to an amount in excess of the property's fair market value. § 362(d)(1). Thus, "always" overstates the tax consequences.

**Answer "A" is a correct statement and, therefore, not the right answer.** Even if a corporate transferor in a § 351 transaction immediately transfers to its shareholders the stock it received from the corporate transferee, the control test is not failed. § 351(c)(1).

**Answer "B" is a correct statement and, therefore, not the right answer.** The holding period in the property transferred is added to the holding period of the stock received in a § 351 transaction if the stock basis is determined by reference to the basis of the transferred property and if the transferred property is a capital asset or a § 1231 asset. § 1223(1). Inventory is not a capital asset, nor is it a § 1231 asset. §§ 1221(a)(1), 1231(b)(1)(A). Therefore, the holding period in the inventory does not tack to the stock.

**Answer "D" is a correct statement and, therefore, not the right answer.** In a failed § 351 transaction the corporation takes bases in the assets transferred to it in accordance with § 1012. § 1.1032-1(d). The basis under § 1012(a) is cost.

58.   **The best answer is "C."** Section 351 applies if property is transferred to a corporation solely in exchange for stock and if the transferors have control immediately after the transfer. § 351(a). Control exists if the transferors possess stock representing at least 80% of the voting power and at least 80% of the shares of nonvoting stock (none here). § 368(c). Stock received for services is not considered stock received for property. § 351(d)(1). This excludes the stock received by O'Hara in the measurement of control. The other three shareholders, own 90% of the stock and therefore have control. Therefore, § 351 applies to their property exchanges.

The fundamental basis rule under § 351 is that the basis in the stock received is the same as the basis in the property transferred. § 358(a)(1). That rule applies here, resulting in a stock basis to Newcomb of $600,000.

The holding period in the stock includes the holding period in the transferred property if the basis of the stock is determined by reference to the basis of the transferred property (which is true here for Newcomb) and if the asset transferred is either a capital asset or § 1231 property. § 1223(1). The Machine is depreciable property used in Newcomb's business held for more than one year and is thus § 1231 property. § 1231(b)(1). Therefore, the holding period for Newcomb's stock includes the four-year holding period in the Machine.

**Answer "A" is incorrect.** O'Hara's receipt of stock in exchange for services is ineligible for § 351 treatment. Because, as discussed above, the other shareholders have control and satisfy the requirements of § 351, nonrecognition treatment still applies to them.

**Answer "B" is incorrect.** Although Massey's stock basis is $220,000 under § 358(a)(1), the holding period in the stock is new because inventory is neither a capital asset nor § 1231 property as required by § 1223(1). § 1221(a)(1); § 1231(b)(1)(A).

**Answer "D" is incorrect.** An "exchange" occurs when the consideration moving in both directions is other than cash (or constructive cash). A "purchase" and "sale" occurs when the consideration given in exchange for property is cash (or constructive cash). Here the consideration given by Lincoln for the stock is cash, so the transaction is not an exchange. § 1.1002-1(d).

59. **The best answer is "C."** Where a corporation takes a carryover basis (i.e., no basis increment for gain recognized by the transferring shareholder) in depreciable property transferred to it by a shareholder in a § 351 transaction, it continues the depreciation schedule that was being used by such shareholder. § 168(i)(7)(A)-(B)(i).

**Answer "A" is a correct statement and, therefore, not the right answer.** Had the services been worth $300,000, the corporation would have been worth the following amount:

| Item Transferred | Value | % |
| --- | --- | --- |
| Cash | $100,000 | 7.8% |
| Inventory | 200,000 | 15.6% |
| Machine | 680,000 | 53.2% |
| Services | 300,000 | 23.4% |
| | $1,280,000 | 100.0% |

Because the services were worth 23.4% of the total value transferred to the corporation, O'Hara would presumably get 23.4% of the stock. Stock received in exchange for services does not count in measuring control. § 351(d)(1). Control requires the control group to possess stock holding at least 80% of the voting power and to possess stock representing at least 80% of the nonvoting shares. § 368(c). (There are no nonvoting shares here). Excluding O'Hara's stock, the other three shareholders only have 76.6% of the stock, thereby failing the control test. As a result the transaction is fully taxable to all shareholders. § 1001(c). Newcomb's realized gain on the exchange of the Machine for stock is $680,000 (value of stock received) - $600,000 (basis in Machine) = $80,000. § 1001(a). The entire gain would be recognized.

**Answer "B" is a correct statement and, therefore, not the right answer.** O'Hara has ordinary income of $20,000. § 83(a). O'Hara's stock basis would be fair market value under tax cost basis principles. § 1.83-4(b)(1). The stock would have a new holding period because no provision of § 1223 applies.

**Answer "D" is a correct statement and, therefore, not the right answer.** As noted above, immediately after the capitalization transaction the control group must have control for § 351 to apply. Where a member of the control group contracts before the capitalization transaction to transfer any stock received to other than a member of the control group, "immediately after" is tested after the contract is performed under step-transaction principles. *Intermountain Lumber Co.*, 65 T.C. 1025 (1976). Since O'Hara is not a member of the control group, Newcomb's sale of the stock to O'Hara brings the control group's stock ownership down to 30%, which fails the control test. As a result § 351 would not apply to any of the shareholders.

60. **The best answer is "A."** Where the shareholder's aggregate basis in the transferred

properties exceeds their aggregatefair market value, the corporation reduces its bases in the properties with built-in losses until the aggregate basis equals the aggregate fair market value to avoid loss doubling. § 362(e)(2). Here the corporation's basis in the Inventory is reduced to $200,000.

**Answer "B" is incorrect.** Phoenix amortizes organizational expenses under § 248(a), which will allow $5,000 to be expensed immediately (the amount of the organizational expenditures is less than $50,000 so there is no phase-out). The remaining $15,000 ($20,000 - $5,000) is amortized pro rata over 180 months beginning with the month the corporation begins business, here August 1. Therefore, the total amortization deduction is: $5,000 +($15,000/180 x 5 months) = $5,417 (rounded).

**Answer "C" is incorrect.** The anti-loss-doubling rule discussed above only applies if the aggregate basis of the property transferred exceeds the aggregate value. After combining the Inventory and the Machine, the aggregate basis is $820,000 ($220,000 + $600,000). The aggregate value is $880,000 ($200,000 + $680,000). Therefore, § 362(e)(2) does not apply and the basis of the Inventory is not reduced.

**Answer "D" is incorrect.** The corporation's holding period in the Inventory includes Massey's holding period. § 1223(2). Therefore, the corporation will be deemed to have held Inventory "long-term." However, the Inventory is not a capital asset. § 1221(a)(1). Therefore, its disposition does not generate a capital gain or loss. § 1222(1)-(4).

61. **The best answer is "B."** The stock basis is: $2,540,000 (aggregate basis of properties transferred) - $1,900,000 (constructive cash received as liability relief) + 0 (gain recognized) = $640,000. § 358(a)(1), (d)(1).

**Answer "A" is incorrect.** To be eligible for § 351 treatment the transferring shareholder must have control immediately after the capitalization transaction. § 351(a). Control requires the transferring shareholder to possess stock having at least 80% of the total voting power and to possess at least 80% of the nonvoting shares. § 368(c). (There are only voting shares here.) As a sole shareholder Eddington has 100% of the stock and therefore satisfies the control test. However, after the subsequent stock transfer Eddington has only 75% of the stock, too little to have control. Whether Eddington is deemed to have 100% of the stock immediately after the capitalization transaction or only 75% is determined by whether Eddington had "freedom of action." That is, was Eddington legally bound prior to the transaction to transfer the stock? *Intermountain Lumber Co.*, 65 T.C. 1025 (1976). Since Eddington had the ability to choose whether to alienate the stock after the capitalization transaction, freedom of action was retained and "immediately after" is measured before the gift. Therefore, Eddington is entitled to § 351 relief. The same would be true even if Eddington had promised to make the gift before the § 351 transaction because gifts are not enforceable by the donee.

**Answer "C" is incorrect.** The stock received in a § 351 transaction is not allocated as consideration received for each of the individual assets. Rather, each share takes an equal amount of the aggregate § 358(a)(1) basis and takes a partitioned holding period based on each transferred asset's relative net fair market value. Rev. Rul. 85-164, 1985-2 C.B. 117. Thus, each share has the following tax attributes:

| Item | Value | Encumbrance | Net Value | % | Holding Period |
|---|---|---|---|---|---|
| Cash | $500,000 | — | $500,000 | 8.20% | 0 |
| Inventory | 900,000 | $100,000 | $800,000 | 13.11% | 0[fn] |
| Operating Asset | 1,600,000 | 1,300,000 | $300,000 | 4.92% | 4 years |
| Raw Land | 5,000,000 | 500,000 | $4,500,000 | 73.77% | 18 years |
| | $8,000,000 | $1,900,000 | $6,100,000 | 100.00% | |

[fn] *Holding period only tacks if the asset transferred is a capital asset or a § 1231 property. Inventory is neither. § 1221(a)(1); § 1231(b)(1)(A).*

If one share was sold one day after the § 351 transaction, 21.31% (8.20% from the cash and 13.11% from the inventory) of the capital gain or loss would be short-term and 78.69% (4.92% from the operating asset and 73.77% from the raw land) would be long-term.

As noted above, the stock basis is $640,000. The basis per share is $640,000 ÷ 6,100 shares = $104.92. The value per share is ($8,000,000 - $1,900,000) ÷ 6,100 shares = $1,000.

**Answer "D" is incorrect.** Recourse liabilities are deemed assumed if, "on the basis of all facts and circumstances, the transferee has agreed to, and is expected to, satisfy such liability . . . , whether or not the transferor has been relieved of such liability[.]" § 357(d)(1)(A). Per the last clause, a novation is not required. There need be no formal agreement since the "agreed to" and "expected to" requirements are based on the "facts and circumstances."

62.    **The best answer is "B."** The total liabilities are now $2,600,000, which exceeds the total basis of $2,540,000. Therefore, Eddington must recognize a gain of $60,000 ($2,600,000 - $2,540,000). § 357(c)(1). The gain is allocated among all of the assets transferred (other than cash) in proportion to their relative fair market values. § 1.357-2. The bases in these assets to Tower is their bases to Eddington plus the gain allocated to them. § 362(a)(1). The gain allocation is:

| Asset | Value | % | Gain Allocation | Original Basis | Revised Basis |
|---|---|---|---|---|---|
| Inventory | $900,000 | 12.00% | $7,200 | $840,000 | $847,200 |
| Operating Asset | 1,600,000 | 21.33% | 12,800 | $1,000,000 | $1,012,800 |
| Raw Land | 5,000,000 | 66.67% | 40,000 | $200,000 | $240,000 |
| | $7,500,000 | 100.00% | $60,000 | | |

The gains on the Operating Asset and Raw Land are § 1231; but the gain on the Inventory is ordinary since inventory is neither a capital asset nor § 1231 property. § 1221(a)(2); § 1231(b)(1).

**Answer "A" is a correct statement and, therefore, not the right answer.** As indicated above, Eddington recognizes a $60,000 gain under § 357(c)(1).

**Answer "C" is a correct statement and, therefore, not the right answer.** As indicated above, Tower take a basis in the inventory of $847,200.

**Answer "D" is a correct statement and, therefore, not the right answer.** Eddington's stock basis is: $2,540,000 (total basis of transferred assets) - $2,600,000 (liability relief) + $60,000 (recognized gain) = $0. § 358(a)(1), (d)(1).

63. **The best answer is "A."** Courts have held that the face amount of a personal note (assuming the note carries an appropriate rate of interest) contributed to a corporation creates stock basis that can help avoid the "liabilities-in-excess-of-basis" forced gain rule of § 357(c)(1)(A). *Peracchi v. Comm'r*, 143 F.3d 487 (9th Cir. 1998). However, the IRS has not acquiesced to this decision. Rev. Rul. 68-629, 1968-2 C.B. 154.

**Answer "B" is incorrect.** Unrecaptured § 1250 gain exists only when realty is depreciable. § 1(h)(6)(A). Raw land is not depreciable. § 1.167(a)-2.

**Answer "C" is incorrect.** As noted above, the stock received in a § 351 transaction is not assigned to the individual assets transferred. Each share takes a partitioned holding period based on each transferred asset's relative net fair market value. Rev. Rul. 85-164, 1985-2 C.B. 117. Also as noted above, the holding period of each share is 21.31% short-term and 73.77% long-term.

**Answer "D" is incorrect.** The Operating Asset is § 1231 property. § 1231(b)(1). Nonetheless, since the gain allocated to this asset is less than the $500,000 of cumulative depreciation ($1,500,000 cost - $1,000,000 adjusted basis) taken on the asset, the gain is ordinary under § 1245.

64. **The best answer is "C."** Where a corporation assumes a liability of the shareholder in a § 351 transaction and the liability originated for a purpose other than a *bona fide* business purpose, all of the liabilities assumed (not just the liability "tainted" by a lack of *bona fide* business purpose) are treated as boot. § 357(b)(1); § 1.357-1(c).

**Answer "A" is incorrect.** Eddington recognizes the lesser of the realized gain and the amount of the boot. § 351(b)(1). This is done on an asset-by-asset basis. Rev. Rul. 68-55, 1968-1 C.B. 140. The analysis is below. Note: The boot deemed received as constructive cash is offset by the cash contributed. Therefore, for these purposes the boot is $1,400,000 ($1,900,000 - $500,000).

| Asset | Value | % | Boot Allocated |
|---|---|---|---|
| Inventory | $900,000 | 12.00% | $168,000 |
| Operating Asset | 1,600,000 | 21.33% | 298,667 |
| Raw Land | 5,000,000 | 66.67% | 933,333 |
| | $7,500,000 | 100.00% | $1,400,000 |

| | Inventory | Operating Asset | Raw Land |
|---|---|---|---|
| Amount realized (value) | $900,000 | $1,600,000 | $5,000,000 |
| Adjusted basis | (840,000) | (1,000,000) | (200,000) |
| Realized gain | $60,000 | $600,000 | $4,800,000 |
| Boot allocated | $168,000 | $298,667 | $933,333 |
| Recognized gain | $60,000 | $298,667 | $933,333 |

**Answer "B" is incorrect.** As indicated above, if any single liability is tainted by § 357(b)(1), all liabilities assumed by the corporation with respect to the same shareholder are treated as boot.

**Answer "D" is incorrect.** As indicated above, the recognized gain on the Operating Asset is $298,667.

65.   **The best answer is "A."** In *Henry C. Beck Co.*, 52 T.C. 1 (1969), the Tax Court held that earnings and profits "is an economic concept which the tax law has utilized . . . to approximate a corporation's power to make distributions which are more than just a return of investment." In other words, earnings and profits is the maximum amount a corporation can distribute without some of the distribution representing invested capital.

**Answer "B" is incorrect.** Although earnings and profits can be computed by starting with taxable income and making adjustments, earnings and profits uses substantially different rules for measuring the amount and timing of income and deductions. It is not even correct to say that *accumulated* earnings and profits equals the corporation's cumulative current earnings and profits less the cumulative amount it has distributed that has been characterized as a dividend because earnings and profits can be extinguished by stock redemptions that are not treated as dividends.

**Answer "C" is incorrect.** As a general rule a corporation must use the same overall method of accounting in computing earnings and profits as it does in computing taxable income. § 1.312-6(a).

**Answer "D" is incorrect.** Accumulated earnings and profits is very similar in concept to financial accounting's retained earnings. As a general rule, retained earnings equals the cumulative amount of net income (or loss) a corporation has earned (or suffered) less the cumulative amount of nonliquidating dividends it has paid out. Although there are significant differences in the way income and expenses are measured and in the timing of their recognition, financial accounting and earnings and profits have the same objective: to measure the maximum amount a corporation can distribute to shareholders without reducing invested capital.

66.   **The best answer is "B."** The characterization of a nonliquidating distribution as a dividend for tax purposes depends on whether the source of the distribution is earnings and profits. § 301(a), (c)(1); § 316 (a). Under the alternative minimum tax the important adjusted current earnings adjustment of § 56(c)(1) cannot be determined without current earnings and profits.

**Answer "A" is incorrect.** There is relatively little statutory guidance on the computation of earnings and profits. There are a few relevant provisions in § 312, but most guidance comes from revenue rulings and the Regulations.

**Answer "C" is incorrect.** The IRS will not provide computational guidance with respect to earnings and profits. Each year Rev. Proc. 20xx-3 (the so-called "no-ruling revenue procedure") lists earnings and profits as a matter with respect to which it will not issue a private letter ruling. *See, e.g.,* Rev. Proc. 2011-3, 2011-1 I.R.B. 111, § 3.01(36).

**Answer "D" is incorrect.** The overall method of accounting used for determining earnings and profits is the same as that used for determining taxable income, whether that be the cash or accrual method. § 1.312-6(a).

67.    **The best answer is "B."** Since federal income taxes reduce a corporation's ability to make distributions without reducing invested capital, they must be subtracted in computing earnings and profits. Like virtually any other accrual-method expense, federal income tax must be recognized in the year all events have occurred that fix the fact of the liability. § 1.461-1(a)(2). *See*, Rev. Rul. 57-332, 1957-2 C.B. 231; Rev. Rul. 70-609, 1970-2 C.B. 78; Rev. Rul. 79-69, 1979-1 C.B. 134. Here that is Year 1.

       **Answer "A" is incorrect.** Since exempt interest provides the wherewithal to make distributions without reducing invested capital, it is included in earnings and profits. § 1.312-6(b).

       **Answer "C" is incorrect.** Losses are deducted in determining earnings and profits when realized because that is when the corporation's wherewithal to make distributions without reducing invested capital is diminished. This is true even though recognition is disallowed for taxable income purposes (e.g., by § 1211 in the context of capital losses). The corollary is that a loss deferred for taxable income purposes (e.g., a capital loss carryforward) has no impact on future years' earnings and profits. § 1.312-7(b).

       **Answer "D" is incorrect.** Earnings and profits are not reduced for deductions involving no expenditure since such deductions do not decrease the corporation's wherewithal to make distributions without reducing invested capital. This principle is illustrated in § 1.312-6(c)(1) and *Weyerhaeuser*, 33 B.T.A. 594 (1935).

68.    **The best answer is "C."** Losses are deducted in determining earnings and profits when realized because that is when the corporation's wherewithal to make distributions without reducing invested capital is diminished. Loss carryovers (e.g., that provided by § 172 in the context of net operating losses) have no impact on earnings and profits. § 1.312-7(b).

       **Answer "A" is a correct statement and, therefore, not the right answer.** Since life insurance premiums decrease a corporation's wherewithal to make distributions without impairing invested capital, they reduce earnings and profits. Rev. Rul. 54-230, 1954-1 C.B. 114. Similarly, life insurance proceeds increase earnings and profits.

       **Answer "B" is a correct statement and, therefore, not the right answer.** A taxpayer must use the same overall method of accounting to compute earnings and profits as it does to compute taxable income. § 1.312-6(a). Tax payments reduce a corporation's wherewithal to make distributions without impairing invested capital. Therefore, earnings and profits are reduced in the year the payments are made. Rev. Rul. 79-69, 1979-1 C.B. 134.

       **Answer "D" is a correct statement and, therefore, not the right answer.** There is no reduction in earnings and profits for deductions involving no expenditure since such deductions do not reduce the corporation's wherewithal to make distributions without reducing invested capital. Once the basis of a depletable asset has been reduced to zero, there is no further reduction in the corporation's assets associated with future depletion. The fact that the percentage depletion method continues to allow depletion deductions for taxable income purposes is irrelevant. § 1.312-6(c)(1).

69.    **The best answer is "C."** Earnings and profits are reduced by expenditures that reduce the corporation's wherewithal to make distributions without impairing invested capital. Because the $125,000 charitable contribution reduces such wherewithal, earnings and profits are

reduced by that full amount. Rev. Rul. 75-515, 1975-2 C.B. 117. This is true even though, for taxable income purposes, the charitable contribution deduction is limited to 10% of the corporation's pre-charitable-deduction taxable income, here $100,000 (10% x $1,000,000). § 170(b)(2)(A), (2)(C)(i).

**Answer "A" is incorrect.** The contrary-to-public-policy limitation on deductions, to the extent it survives, relates to whether a deduction should be allowed in the determination of taxable income. A deduction would reduce the taxpayer's tax liability, subsidize anti-social conduct and shift the tax burden to other taxpayers. In the context of earnings and profits the issue is whether the payment reduces the corporation's wherewithal to make distributions without impairing invested capital. Civil tax penalties reduce such wherewithal and therefore are deductible in determining earnings and profits. The principle is illustrated in Rev. Rul. 57-332, 1957-2 C.B. 231.

**Answer "B" is incorrect.** The corporation's wherewithal to make distributions without impairing invested capital is reduced, when measured on the cash basis, in the year the tax payment is made, regardless of the year with respect to which the deficiency arose. Rev. Rul. 70-609, 1970-2 C.B. 78.

**Answer "D" is incorrect.** The LIFO inventory method is prohibited in determining earnings and profits since it is deemed to distort the extent to which a corporation's wherewithal to make distributions without impairing invested capital is reduced. § 312(n)(4).

70. **The best answer is "D."** The installment sale method is prohibited in determining earnings and profits because it is deemed to improperly understate the extent to which a corporation's wherewithal to make distributions without impairing invested capital is increased by the gross income derived from the transaction under § 61(a)(3). § 312(n)(5). Current earnings and profits would be increased by $200,000, not $50,000.

**Answer "A" is a correct statement and, therefore, not the right answer.** The corporation's wherewithal to make distributions without impairing invested capital is reduced, when measured on the accrual basis, in the year to which the tax payment relates, regardless of the year in which payment is made. The principle is illustrated in Rev. Rul. 57-332, 1957-2 C.B. 231, and Rev. Rul. 70-609, 1970-2 C.B. 78.

**Answer "B" is a correct statement and, therefore, not the right answer.** Losses are deducted in determining earnings and profits when realized because that is when the corporation's wherewithal to make distributions without reducing invested capital is diminished. Loss carryovers (e.g., that provided by § 172 in the context of net operating losses) have no impact on earnings and profits. § 1.312-7(b). If the corporation has no taxable income or loss other than the $300,000 net operating loss (and assuming no difference between the measurement of that loss for taxable income and earnings and profits purposes), current earnings and profits would be negative $300,000.

**Answer "C" is a correct statement and, therefore, not the right answer.** Under the same rationale as provided for "B," the loss is taken into account immediately for earnings and profits purposes even though § 1211 disallows the loss for taxable income purposes.

71. **The best answer is "A."** Organizational expenditures are deemed to have an indefinite useful life. Although § 248 provides a deduction for taxable income purposes, that deduction is not grounded on measuring the reduction in a corporation's wherewithal to make distributions without impairing invested capital. Rather, expensing is allowed for policy

reasons. Therefore, there is no § 248 deduction for earnings and profits purposes. § 312(n)(3).

**Answer "B" is a correct statement and, therefore, not the right answer.** The completed-contract method is deemed to improperly understate a corporation's wherewithal to make distributions without impairing invested capital. Therefore, the method is prohibited and the percentage-of-completion method must be used. § 312(n)(6).

**Answer "C" is a correct statement and, therefore, not the right answer.** Accelerated depreciation is allowed in determining taxable income for policy reasons — principally to provide economic stimulus. Such accelerated depreciation is deemed to understate a corporation's actual wherewithal to make distributions without impairing invested capital. Therefore, the straight-line method over the asset's useful life (versus over its typically foreshortened recovery period) is required for earnings and profits purposes. § 312(k)(3)(A).

**Answer "D" is a correct statement and, therefore, not the right answer.** Similar to the rationale given for "C," the immediate § 179 deduction is principally grounded on economic stimulus. The deduction for earnings and profits purposes is decelerated to better reflect a corporation's wherewithal to make distributions without impairing invested capital. § 312(k)(3)(B).

72.    **The best answer is "B."** Gains increase earnings and profits only to the extent recognized. § 1.312-6(b). Therefore the realized but unrecognized § 1031 gain has no impact. The tax and penalty payments will have no impact on Elwyn's earnings and profits because taxes and penalties are accrued, for earnings and profits purposes, in the year to which they relate. Rev. Rul. 57-332, 1957-2 C.B. 231; Rev. Rul. 70-609, 1970-2 C.B. 78. Thus, the Year 1 earnings and profits is impacted by these payments. Finally, even though the loss on the sale of its property to its sole shareholder was disallowed for taxable income purposes under § 267, the loss reduced the corporation's wherewithal to make distributions without impairing invested capital. § 1.312-7(b). Therefore, current earnings and profits is reduced by $125,000. For these reasons, **answers "A," "C" and "D" are incorrect.**

73.    Depreciation deductions are taken under the alternative depreciation system for earnings and profits purposes. § 312(k)(3)(A). The asset is depreciated using the straight-line method over its class life utilizing the half-year convention. Therefore, only a half year's depreciation is available in Year 4, the year of disposition. § 168(g)(2). The § 179 amount is deducted over five years. § 312(k)(3)(B). The total depreciation is:

|            |          |                         |
| ---------- | -------- | ----------------------- |
| MACRS      | $6,250   | ($100,000/8 x 50%)      |
| § 179      | 50,000   | ($250,000/5)            |
|            | $56,250  |                         |

74.    The § 248 deduction is disallowed in computing earnings and profits since organizational expenditures have an indefinite useful life. The tax policy deduction for taxable income purposes understates the corporation's wherewithal to make distributions without impairing invested capital. § 312(n)(3).

75.

| | | | | | |
|---|---|---|---|---|---|
| Amount realized: | | | | $325,000 | |
| Adjusted basis: | Cost | | $350,000 | | |
| | § 179 | | (250,000) | | |
| | MACRS: | Year 1 | $20,000 | | |
| | | Year 2 | 32,000 | | |
| | | Year 3 | 19,200 | | |
| | | Year 4 | 5,760 | (76,960) | ($11,520 x 50%) |
| | | | | (23,040) | |
| Gain: | | | | $301.960 | |

76.

| | | | | | |
|---|---|---|---|---|---|
| Amount realized: | | | | $325,000 | |
| Adjusted basis: | Cost | | $350,000 | | |
| | § 179 | | (200,000) | | ($50,000 x 4 years) |
| | MACRS: | Year 1 | $6,250 | | ($100,000/8 x 50%) |
| | | Year 2 | 12,500 | | ($100,000/8) |
| | | Year 3 | 12,500 | | ($100,000/8) |
| | | Year 4 | 6,250 | (37,500) | ($100,000/8 x 50%) |
| | | | | (175,000) | |
| Gain: | | | | $212,500 | |

77.

| Item | |
|---|---|
| Cash ordinary operating income | $1,000,000 |
| Long-term capital gain | 100,000 |
| Short-term capital loss | (100,000) |
| Net operating loss carryforward | (200,000) |
| Dividends from 10%-owned domestic corporation | 50,000 |
| Dividends-received deduction | (35,000) |
| § 248 deduction | (15,000) |
| § 179 deduction | (30,000) |
| MACRS deduction | (10,000) |
| | $760,000 |

78.

| Item | | |
|---|---|---|
| Cash ordinary operating income | $1,000,000 | |
| Long-term capital gain | 100,000 | |
| Short-term capital loss | (160,000) | *(get full loss; § 1.312-7(b))* |
| Net operating loss carryforward | 0 | *(not reduce earnings and profits; § 1.312-6(b))* |
| Dividends | 50,000 | |
| Dividends-received deduction | 0 | *(no deduction; Weyerhaeuser, 33 B.T.A. 594 (1935))* |
| Loss disallowed under § 267 | (60,000) | *(get full loss; § 1.312-7(b))* |
| § 248 deduction | 0 | *(no deduction; § 312(n)(3))* |
| Penalty paid to IRS | (40,000) | *(get deduction; Rev. Ruls. 57-332, 70-609)* |

| | | |
|---|---|---|
| Estimated taxes paid | (110,000) | *(get deduction; id.)* |
| § 179 deduction | (6,000) | *(take over five years; § 312(k)(3)(B))* |
| MACRS deduction | (10,000) | *(same because elected § 168(g) for tax; § 312(k)(3)(A))* |
| Life insurance premiums | (25,000) | *(get deduction; Rev. Rul. 54-230)* |
| | $739,000 | |

79.

| | |
|---|---|
| Beginning accumulated deficit | ($900,000) |
| Current earnings and profits | 739,000 |
| Ending accumulated deficit | ($161,000) |

80. Where beginning accumulated earnings and profits is negative, but current earnings and profits is positive, distributions are characterized as dividends to the extent of current earnings and profits. § 1.316-2(b); Rev. Rul. 74-164, 1974-1 C.B. 74. Earnings and profits are reduced by the amount of the distribution characterized as a dividend. § 312(a)(1).

| | |
|---|---|
| Current earnings and profits | $739,000 |
| Dividend | (500,000) |
| | 239,000 |
| Beginning accumulated deficit | (900,000) |
| Ending accumulated deficit | ($661,000) |

81. **The best answer is "C."** Section 301(a) distributions (i.e., dividends) reduce earnings and profits before § 302(a) distributions (i.e., redemptions). Rev. Rul. 74-339, 1974-2 C.B. 103.

**Answer "A" is a correct statement and, therefore, not the right answer.** The tax law respects the legal priority of preferred stock to dividends and therefore allocates earnings and profits first to distributions on preferred stock and second to distributions on common stock. Rev. Rul. 69-440, 1969-2 C.B. 46.

**Answer "B" is a correct statement and, therefore, not the right answer.** For tax purposes, a dividend is a distribution sourced from earnings and profits. § 316(a). Therefore, without earnings and profits there can be no "dividend."

**Answer "D" is a correct statement and, therefore, not the right answer.** All distributions are first allocated a pro rata amount of current earnings and profits. Accumulated earnings and profits are then allocated, in order of time, to the distributions to the extent the total distributions exceed the current earnings and profits during a year. § 1.316-2. This increases the likelihood that earlier distributions during the year carry out more earnings and profits than later distributions during the year.

82. **The best answer is "B."** Since current earnings and profits cannot be determined until the end of the year and since current earnings and profits must be allocated to every distribution during the year proportionately, the amount of each distribution which constitutes a dividend cannot be determined until the end of the year. § 316(a)(2).

**Answer "A" is incorrect.** Nonliquidating distributions (other than redemptions) first carry out a pro rata share of current earnings and profits and then, to the extent the distribution exceeds the available current earnings and profits, such distributions carry out accumulated earnings and profits in order of time. Accumulated earnings and profits do not flow out on a pro rata basis. § 1.316-2.

**Answer "C" is incorrect.** In a redemption earnings and profits are reduced by the amount of the distribution, but not in excess of the redeemed stock's pro rata share of earnings and profits. If a corporation with earnings and profits of $8,000,000 redeems 10% of its stock for $1,000,000, earnings and profits is reduced by the lesser of the amount of the distribution ($1,000,000) or the redeemed stock's pro rata share of earnings and profits, $800,000 (10% x $8,000,000). § 312(n)(7). Thus, earnings and profits is reduced by $800,000.

**Answer "D" is incorrect.** The negative current earnings and profits for the year are prorated to the date of the distribution. If, after such proration, the balance in earnings and profits is positive, the amount of the distribution on that day is a dividend to the extent of the positive balance. Assume that accumulated earnings and profits at the beginning of the year is $1,500,000 and that current earnings and profits at the end of the year is ($1,200,000). Further assume that the only distribution during the year occurs on August 31 in the amount of $900,000. Current earnings and profits prorated to August 31 would be ($800,000) (8/12 x $1,200,000). The net balance in earnings and profits would be $700,000 ($1,500,000 accumulated - $800,000 prorated current). Therefore $700,000 of the $900,000 distribution would be a dividend. At that point net earnings and profits would be zero. The accumulated earnings and profits at the end of the year would be ($400,000) (4/12 x ($1,200,000)).

83.    **The best answer is "D."** A dividend for tax purposes is any distribution to a shareholder by a corporation with respect to its stock sourced from earnings and profits. § 301(a), (c)(1); § 316(a). Current earnings and profits is allocated to all distributions during the year proportionately. Accumulated earnings and profits is allocated to distributions in order of time to the extent that the amount of the distribution exceeds the amount of current earnings and profits allocated to the distribution. § 1.316-2.

The total amount distributed during the year is $3,000,000, which exceeds the available earnings and profits, $1,800,000 ($1,000,000 accumulated, $800,000 current). Current earnings and profits is allocated to the distributions proportionately as follows:

| Date | Amount of Distribution | % | Allocation of Current Earnings & Profits | Remaining Distribution |
|---|---|---|---|---|
| March 1 | $600,000 | 20% | $160,000 | $440,000 |
| November 1 | 2,400,000 | 80% | 640,000 | 1,760,000 |
| | $3,000,000 | 100% | $800,000 | $2,200,000 |

Accumulated earnings and profits is then allocated to the distributions in order of time to the extent of the remaining distribution as follows:

| Date | Remaining Distribution | Allocation of Accumulated Earnings & Profits |
|---|---|---|
| March 1 | $440,000 | $440,000 |
| November 1 | 1,760,000 | 560,000 |
| | $2,200,000 | $1,000,000 |

The dividend to each shareholder therefore is:

| Shareholder | Earnings & Profits Current | Accumulated | "Dividend" |
|---|---|---|---|
| McGraw | $160,000 | $440,000 | $600,000 |
| O'Leary | 640,000 | 560,000 | 1,200,000 |
| | $800,000 | $1,000,000 | $1,800,000 |

**Answer "A" is incorrect.** Even if the board of directors directed the distributions to be made out of retained earnings for financial accounting purposes, that direction does not control the characterization of the distributions for federal income tax purposes. For tax purposes the general rule is that every distribution is made out of earnings and profits to the extent thereof. § 316(a). Since Harmony only had earnings and profits of $1,800,000, only

$1,800,000 of the $3,000,000 in distributions could be dividends for tax purposes.

**Answer "B" and answer "C" are incorrect** because they differ from the proper computation described above. Answer "B" simply allocated all of the earnings and profits to the controlling shareholder; answer "C" allocated both current and accumulated earnings and profits in proportion to the size of the distributions, which is correct only for current earnings and profits.

84.    Serenity recognizes no gain or loss on the distribution. § 311(a)(2). It reduces its earnings and profits to zero [($800,000 current earnings and profits + $0 accumulated earnings and profits) - $2,000,000; cannot be reduced below zero]. § 312(a)(1).

85.    The amount of Shep's distribution is $1,200,000 (60% x $2,000,000). § 301(b)(1). Current earnings and profits is allocated to distributions on a pro rata basis. § 1.316-2(b). Therefore, Shep's share of current earnings and profits is $480,000 (60% x $800,000). (There are no accumulated earnings and profits to allocate.) That amount is characterized as dividend income. § 301(a), (c)(1). Shep's stock basis is then reduced to zero [$500,000 beginning basis - ($1,200,000 amount of the distribution - $480,000 dividend portion)]. § 301(c)(2). The remaining distribution, $220,000 [$1,200,000 amount of the distribution - $480,000 dividend portion - $500,000 stock basis reduction] is a long-term capital gain. § 301(c)(3)(A).

86.    In accordance with the authorities provided "B," the amount of the distribution is $800,000 (40% x $2,000,000). Alliance's dividend is $320,000 (40% x $800,000). Alliance reduces its stock basis to $120,000 [$600,000 beginning basis - ($800,000 amount of the distribution - $320,000 dividend portion)]. Alliance is entitled to a dividends-received deduction of $256,000 (80% x $320,000). § 243(a)(1), (c).

87.    **The best answer is "C."** Oriental is entitled to a preferred stock dividend of $500,000 (10% stated dividend rate x $5,000,000 par). With respect to distributions, earnings and profits flow in accordance with each class of stock's legal priority. Rev. Rul. 69-440, 1969-2 C.B. 46. Therefore, the first $500,000 of earnings and profits is allocated to the preferred stock and constitutes the amount of the distribution to Oriental. § 301(b)(1). It is all dividend income. § 301(a), (c)(1).

**Answer "A" is a correct statement and, therefore, not the right answer.** Section 311(a)(2) expressly so states with respect to property, which includes cash. § 317(a).

**Answer "B" is a correct statement and, therefore, not the right answer.** The amount of the distribution to Patty is $100,000 ($600,000 total distribution - $500,000 preferred stock dividend). § 301(b)(1). The current earnings and profits remaining after the preferred stock dividend is $500,000 [($1,000,000 current earnings and profits + $0 accumulated earnings and profits) - $500,000 preferred stock dividend]. § 312(a)(1). This is sufficient to cover the entire amount of the distribution, so the dividend to Patty is $100,000. § 301(a), (c)(1).

**Answer "D" is a correct statement and, therefore, not the right answer.** Current earnings and profits is allocated to distributions pro rata regardless of the amount of the accumulated deficit. § 1.316-2(b); Rev. Rul. 74-164, 1974-1 C.B. 74. Therefore, the tax consequences of the distributions would remain unchanged.

88.    **The best answer is "D."** The negative current earnings and profits of ($1,000,000) would have been prorated to the date of the distribution, December 31, the end of the taxable year.

Rev. Rul. 74-164, 1974-1 C.B. 74. The available earnings and profits on December 31 would have been zero [$1,000,000 accumulated earnings and profits − (365/365 x $1,000,000 negative current earnings and profits)]. Therefore, none of the distributions would have been characterized as dividends.

**Answer "A" is a correct statement and, therefore, not the right answer.** Shangri-La reduces its earnings and profits by the amount of the distribution to $400,000 [$1,000,000 available earnings and profits - ($500,000 preferred stock dividend to Oriental + $100,000 common stock dividend to Patty)]. § 312(a)(1).

**Answer "B" is a correct statement and, therefore, not the right answer.** As noted above, the amount of the distribution to Patty is less than the amount of available earnings and profits. Therefore, all of Patty's distribution is a dividend and Patty's stock basis is not reduced.

**Answer "C" is a correct statement and, therefore, not the right answer.** As was true in "B," the amount of the distribution to Oriental is less than the amount of available earnings and profits. Therefore, Oriental's stock basis is not reduced.

89.  **The best answer is "A."** Earnings and profits flows to ordinary distributions before it flows to redemptions. Rev. Rul. 74-339, 1974-2 C.B. 103. Negative current earnings and profits is prorated to the date of the distribution, here December 31. Rev. Rul. 74-164, 1974-1 C.B. 74. The available earnings and profits on December 31 are $2,000,000 ($3,200,000 accumulated earnings and profits - 365/365 x $1,200,000 negative current earnings and profits). The available earnings and profits is greater than the amount of the distribution, $900,000, so all of the distribution is characterized as dividend income. § 301(b)(1); § 316(a); § 1.316-2(b). Therefore, Medford's available earnings and profits before the redemption is $1,100,000 ($2,000,000 available earnings and profits - $900,000 amount of the distribution).

The redemption of Ralph's stock receives sale or exchange treatment under § 302(a) because it is a substantially disproportionate redemption. § 302(b)(2). After the redemption Ralph has less than 50% of the voting power. (He owns 100 of the then-outstanding 900 shares or 11.1%.) His post-redemption voting power of 11.1% is less than 80% of his voting power before the redemption (80% of 20%, his pre-redemption voting power, is 16%; 11.1% is less than 16%).

Medford's earnings and profits is reduced by the amount of the redemption distribution, but not in excess of the redeemed stock's pro rata share of the pre-redemption earnings and profits. § 312(a)(1), (n)(7). Thus, Medford's earnings and profits is reduced by the lesser of $600,000 or $110,000 [10% (Ralph redeemed half of his 20%) x $1,100,000 available earnings and profits]. Medford's end-of-year earnings and profits is, therefore, $990,000 ($1,100,000 earnings and profits available before the redemption - $110,000 attributable to the redeemed stock).

**Answer "B" is a correct statement and, therefore, not the right answer.** Since all of the $900,000 distribution is characterized as a dividend, none of the amount of the distribution to any of the shareholders reduces stock basis. § 301(a), (c).

**Answer "C" is a correct statement and, therefore, not the right answer.** The amount of the distribution to Ralph is $180,000 (20% x $900,000). § 301(b)(1). All of that distribution is dividend income, as noted in "A."

**Answer "D" is a correct statement and, therefore, not the right answer.** Section 311(a)(2) expressly so states.

90.     **The best answer is "B."** In testing for whether a redemption receives sale or exchange treatment the constructive ownership rules of § 318 apply. § 302(c)(1). Spouses are deemed to own each other's stock. § 318(a)(1)(A)(i). Therefore, Ralph is deemed to own 100% of the stock both before and after the redemption. In such a situation the redemption is never accorded sale or exchange treatment. *U.S. v. Davis*, 397 U.S. 301 (1970). Instead, the redemption is characterized under § 301(a). § 302(d). Since the $2,000,000 of available earnings and profits exceeds the total distribution of $1,500,000 ($900,000 distribution + $600,000 redemption), all of the $600,000 distributed to Ralph in the redemption would be characterized as a dividend.

**Answer "A" is incorrect.** The available earnings and profits would have been $3,196,712 [$3,200,000 accumulated earnings and profits − (1/365 x $1,200,000 negative current earnings and profits)].

**Answer "C" is incorrect.** Regardless of the date of the redemption, earnings and profits is allocated first to non-redemption distributions. Rev. Rul. 74-339, 1974-2 C.B. 103.

**Answer "D" is incorrect.** A corporation uses the same overall method of accounting in computing earnings and profits as it does in computing its taxable income. § 1.312-6(a). There are extensive differences in the way gross income, deductions, basis, etc., are measured between the cash- and accrual-methods of accounting. Therefore, it is highly unlikely that earnings and profits measured under the cash method would be the same as earnings and profits measured on the accrual method.

91.     Birtchnell recognizes a gain on the distribution of the warehouse. § 311(b)(1). The gain for earnings and profits purposes is measured using the basis for earnings and profits purposes. § 312(f)(1). The gains are:

|                            | Taxable Income | Earnings & Profits |
|----------------------------|---------------:|-------------------:|
| Deemed amount realized     | $2,500,000     | $2,500,000         |
| Adjusted basis             | (2,000,000)    | (2,100,000)        |
| Realized and recognized gain | $500,000     | $400,000           |

The marginal federal income tax on the gain is $170,000 (34% x $500,000). This reduces earnings and profits based on the principles of Rev. Rul. 57-332, 1957-2 C.B. 231, Rev. Rul. 70-609, 1970-2 C.B. 78, and Rev. Rul. 79-69, 1979-1 C.B. 134. Therefore, the available earnings and profits is $530,000 ($300,000 earnings and profits before the distribution + $400,000 gain on the distribution - $170,000 tax on that gain).

The amount of the distribution is $600,000 ($2,500,000 value of the warehouse - $1,900,000 encumbrance on the warehouse). § 301(b)(1), (b)(2)(B). The amount of the distribution is characterized as a dividend to the extent of available earnings and profits. § 301(a), (c)(1); § 316(a). Therefore, the dividend to John is $530,000. John then reduces his stock basis to $630,000 [$700,000 beginning basis - ($600,000 amount of the distribution - $530,000 dividend portion)]. § 301(c)(2).

John takes a fair market value basis in the warehouse of $2,500,000. § 301(d). His holding period in the warehouse is new because no provision of § 1223 applies.

92.     Now there would be a loss on the distribution as follows:

|  | Taxable Income | Earnings & Profits |
|---|---|---|
| Deemed amount realized | $2,500,000 | $2,500,000 |
| Adjusted basis | (2,700,000) | (2,800,000) |
| Realized loss | ($200,000) | ($300,000) |

Realized losses on distributions to shareholders with respect to their stock are not recognized by the corporation. § 311(a)(2). Such nonrecognized losses are also not taken into account for earnings and profits purposes. § 1.312-6(b). Therefore, the available earnings and profits remains $300,000.

John has a dividend of $300,000 and reduces his stock basis to $400,000 [$700,000 beginning basis - ($600,000 amount of the distribution - $300,000 dividend portion)].

John still takes a fair market value basis in the warehouse of $2,500,000 and his holding period in the warehouse is still new.

93.     **The best answer is "A."** Current earnings and profits (CE&P) are allocated proportionately to all distributions during the year, regardless of when the distributions occur. Accumulated earnings and profits (AE&P) are allocated on a first-in-first-out basis to the extent that the amount distributed to a shareholder exceeds the current earnings and profits allocated to that shareholder's distribution. § 1.316-2. A distribution is a dividend to the extent it is sourced from earnings and profits. § 316(a). Applying these rules:

| Shareholder | Date of Distribution | Amount of Distribution | % | Allocation of CE&P | Allocation of AE&P | Dividend |
|---|---|---|---|---|---|---|
| Adams | March 1 | $300,000 | 60% | $72,000 | $228,000 | $300,000 |
| Blunt | June 15 | 150,000 | 30% | 36,000 | 82,000 | 118,000 |
| Crisp | December 31 | 50,000 | 10% | 12,000 | 0 | 12,000 |
|  |  | $500,000 | 100% | $120,000 | $310,000 | $430,000 |

Under § 301(c)(1)-(3)(A):

- First, the distribution is a dividend to the extent sourced from earnings and profits;

- Second, the remaining distribution is a recovery of stock basis to the extent thereof;

- Third, the remaining distribution is a gain.

Applying these rules:

| SH | Am't of Distrib'n | Dividend | Remaining Distrib'n | Beginning Basis | Recovery of Basis | Ending Basis | Gain |
|---|---|---|---|---|---|---|---|
| Adams | $300,000 | $300,000 | $0 | $20,000 | $0 | $20,000 | $0 |
| Blunt | 150,000 | 118,000 | 32,000 | $250,000 | $32,000 | $218,000 | $0 |
| Crisp | 50,000 | 12,000 | 38,000 | $25,000 | $25,000 | $0 | $13,000 |
|  | $500,000 | $430,000 | $70,000 |  |  |  |  |

Crisp, therefore, will recognize a $13,000 gain as a result of the distribution.

**Answer "B" is incorrect.** Sometimes students believe that total earnings and profits, $430,000 (120,000 current earnings and profit + 310,000 accumulated earnings and profit), are allocated first-in-first-out. Under this erroneous assumption Crisp would have a gain of $25,000 as follows:

| Shareholder | Amount of Distrib'n | Allocation of E&P | Remaining Distrib'n | Beginning Basis | Recovery of Basis | Ending Basis | Gain |
|---|---|---|---|---|---|---|---|
| Adams | $300,000 | $300,000 | $0 | $20,000 | $0 | $20,000 | $0 |
| Blunt | 150,000 | 130,000 | 20,000 | $250,000 | $20,000 | $230,000 | $0 |
| Crisp | 50,000 | 0 | 50,000 | $25,000 | $25,000 | $0 | $25,000 |
| | $500,000 | $430,000 | $70,000 | | | | |

**Answer "C" is incorrect.** Sometimes students believe that total earnings and profits are allocated proportionately. Under this erroneous assumption Crisp would have a gain of zero as follows:

| SH | Amount of Distrib'n | % | Allocat'n of E&P | Remain'g Distrib'n | Beginning Basis | Recovery of Basis | Ending Basis | Gain |
|---|---|---|---|---|---|---|---|---|
| Adams | $300,000 | 60% | $258,000 | $42,000 | $20,000 | $20,000 | $0 | $22,000 |
| Blunt | 150,000 | 30% | 129,000 | 21,000 | $250,000 | $21,000 | $229,000 | $0 |
| Crisp | 50,000 | 10% | 43,000 | 7,000 | $25,000 | $7,000 | $18,000 | $0 |
| | $500,000 | 100% | $430,000 | $70,000 | | | | |

**Answer "D" is incorrect.** Sometimes students believe that stock basis is recovered before any portion of the distribution is treated as sourced from earnings and profits. Students typically also assume that total earnings and profits flow out on a first-in-first-out basis. Under these assumptions: Crisp first allocates her $50,000 distribution to the recovery of her $20,000 stock basis, bringing that basis to zero. The remaining $30,000 of the distribution is deemed sourced from earnings and profits to the extent allocated to Crisp. As noted under the discussion of "A", a first-in-first-out assumption would allocate no earnings and profits to Crisp. Therefore, the $30,000 of remaining distribution would be characterized as a gain.

94.    **The best answer is "D."** For federal income tax purposes a "dividend" is a distribution of property by a corporation to shareholders with respect to its stock sourced from "earnings and profits" (which is a federal income tax concept); and all distributions are deemed sourced from earnings and profits to the extent thereof. § 301(a), (c)(1); § 316(a). A dividend under state law is also a distribution to shareholders by a corporation with respect to its stock, but the board of directors can identify the source of the dividend as either earned surplus (essentially, cumulative undistributed earnings, analogous to financial accounting's retained earnings) or paid-in capital in excess of par (i.e., invested capital in excess of the stock's par value — a liquidating dividend). The board of director's identification of source, while effective for state law purposes, is irrelevant to the determination of whether a dividend has been distributed for federal income tax law purposes. The Code conclusively presumes that all dividends are sourced from earnings and profits to the extent thereof. For the same reason, **answer "A" is incorrect.**

    **Answer "B" is incorrect.** Although the board of directors is directing the distribution be paid out of earnings and, for federal income tax purposes, dividends are defined as distributions made from earnings and profits, the rules governing the computation of earned surplus under state law (which derive from financial accounting rules) and the rules governing the computation of earnings and profits under federal income tax law are significantly different. Therefore, a distribution out of earned surplus (state law) may or may not be sourced from earnings and profits (federal income tax law).

    **Answer "C" is incorrect.** Financial accounting rules used to measure "net income" (and therefore retained earnings) for state law purposes are significantly different from those used to measure earnings and profits for federal income tax purposes. Therefore, financial accounting rules would not require a corporation's financial statements to classify a particular distribution as from retained earnings simply because the federal income tax law requires the distribution to be classified as a dividend, which by definition means that the source of the distribution is earnings and profits.

95.    A "constructive dividend" is a distribution by a corporation to its shareholders with respect to its stock that was not authorized in accordance with state law requirements by formal action of the board of directors and which is not made for the corporation's benefit. *U.S. v. Mews*, 923 F.2d 67 (7th Cir. 1991). Technically, the phrase should be "constructive *distribution*" because a "distribution" is not a "dividend" unless sourced from earnings and profits. If the available earnings and profits is less than the amount of the "constructive dividend," only a portion of the distribution will be a "dividend" for tax purposes.

96.    To the corporation the calf blood was considered a worthless byproduct. It had tried and failed to develop the business to exploit the blood commercially. In the exercise of bona fide business judgment, unaffected by family relationships, the board allowed Michael to remove the blood and exploit it commercially, if possible. The corporation parted with no value when

it allowed Michael to remove the blood. It is even possible that the corporation secured a financial advantage by avoiding the full cost of disposing of the blood. Therefore, this was not a distribution of property to Michael in his capacity as shareholder and for that reason cannot be a "constructive dividend." *McCabe Packing Co. v. U.S.*, 809 F. Supp. 614 (C.D. Ill. 1992).

97.   Such expenditures are not ordinary and necessary business expenses of the corporation and therefore cannot be deducted by the corporation and cannot be characterized as for the corporation's benefit. The primary beneficiary of the corporate expenditures is the shareholder, which makes the costs of creating and operating the horticultural showplace a constructive dividend. *Greenspon v. Comm'r*, 229 F.2d 947 (8th Cir. 1956).

98.   The fine was the personal liability of the CEO. Characterization of the payment as an indemnification is unsustainable because indemnification for illegal conduct is not permissible under state law. The corporation's payment of $40,000 to the IRS discharges the CEO's personal liability and therefore is a constructive dividend. *Sachs v. Comm'r*, 227 F.2d 879 (8th Cir. 1960); § 1.301-1(m).

99.   **The best answer is "B."** The home-building expenses are not ordinary and necessary expenses of the corporation. The corporation derived no benefit from the expenditures. Therefore, they are not deductible to the corporation. § 162(a). They will be characterized as constructive dividends to the shareholder. *Hagaman v. Comm'r*, 958 F.2d 684 (6th Cir. 1992). Further, the unreasonable portion of the compensation paid to the children is not deductible. § 162(a)(1). These payments will also be characterized as constructive dividends to the shareholder. *Quarrier Diner, Inc.*, 22 T.C.M. (CCH) 276 (1963). The shareholder will then be deemed to have made gifts to the children in the amounts of the constructive dividends (which may create a gift tax liability for the shareholder). As a result of these recharacterizations, the excess compensation will be removed from the children's personal tax returns, which will likely result in tax refunds. The value of the homes and the excess compensation received are not taxable to the children since they constitute gifts. § 102(a).

      **Answer "A" is not correct.** As stated above, the home-building expenses will not be deductible to the corporation, but neither will the excess compensation to the children. This is a "red herring" answer in that it may distract a student by suggesting that any compensation is reasonable so long as it does not violate the prohibition against deducting remuneration in excess of $1 million annually with respect to certain employees (which, in any case, applies only to publicly held corporations). § 162(m). The restriction of § 162(m) and the "reasonable allowance for salaries" provision of § 162(a)(1) are independent standards that must both be met for compensation to be deductible.

      **Answer "C" is not correct** because the children are not shareholders in the corporation and, therefore, cannot receive dividends (distributions with respect to stock), constructive or otherwise.

      **Answer "D" is not correct.** These amounts will be characterized as dividends under § 301(c)(1) to the extent of the corporation's amount of earnings and profits. Only if the earnings and profits are exhausted would any portion of the constructive distributions reduce the shareholder's basis in her stock under § 301(c)(2).

100.  The IRS will characterize the misappropriated revenues as constructive dividends to Hildi.

*O'Neal v. U.S.*, 77 AFTR 2d 96-2491 (M.D. Fla. 1996). The bargain components of the land sales will be characterized as constructive dividends. § 1.301-1(j). The excess compensation will be characterized as a constructive dividend. *Quarrier Diner, Inc.*, 22 T.C.M. (CCH) 276 (1963). Absent other underreporting, the 20% understatement of gross income will not cause the statute of limitations to be extended to six years from the normal three. § 6501(e)(1)(A). However, if the failure to report that gross income on both Hildi's and Tyrant's tax returns constitutes fraud, the statute of limitations with respect to the year involved never starts to run. § 6501(c)(1).

101.    The misappropriated revenues have two possible characterizations: embezzlement or constructive dividend. The repayment of embezzled amounts are treated as § 162 deductions. The return of constructive dividends is characterized as a nondeductible contribution to capital. *O'Neal, supra.*

The return of the excess compensation is deductible under § 162 only if, before the excess salary was received by the employee, the employee was legally obligated to return any amount subsequently held to be unreasonable compensation for tax purposes. Rev. Rul. 69-115, 1969-1 C.B. 50. Therefore, Hildi would not be able to deduct any repayment. Instead, the repayment will be treated as a contribution to capital. The IRS is also likely to assert that Hildi is ineligible for § 1341 relief. *Id.* Courts have tended to disagree. E.g., *Van Cleave v. U.S.*, 718 F.2d 193 (6th Cir. 1983).

102.    North Hollow recognizes no gain or loss on the distribution of the stock. § 311(a)(1). Nor are earnings and profits reduced. § 312(d)(1)(B).

103.    Michelle has no gain or loss on the stock distribution. § 305(a). She allocates the stock basis between the two blocks of stock in proportion to their relative fair market values. § 307(a); § 1.307-1(a). Since the new stock is identical to the old stock, the basis can be allocated in proportion to the number of shares. There were 100,000 shares outstanding before the stock distribution (inferred from the fact that the 10,000 shares distributed comprised 10% of the previously outstanding shares). Michelle held 20,000 shares (20% of the shares previously outstanding, as just determined) and received 2,000 shares in the distribution. Her basis in the new stock is $10,000 ($110,000 basis in the old shares x [2,000 new shares/(20,000 old shares + 2,000 new shares)]). The holding period of the new stock is three years. § 1223(4).

104.    Since the fair market value of the rights is less than 15% of the value of the stock already held (the distribution was one right per 10 outstanding shares, which is only 10%, and the value of a right would be less than the value of a share), and since Michelle made no election with respect to the distribution, the basis allocated to the stock rights is zero. § 307(b)(1).

105.    Section 305(b)(2) generally treats a stock distribution as a property distribution subject to taxation under § 301 if some shareholders receive cash and others receive stock or rights. An exception exists where cash is distributed in lieu of fractional shares to save the corporation the trouble and cost of issuing fractional shares. § 1.305-3(c)(1). The fractional shares are deemed distributed and then redeemed in a transaction qualifying for sale or exchange treatment. § 1.305-3(c)(2).

106.    The distribution is taxable as a property distribution under § 301 because distributing preferred to common shareholders alters the pre-distribution allocation of voting power and distribution rights between the common and preferred stockholders. § 305(b)(4). The amount of the distribution is the fair market value of the preferred stock received. § 301(b)(1); § 1.305-1(b)(1). To the extent of Jersey Corp.'s earnings and profits allocable to the distribution to Martin, the distribution will be a dividend. § 301(a), (c)(1); § 316(a). The remaining amount of the distribution, if any, will reduce Martin's basis in his stock. § 301(c)(2). Once that basis has been exhausted, any remaining distribution will be a capital gain. § 301(c)(3)(A).

107.    **The best answer is "C."** The Court said "A 'stock dividend' shows that the company's accumulated profits have been capitalized, instead of distributed to the stockholders or retained as surplus available for distribution[.] Far from being a realization of profits [by the shareholder, the corporation's income] no longer is available for actual distribution. [The] controlling fact is that the stockholder has received nothing out of the company's assets for his separate use and benefit; on the contrary, every dollar of his original investment,

together with . . . accumulations . . . from employment of his money . . . , still remains the property of the company[. The shareholder] has received nothing that answers the definition of income[.]"

**Answer "A" is incorrect.** The distribution is governed by § 305(b)(1) and is treated as a property distribution under § 301 rather than as a tax-free stock distribution under § 305(a). Section 1.305-2(a)(1) states that, "[u]nder section 305(b)(1), if any shareholder has the . . . option with respect to whether a distribution shall be made either in money . . . , or in stock . . . , then, with respect to *all* shareholders, the distribution of stock . . . is treated as a distribution of property to which section 301 applies regardless of whether the distribution is actually made in whole or in part in stock[.]" (Emphasis added.)

**Answer "B" is incorrect.** The distribution is governed by § 305(b)(3), which covers distributions which have "the result of" receipt of preferred stock by some common shareholders and receipt of common stock by others. Thus, the distribution will be treated as a property distribution under § 301. § 1.305-4(b) Ex. 2.

**Answer "D" is incorrect.** Section 1.305-1(a) states that eligibility for tax-free treatment under § 305(a) is not impacted by the fact that treasury stock was used in the distribution.

108.   There are two family attribution rules. An individual is deemed to own the stock actually owned by the individual's spouse. § 318(a)(1)(A)(i). An individual is also deemed to own the stock actually owned by the individual's children, grandchildren and parents. § 318(a)(1)(A)(ii). Stock deemed owned by an individual by virtue of one of the family attribution rules cannot be re-attributed to another family member. § 318(a)(5)(B). Son is therefore deemed to own the stock of Father, Mother, and Son's daughter and grandson. Father's brother's stock is not attributable to Father; and even if it were, it could not be reattributed to Son. The same is true with respect to Mother's nephew. Although Father's father's (Mother's father's) stock can be attributed to Father (Mother), such stock could also not be reattributed to Son. Therefore, Son actually and constructively owns the following stock:

| | | | |
|---|---|---|---|
| Actually: | | | 2 |
| Constructively: | Father | 36 | |
| | Mother | 40 | |
| | Son's daughter | 3 | |
| | Son's grandson | 5 | |
| | Father's brother | 0 | |
| | Father's father | 0 | |
| | Mother's father | 0 | |
| | Mother's nephew | 0 | 84 |
| | | | 86 |

109.   In *Cerone*, 87 T.C. 1 (1986), the Tax Court said:

> Before the enactment of the 1954 Code, the attribution rules were sometimes applied, and sometimes not applied; to avoid that uncertainty, section 302 expressly made the attribution rules applicable for purposes of determining whether a distribution in redemption should be treated as a dividend. . . . Congress sought to provide definite and specific rules and to avoid the uncertainties which had arisen under the earlier law. . . . If the applicability of the attribution rules depended upon the feelings or attitudes among the members of a family, it would then be necessary to inquire into whether there was hostility or animosity among them, whether such discord was serious, and whether it would actually or likely impair the ability of one member of the family to influence the conduct of other members. By the terms of the statute, the attribution rules are applicable irrespective of the personal relationships which exist among the members of a family, and an interpretation of the statute which made their applicability depend upon whether there was discord among the members of the family — or the extent of any such discord — would frustrate the legislative objective.

Therefore, the existence of discord between Son and Mother is irrelevant in determining the amount of Mother's stock that Son constructively owns.

110.    **The best answer is "A."** Stock owned by a partnership is considered owned proportionately by its partners. § 318(a)(2)(A). Therefore, Philip is deemed to own 2.16 shares (6% of 36 shares) of the E stock through P.

If at least 50% percent in value of the stock in a corporation is owned by any person, such person is considered to own the stock owned by such corporation in proportion to the value of the stock owned. § 318(a)(2)(C). Since Philip owns less than 50% of C, he is not deemed to own any of the E stock owned by C. Since Philip owns 70% of D, he is deemed to own 30.1 shares (70% of 43 shares) of the E stock through D.

Stock owned by a trust is considered owned by its beneficiaries in proportion to their actuarial interests. § 318(a)(2)(B)(i). Therefore, Philip is deemed to own .77 shares (11% of 7 shares) of the E stock through T.

In the aggregate Philip is deemed to own the following number of shares of E stock:

| P | 2.16 |
|---|------|
| D | 30.10 |
| T | .77 |
|   | 33.03 |

Philip's wife is deemed to own the shares owned by Philip. § 318(a)(1)(A)(i). Therefore, she is also deemed to own 33.03 shares.

Stock owned by a child is deemed owned by the parent. § 318(a)(1)(A)(ii). However, stock deemed owned by an individual by virtue of one of the family attribution rules cannot be re-attributed to another family member. § 318(a)(5)(B). Therefore, Philip's mother-in-law is not deemed to own any of the stock deemed owned by Philip (i.e., Philip to Wife to Wife's mother).

Based on the above analysis, **answer "B" and answer "C" are incorrect.**

**Answer "D" is incorrect.** If at least 50% percent in value of the stock in a corporation is owned by any person, the corporation is considered to own the stock owned by such person. § 318(a)(3)(C). Since Philip owns less than 50% of C, C is not deemed to own any of the stock owned by Philip.

111.    Philip is deemed to own stock on which he has an option. § 318(a)(4). Therefore, Philip is deemed to own 165 shares. A partnership is deemed to own the stock owned by its partners. § 318(a)(3)(A). Therefore, P is deemed to own all of Philip's 165 IBM shares.

If at least 50% percent in value of the stock in a corporation is owned by any person, the corporation is considered to own the stock owned by such person. § 318(a)(3)(C). Since Philip owns less than 50% of C, C is not deemed to own any of the IBM stock owned by Philip. However, since Philip owns 70% of D, D is deemed to own all of Philip's 165 IBM shares.

Stock owned by a beneficiary is deemed owned by the trust. § 318(a)(3)(B)(i). Therefore, T is deemed to own all of Philip's 165 IBM shares.

112.    Stock owned by a partnership is considered owned proportionately by its partners. § 318(a)(2)(A). It was noted above that P is deemed to own all of Philip's 165 IBM shares.

However, stock attributed to an entity from an equity holder cannot be reattributed to another equity holder. § 318(a)(5)(C). Therefore, Sharon is not deemed to own any of the stock constructively owned by P (i.e., Philip to P to Sharon).

113. **The best answer is "A."** Gerald's wife is deemed to own the stock owned by her father. § 318(a)(1)(A)(ii). Gerald is deemed to own the stock owned by his wife. § 318(a)(1)(A)(i). However, stock deemed owned by an individual by virtue of one of the family attribution rules cannot be reattributed to another family member. § 318(a)(5)(B). Therefore, Gerald is not deemed to own any of the stock owned by his wife's father.

   **Answer "B" is incorrect.** Sibling attribution does not exist under § 318. Therefore, Maria is not deemed to own any of the stock owned by her brother.

   **Answer "C" is incorrect.** Adopted children are treated the same as children by blood. § 318(a)(1)(B). A parent is deemed to own the stock owned by a child. § 318(a)(1)(A)(ii). Therefore, the adopting parent is deemed to own the stock owned by the adopted child.

   **Answer "D" is incorrect.** Stock owned by a person's former spouse is not deemed owned by that person. § 318(a)(1)(A)(i).

114. Sibling attribution does not exist under § 318, so Cori's Gamma stock can be attributed to Gwen only through Pittsford. Pittsford is deemed to own Cori's Gamma stock. § 318(a)(3)(A). Normally Gwen would be deemed to own a proportionate amount of any stock owned by Pittsford. § 318(a)(2)(A). However, stock attributed to an entity from an equity holder cannot be reattributed to another equity holder. § 318(a)(5)(C). Therefore, Gwen is not deemed to own any of the Gamma stock owned by Cori.

115. Cori is deemed to own 50% of Pittsford's Alpha stock. § 318(a)(2)(A). Mendon is deemed to own any stock owned by Cori. § 318(a)(3)(A). Therefore, Mendon is deemed to own 50% of Pittsford's Alpha stock.

116. **The best answer is "B."** Section 318(a)(4) expressly so states.

   **Answer "A" is incorrect.** The constructive ownership rules only apply when expressly invoked by the Code. § 318(a).

   **Answer "C" is incorrect.** Family attribution can be waived in the context of § 302(b)(3) redemptions (complete termination of interest). § 302(c)(2). The requirements for waiver are: 1) immediately after the redemption the distributee has no interest in the corporation (including an interest as officer, director, or employee), other than as a creditor; 2) the distributee does not acquire such an interest (other than by inheritance) within ten years from the date of the redemption; 3) the distributee agrees to notify the IRS if an interest in the corporation is acquired within that 10-year period; and 4) the distributee retains the records required by the IRS.

   **Answer "D" is incorrect.** The statement is correct only if the stock owned by the individual represents at least 50% of the value of all of the corporate stock. § 318(a)(2)(C).

117. **The best answer is "B."** *Himmel v. Comm'r*, 338 F.2d 815 (2d Cir. 1964), expressly so states.

**Answer "A" is incorrect.** The tax consequences to an individual of a redemption of stock held long-term at a gain are generally more favorable. § 1(h). The redemption generally qualifies for the same 15% tax rate as is applicable to dividends. However, in a redemption that gain is determined after subtracting the stock's basis, which makes the gain less than the amount of the distribution. § 1001(a). A capital gain on the redemption may also be offset by current or carried-over capital losses. § 1211.

**Answer "C" is incorrect.** These redemptions are tested by evaluating their impact on the redeeming shareholder, not on the corporation. Under § 302(b)(4), partial liquidations *are* tested for redemption status by evaluating the redemption's impact on the corporation. § 302(e)(1)(A).

**Answer "D" is incorrect.** State law characterization of a transaction as a redemption is not determinative of the federal income tax consequences. State law governs tax consequences only when the Code expressly so provides. *Burnet v. Harmel*, 287 U.S. 103 (1932).

118. If a redemption is respected as such by the tax law, the shareholder will receive sale or exchange treatment, which normally results in a capital gain or loss, often long-term. § 302(a). Otherwise the shareholder will receive the standard distribution treatment. § 302(d). Under that treatment the distribution is first treated as sourced from earnings and profits to the extent thereof and is characterized as a dividend. Any remaining distribution is treated as a non-taxable recovery of stock basis to the extent thereof. Finally, any remaining distribution is treated as a gain from the disposition of the stock. § 301(c).

119. A redemption will be respected only if it satisfies one of the following four tests: 1) The distribution is not essentially equivalent to a dividend; 2) the distribution is substantially disproportionate; 3) the distribution completely terminates the shareholder's equity interest; or 4) the distribution is in partial liquidation of the corporation. For a redemption to not be essentially equivalent to a dividend, the redeeming shareholder's rights to vote, to share in earnings, and to share in assets upon liquidation must each contract and that shareholder's post-redemption voting power must be less than 50%. To be substantially disproportionate, the redeeming shareholder's post-redemption voting power must be less than 50%, and that shareholder's post-redemption voting power must be less than 80% of its pre-redemption voting power. Here, the facts state that this is not a partial liquidation. § 302(b); *U.S. v. Davis*, 397 U.S. 301 (1970).

120. Yes. § 302(c). Under the rules of § 318(a), spouses are deemed to own each other's stock. Therefore, Husband is deemed own 70 shares (his 20 shares and Wife's 50 shares) of the Beverly stock before the redemption and 50 shares (Wife's 50 shares) after the redemption.

121.   No. First, Husband did not completely terminate his equity interest in Beverly because, after the redemption of the stock he actually owned, he is still deemed to own Wife's 50 shares under the analysis in "C." § 302(b)(3).

This was also not a substantially disproportionate distribution. Husband's pre-redemption voting power was 70% [(his 20 shares + Wife's 50 shares)/100 shares outstanding]. His post-redemption voting power is 62.5% (Wife's 50 shares/80 shares outstanding), which fails the "less than 50%" test. In addition, the ratio of Husband's post-redemption voting power to his pre-redemption voting power is 89.3% (62.5%/70%), which fails the "less than 80%" test. § 302(b)(2)

The distribution also fails the "not essentially equivalent to a dividend" test. Although Husband's rights to vote, to share in earnings, and to share in assets upon liquidation contracted, his post-redemption voting power, 62.5%, was not less than 50%. § 302(b)(1).

122.   The amount of the distribution is $800,000 and earnings and profits are $600,000. Therefore, Husband has a dividend of $600,000 based on the analysis in "A." The remaining distribution ($200,000) fully recovers Husband's stock basis ($50,000). The rest of the distribution ($150,000) is treated as a gain from the sale or change of the stock, which is a capital asset and which has been held more than six years. Therefore, Husband has a $150,000 long-term capital gain. If Husband has no other capital asset transaction during the tax year, it is probable that both the $600,000 dividend portion and the $150,000 long-term capital gain portion will be taxed at a favorable 15% rate. § 1(h).

123.   **The best answer is "D."** *Himmel v. Comm'r*, 338 F.2d 815 (2d Cir. 1964), expressly so holds.

**Answer "A" is incorrect.** The constructive ownership rules of § 318 apply to analyses under § 302(b). § 302(c)(1). Spouses are deemed to own each other's stock. § 318(a)(1)(A)(i). Therefore, the existence of the shareholding spouse would impact the characterization of the redemption.

**Answer "B" is incorrect.** A shareholder is not deemed to own a nephew's stock. Therefore, the existence of a shareholding nephew would not impact the characterization of the redemption.

**Answer "C" is incorrect.** A shareholder is deemed to own optioned stock. § 318(a)(4). Therefore, the existence of optioned stock would impact the characterization of the redemption.

124.   **The best answer is "C."** The basis of the redeemed stock "jumps" to the redeeming shareholder's other stock in the same corporation. If the shareholder owns no stock in that corporation after the redemption, the basis "jumps" to the stock attributed to the redeeming shareholder under § 318. § 1.302-2(c).

**Answer "A" is a correct statement and, therefore, not the right answer.** Section 302(a) expressly so states.

**Answer "B" is a correct statement and, therefore, not the right answer.** The general rule is that earnings and profits are reduced by the amount of the distribution (in this context, the amount paid for the redeemed stock). § 312(a)(1). However, § 312(n)(7) limits the reduction to the redeemed stock's proportionate share of the earnings and profits. Thus, if 15% of the stock is redeemed and the redemption is characterized as a sale or exchange, the corporation's earnings and profits will be reduced by the lesser of the amount paid for stock or 15% of the available earnings and profits.

**Answer "D" is a correct statement and, therefore, not the right answer.** *US v. Davis*, 397 U.S. 301 (1970), expressly so states; *Johnston*, 77 T.C. 679 (1981); Rev. Rul. 75–502, 1975–2 C.B.111.

125. **The best answer is "B."** This answer is a "red herring." The holding period of all property acquired is new by default. There is no express statutory authority for this proposition; it is simply a fundamental aspect of the tax system. Section 1223 overrides the default rule and allows for a "tacked" holding period in the circumstances specified by that provision.

**Answer "A" is a correct statement and, therefore, not the right answer.** Section 302(d) expressly so states.

**Answer "C" is a correct statement and, therefore, not the right answer.** Section 301(d) expressly so states.

**Answer "D" is a correct statement and, therefore, not the right answer.** Section 312(a)(3) and (b)(2) expressly so state.

126. **The best answer is "A."** Earnings and profits are reduced by the fair market value of the distributed appreciated property. § 312(a)(3), (b)(2).

**Answer "B" is a correct statement and, therefore, not the right answer.** Earnings and profits are reduced by the marginal tax attributable to the gain resulting to the corporation from the distribution of the appreciated property. *See*, Rev. Rul. 57-332, 1957-2 C.B. 231; Rev. Rul. 70-609, 1970-2 C.B. 78; Rev. Rul. 79-69, 1979-1 C.B. 134.

**Answer "C" is a correct statement and, therefore, not the right answer.** In a § 302(b)(3) redemption the family attribution rules are waived if: 1) immediately after the redemption the distributee has no interest in the corporation (including an interest as officer, director, or employee), other than as a creditor; 2) the distributee does not acquire such interest (other than by inheritance) within ten years from the date of the redemption; 3) the distributee agrees to notify the IRS if an interest in the corporation is acquired within the ten-year period; and 4) the distributee retains the records required by the IRS. § 302(c)(2).

**Answer "D" is a correct statement and, therefore, not the right answer.** Section 303(a)(1) expressly so states. Only the amount needed to pay the gratuitous transfer taxes and the funeral and estate administrative expenses is eligible. The stock holding from which the redeemed stock comes must comprise at least 35% of the excess of the value of the gross estate over certain estate expenses, losses and liabilities. § 303(b)(2)(A). Stock aggregation rules for the purposes of the 35% test are available. § 303(b)(2)(B).

127. **The best answer is "C."** While in S status, a corporation does not increase its earnings and profits. § 1371(c)(1).

**Answer "A" is a correct statement and, therefore, not the right answer.** Section 312(b)(1) expressly so states.

**Answer "B" is a correct statement and, therefore, not the right answer.** A redemption that fails the § 302(b) tests is treated as a § 301 distribution. § 302(d). Under § 301(a), (c)(1)-(c)(3)(A), the amount of the distribution is first a dividend to the extent of the earnings and profits allocated to the distribution (here none), then a recovery of stock basis and finally a capital gain. This result is the same as would have obtained had the redemption satisfied one of the § 302(b) tests and been accorded sale or exchange treatment.

**Answer "D" is a correct statement and, therefore, not the right answer.** Section 301 distributions are allocated earnings and profits before § 302(a) distributions. Rev. Rul. 74-339, 1974-2 C.B. 103. Thus, there would be no earnings and profits remaining after the § 301 distributions on these facts.

128.  **The best answer is "B."** With 90% the shareholder controls not only the routine corporate operating decisions but also the major corporate decisions that require a super-majority vote (e.g., merger, sale of substantially all of the assets). The courts generally view a reduction in the control right from super-majority control to simple operating control to be sufficient to satisfy the "not essentially equivalent to a dividend" test. *Wright v. U.S.*, 482 F.2d 600 (8th Cir. 1973). The IRS disagrees, but has had little success in litigation. Rev. Rul. 78-401, 1978-2 C.B. 127. However, the courts have not followed this position.

**Answer "A" is incorrect.** Stock represents three distinct rights: the right to participate in control, in earnings, and in assets upon liquidation. *Himmel v. Comm'r*, 338 F.2d 815 (2d Cir. 1964). When testing for sale or exchange treatment under § 302(b)(1), the primary right addressed is control. *Johnston*, 77 T.C. 679 (1981); Rev. Rul. 75-502, 1975-2 C.B. 111. Both 60% and 55% voting power give the shareholder operating control of the corporation. Therefore, there has not been a sufficient reduction in the control right to satisfy the "not essentially equivalent to a dividend" test.

**Answer "C" is incorrect.** Since control is not reduced by the redemption of preferred stock, the "not essentially equivalent to a dividend" test is failed. *Furr v. Comm'r*, 34 T.C.M. (CCH) 433 (1975).

**Answer "D" is incorrect.** The shareholder is deemed to own the stock owned by the granddaughter. §§ 302(c)(1), 318(a)(1)(A)(ii). Since the shareholder and the granddaughter are the only stockholders, the shareholder is deemed to own 100% of the stock both before and after the redemption. No change in control has occurred, so the redemption fails the "not essentially equivalent to a dividend" test. *U.S. v. Davis*, 397 U.S. 301 (1970).

129.  **The best answer is "C."** To satisfy the "not essentially equivalent to a dividend" tests of § 302(b)(1) there must be a meaningful reduction in the shareholder's interest in the corporation. *U.S. v. Davis*, 397 U.S. 301 (1970). The interest of a shareholder consists of three rights: the right to participate in control, in earnings, and in assets upon liquidation. *Himmel v. Comm'r*, 338 F.2d 815 (2d Cir. 1964). The principal right that must be meaningfully reduced is control. *Johnston*, 77 TC 679 (1981); Rev. Rul. 75-502, 1975-2 C.B. 111. A sole shareholder owns 100% of the stock both before and after the redemption. Therefore, the "not essentially equivalent to a dividend" test is failed.

**Answer "A" is incorrect.** Before the redemption Sharon owned stock representing 28% of the voting power. After redeeming 25.2 shares (90% x 28 shares) her remaining 2.8 shares represent a voting power of 3.7% [2.8/(100 - 25.2)]. Before the redemption she could join with only one other shareholder and exercise control of the corporation. After the redemption this is no longer the case since her 3.7% combined with any other single shareholder's 32.1% [24/ (100 - 25.2)] is only 35.8%. This reduction in the ability to influence the corporation constitutes a meaningful reduction in the shareholder's interest and therefore satisfies the "not essentially equivalent to a dividend" test. Rev. Rul. 76-364, 1976-2 C.B. 91.

**Answer "B" is incorrect.** As a general rule, if a shareholder has no meaningful control right, any reduction in the shareholder's stock interest is considered meaningful. Rev. Rul. 76-385, 1976-2 C.B. 92.

**Answer "D" is incorrect.** The redemption of nonvoting, nonconvertible preferred stock by a shareholder who owns no common stock (and who therefore exercises no control) qualifies for sale or exchange treatment under § 302(b)(1). § 1.302-2(a); Rev. Rul. 77-426, 1977-2 C.B. 87.

130. **The best answer is "D."** Mother is deemed to own all of the stock owned by her children and grandchildren. § 302(c)(1); § 318(a)(1)(A)(ii). Therefore, both before and after the redemption she is deemed to own 100% of the stock. The § 302(b)(1) and (2) tests for sale or exchange treatment require the shareholder to not have control after the redemption. The § 302(b)(3) test requires the shareholder to have no interest in the corporation (other than as a creditor) after the redemption. Since this is not the case, and since no waiver of family attribution was elected which would have allowed § 302(b)(3) to be satisfied, Mother is not eligible for sale or exchange treatment. Because "D" is the best answer, **answers "A", "B" and "C" are not correct.**

131. **The best answer is "A."** The status of corporate employee constitutes an interest in the corporation. § 302(c)(2)(A)(i). Serving as a paid corporate consultant is deemed similar to providing services as an employee. Rev. Rul. 70-104, 1970-1 C.B. 66.

**Answer "B" is incorrect.** The status of executor of a shareholding family member's estate does not constitute an interest in the corporation. Rev. Rul. 75-2, 1975-1 C.B. 99.

**Answer "C" is incorrect.** The status of landlord does not constitute an interest in the corporation. Rev. Rul. 70-639, 1970-2 C.B. 74.

**Answer "D" is incorrect.** Stock reacquired by bequest or inheritance does not cause the family attribution waiver to be lost. § 302(c)(2)(A)(ii).

132. **The best answer is "C."** The status of corporate director constitutes an interest in the corporation. § 302(c)(2)(A)(i). Her power to appoint a member is deemed equivalent to her holding the directorship herself. Rev. Rul. 59-119, 1959-1 C.B. 68.

**Answer "A" is a correct statement and, therefore, not the right answer.** The status of corporate creditor does not constitute an interest in the corporation for the purpose of the family attribution waiver rules. § 302(c)(2)(A)(i).

**Answer "B" is a correct statement and, therefore, not the right answer.** Acquiring corporate assets pursuant to her rights as a creditor does not constitute an interest in the corporation. § 1.302-4(e).

**Answer "D" is a correct statement and, therefore, not the right answer.** The statute of limitations on assessment with respect to any deficiency related to the redemption does not run until one year after the redeeming shareholder notifies the IRS that the requirements for the family attribution waiver have been violated. § 302(c)(2)(A). Because Mother never notified the IRS about her becoming the CEO, the statute of limitations period has not run and the IRS can still assert a deficiency.

133. **The best answer is "C."** The family attribution waiver rules only apply to § 302(b)(3) redemptions. § 302(c)(2)(A).

**Answer "A" is a correct statement and, therefore, not the right answer.** Trust is deemed to own the stock owned by its beneficiaries, here only Child. § 318(a)(3)(B)(i). Child is deemed to own the stock owned by Parent. § 318(a)(1)(A)(ii). After the redemption Parent owns all of the stock. Therefore, Trust is deemed to own all of the stock.

**Answer "B" is a correct statement and, therefore, not the right answer.** Section 302(c)(2)(C) expressly so provides. Trust and Child must both agree to: 1) hold no interest in the corporation (including an interest as officer, director, or employee), other than an interest as a creditor; 2), notify the IRS if an interest is acquired during the next ten years; and 3) maintain certain records. § 302(c)(2)(A).

**Answer "D" is a correct statement and, therefore, not the right answer.** Where a redeemed shareholder no longer holds any stock in the redeeming corporation and sale or exchange treatment was not allowed, such shareholder's remaining stock basis "jumps" to the stock of the person from whom stock ownership was attributed to the redeeming shareholder under § 318. § 1.302-2(c).

134.   **The best answer is "A."** Therefore, **Answer "D" is incorrect.**

Section 302(b)(2)(B) requires that the redeeming shareholder's post-redemption voting power be less than 50%. Algebraically Roy's voting power after the redemption is:

AFTER = (70 − X)/(100 − X), where X is the number of shares Roy redeems

To satisfy the "less than 50%" test:

$$AFTER = (70 − X)/(100 − X) < .5$$

$$70 − X < 50 − .5X$$

$$20 < .5X$$

40 < X, which means that X must be at least 41 since fractional shares are not allowed

**Answer "B" is a correct statement and, therefore, not the right answer.** Section 302(b)(2)(C) requires the redeeming shareholder's voting power to contract by more than 20% as a result of the redemption. Algebraically,

$$AFTER/BEFORE < .8$$

$$BEFORE = 70/100 = .7$$

$$Therefore, [(70 − X)/(100 − X)]/.7 < .8$$

$$(70 − X)/(100 − X) < .56$$

$$70 − X < 56 − .56X$$

$$14 < .44X$$

$$31.8 < X$$

X must be at least 32 since fractional shares are not allowed

**Answer "C" is a correct statement and, therefore, not the right answer.** To enjoy sale or exchange treatment under § 302(b)(2), both the "less than 50% voting power" and the "more than 20% voting power contraction" tests must be satisfied. Therefore, the minimum number of shares Roy must redeem it is the *greater* of 41 and 32, which is 41. The redemption of only 32 shares will not suffice because, although it satisfies the "more than 20% voting power contraction" test, that number would not satisfy the "less than 50% voting power" test.

135.    **The best answer is "C."** Section 302(b)(2)(D) requires the substantially disproportionate redemption tests to be performed after all of a planned series of redemptions are completed. Therefore, the impact of Inez' redemption must be taken into account.

Roy (with Bertha's stock) owned 90% (90/100) before the redemption. After the redemption Roy will be deemed to own 90 - X shares of the stock. The total number of shares outstanding at the end of the series of the redemptions is: 100 - X - 5 (50% redeemed by Inez), or 95 - X. Therefore the test for "more than 20% voting power contraction" is:

$$\text{AFTER/BEFORE} < .8$$

$$[(90 - X)/(95 - X)]/.9 < .8$$

$$(90 - X)/(95 - X) < .72$$

$$90 - X < 68.4 - .72X$$

$$21.6 < .28X$$

$$77.1 < X$$

X must be at least 78
since fractional shares are not allowed

The "less than 50% voting power" test is:

$$\text{AFTER} < .5$$

$$(90 - X)/(95 - X) < .5$$

$$90 - X < 47.5 - .5X$$

$$42.5 < .5X$$

$$85 < X$$

X must be at least 86
since fractional shares are not allowed

To enjoy sale or exchange treatment under § 302(b)(2), both the "less than 50% voting power" and the "more than 20% voting power contraction" tests must be satisfied. The former requires that at least 86 shares be redeemed; the latter requires that at least 81 shares be redeemed. Therefore, at least 86 shares must be redeemed. This will require Roy and Bertha to act together to redeem the necessary shares.

**Answer "A" is incorrect.** Roy and Inez are not within the family attribution rules of § 318(a)(1)(A).

**Answer "B" is incorrect.** The "less than 50% voting power" rule requires that, algebraically:

$$\text{AFTER} = [(70 \text{ Roy's shares} + 20 \text{ Bertha's shares}) - X]/(100 - X) < .5$$

$$90 - X < 50 - .5X$$

$$40 < .5X$$

$$80 < X$$

X must be at least 81
since fractional shares are not allowed

Although not sufficient to allow for sale or exchange treatment under § 302(b)(2) because the "less than 50% voting power" test is failed (Roy redeemed only 65 shares), 65 does satisfy the "more than 20% voting power contraction" test, as follows:

$$\text{AFTER/BEFORE} < .8$$

$$[(90 - X)/(100 - X)]/(90/100) < .8$$

$$(90 - X)/(100 - X) < .72$$

$$90 - X < 72 - .72X$$

$$18 < .28X$$

$$64.3 < X$$

X must be at least 65
since fractional shares are not allowed

**Answer "D" is incorrect.** Because Roy is deemed to own Bertha's stock under § 318(a)(1)(A)(i), even if he redeems all of his stock he will not be able to qualify under § 302(b)(3) unless Bertha also redeems all of her stock or he can waive the family attribution rules under § 302(c)(2)(A). Since the latter is possible and fully under his control, it is incorrect to say that it is impossible for Roy to qualify under § 302(b)(3).

136.    If a shareholder owns at least 20% of the stock of a corporation and if that stock is included in the shareholder's gross estate, then such stock and all similarly qualifying stock are *aggregated* in applying the 35% test of § 303(b)(2)(A). § 303(b)(2)(B). The total value of the Townsend and Whidbey stock is $12,000,000 ($7,000,000 + $5,000,000). The gross estate less the § 2053 deductions is $30,000,000 ($40,000,000 − $10,000,000). Thirty-five percent of that amount is $10,500,000, which is less than the total value of the stock. Therefore, § 303 applies.

137.    The maximum amount of the redemption accorded sale or exchange treatment under § 303 is the sum of the estate tax liability and the funeral and administrative expenses, $11,000,000 ($10,500,000 + $500,000). § 303(a). Since the stock is redeemed for $12,000,000, $1,000,000 is not governed by § 303.

The remaining $1,000,000 has to be tested under § 302(b)(1)-(3). Linnea is clearly eligible for

§ 302(b)(3) since she has completely terminated her interest in both corporations. Therefore, none of the amount received with respect to the stock will be or could be characterized as a dividend.

138. **The best answer is "D."** Since there was no contraction of the corporation's business activity resulting from the condemnation, the distribution of the proceeds fails to qualify as a partial liquidation. Rev. Rul. 67-16, 1967-1 C.B. 77.

**Answer "A" is a correct statement and, therefore, not the right answer.** Section 302(e)(1)(A) expressly so states.

**Answer "B" is a correct statement and, therefore, not the right answer.** *Blascha v. U.S.*, 393 F.2d 983 (Ct. Cl. 1968), expressly so states.

**Answer "C" is a correct statement and, therefore, not the right answer.** Section 1.346-1(b) expressly so states.

139. **The best answer is "B."** The destruction of the line of business results in a contraction in the existing level of business activity. Therefore, the redemption which distributes the insurance proceeds qualifies as a partial liquidation. § 1.346-1(a)(2).

**Answer "A" is incorrect.** The working capital associated with a discontinued line of business can be included in a redemption distribution. Rev. Rul. 60-232, 1960-2 C.B. 115.

**Answer "C" is incorrect.** There is no contraction in the existing level of business activity resulting from the abandonment of the expansion plan. Therefore, the redemption which distributes the expansion reserve does not qualify as a partial liquidation. § 1.346-1(a)(2).

**Answer "D" is incorrect.** Corporate shareholders are precluded from enjoying sale or exchange treatment under the partial liquidation safe harbor. § 302(b)(4)(A).

140. The primary advantage of having the redemption characterized as a dividend under § 302(d) is that the amount received will be taxed at a maximum rate of 15%. § 1(h)(11). The basis of the redeemed stock will jump to other stock in the same corporation held by the redeeming shareholder (or to the stock owned by the related person from whom the redeeming shareholder's stock ownership was attributed under § 318). § 1.302-2(c).

If the redemption is characterized as a sale or exchange under § 302(a), one advantage is that the amount of the gain is reduced by the basis of the stock redeemed. § 1001(a). The gain may be further reduced by current capital losses or capital loss carryovers. § 1222; § 1212(b). The primary disadvantage of sale or exchange treatment is that, since the holding period is short-term, the gain will be taxed at the ordinary tax rates (currently up to 35%) since short-term capital gain is not included in net capital gain. § 1222(11).

141. Neither characterization has a tax rate advantage since corporate shareholders do not enjoy a preferential tax rate on dividends. However, characterization as a dividend has the advantage of allowing a dividends-received deduction of 70% or 80% (because a minority interest is involved). § 243(a)(1), (c). The basis of the redeemed stock will move to other stock in the same corporation held by the redeeming corporate shareholder (or to the stock owned by the related person from whom the redeeming corporate shareholder's stock ownership was attributed under § 318). § 1.302-2(c).

Sale or exchange treatment has two advantages. First, the amount of the gain is reduced by the basis of the stock redeemed. § 1001(a). Second, the gain may be further reduced by current capital losses or capital loss carryovers. § 1222; § 1212(a).

142.  **The best answer is "D." Thus, answer "A," answer "B" and answer "C" are incorrect.** All three alternatives yield "sale or exchange" treatment for Seller.

Answer "A" and answer "B" involve complete terminations of interest under § 302(b)(3). *Zenz v. Quinlivan*, 213 F.2d 914 (6th Cir. 1954), held that the step-transaction doctrine is inapplicable where, at the end of the combined transaction, the redeemed shareholder would qualify for § 302(a) treatment under § 302(b)(3). It further held that the order in which the redemption and sale occurred was irrelevant. The IRS acquiesced in Rev. Rul. 55-745, 1955-2 C.B. 223.

The logic of *Zenz v. Quinlivan* was extended to substantially disproportionate redemptions under § 302(b)(2) in Rev. Rul. 75-447, 1975-2 C.B. 113. In answer "C," Seller qualifies for "sale or exchange" treatment under § 302(b)(2) by satisfying both the 80% and 50% tests as follows:

50% test: After the redemption there are 80 shares outstanding, of which Seller owns 20 (60 of the original 100 were sold to Buyer; 20 were redeemed). Thus, after the redemption Seller owns only 25% of the stock (20/80), which is less than 50%.

80% test: (Voting power after redemption)/(Voting power before redemption) = 25%/100% = 25%, which is less than 80%.

143. **The best answer is "A."** To qualify for "sale or exchange" treatment under § 302(a), one of the tests under § 302(b) must be satisfied. Section 302(b)(4), partial liquidations, is inapplicable here. Because Cori owns some Marcus stock after the redemption, § 302(b)(3) does not apply.

Section 302(b)(2) can apply only if the redemption contracts Cori's ownership in Marcus stock by more than 20% and if the redemption leaves Cori with less than 50% of the voting power in Marcus. The constructive ownership rules of § 318 apply per § 302(c)(1). Even though, under § 318(a)(3)(C), a corporation (e.g., L) is deemed to own a pro rata portion of the stock owned by another corporation (e.g., M) if the former (L) owns at least 50% by value of the stock in the latter (M), this rule does not apply when the stock in question held by the latter (M) is stock in the former (L). § 1.318-1(b)(1). As a result, none of the Marcus stock owned by Garibaldi can be imputed to Cori through Marcus. § 318(a)(2)(C). Therefore, after the redemption Cori owns 48 of the then-outstanding 52 shares of Marcus. This exceeds 50% and represents a contraction of less than 4% (from 96% to 92.3% (48/52)). The transaction is therefore not a substantially disproportionate redemption.

To satisfy § 302(b)(1), there must be a meaningful reduction in the shareholder's interest in the corporation. *U.S. v. Davis*, 397 U.S. 301 (1970). A shareholder's interest consists of three rights: 1) the right to participate in control, 2) the right to participate in earnings, and 3) the right to participate in assets upon liquidation. *Himmel v. Comm'r*, 338 F.2d 815 (2d Cir. 1964). In this context, control is the most important right. *Johnston*, 77 T.C. 679 (1981). The shareholder must not have control after the redemption to qualify under this provision. Rev. Rul. 75-502, 1975-2 C.B. 111. Since Cori has control (92.3%) after the redemption, § 302(b)(1) is not satisfied.

Therefore the redemption will be treated as a § 301(a) distribution. § 302(d).

**Answer "B" is incorrect.** Marcus' redemption of half of its Garibaldi stock still leaves it with 96.1% of the voting power (98 shares remaining/102 shares still outstanding). The redemption will be treated as a distribution under § 301(a) for the same reasons given in "A." However, Marcus owns more than 80% of the Garibaldi stock and therefore is entitled to a 100% dividends-received deduction. § 243(a)(3), (b). For this reason, absent some adverse additional facts, Marcus' taxable income will likely not change as a result of the redemption.

**Answer "C" is incorrect.** "Control" for the purposes of § 304 is satisfied if the shareholder's stock holds at least 50% of the voting power or at least 50% of the total stock value of the corporation. § 304(c)(1). Therefore, Cori controls Marcus and Marcus control Garibaldi. Under the same provision Cori is deemed to control Garibaldi.

**Answer "D" is incorrect.** Section 304(a)(1) states that "if (A) one or more persons are in control of each of two corporations, and (B) in return for property, one of the corporations acquires stock in the other corporation from the person (or persons) so in control, then (unless paragraph (2) applies) such property shall be treated as a distribution in redemption of the stock of the corporation acquiring such stock." It would seem that this provision governs since, as noted above, Cori is deemed to be in control of both Marcus and Garibaldi. However, the provision contains the qualifier, "unless paragraph (2) applies." Section 304(a)(2) states that, "if (A) in return for property, one corporation acquires from a shareholder of another corporation stock in such other corporation, and (B) the issuing corporation controls the acquiring corporation, then such property shall be treated as a distribution in redemption of the stock of the issuing corporation." Thus, this provision also applies since Garibaldi is controlled by Marcus and Garibaldi is acquiring Marcus stock from Cori. The parenthetical in § 304(a)(1) thus requires that provision to yield to § 304(a)(2).

144.    **The best answer is "D."** This transaction is governed by § 304(a)(2). Therefore, the earnings and profits of both corporations are available should the transaction be characterized under § 301(a). § 304(b)(2).

**Answer "A" is incorrect.** For § 304(a)(2) to apply, the subsidiary must acquire the parent's stock from the parent's shareholder. Here the parent is acquiring subsidiary stock from the parent's shareholder. Therefore, § 304(a)(2) does not apply. Instead, as discussed in "D" of the prior question, § 304(a)(1) applies.

**Answer "B" is incorrect.** If Cori still held any Marcus stock, the basis in the Marcus stock redeemed would be allocated to the Marcus stock retained. § 1.304-3(a). But here Cori has no Marcus stock after the redemption. In such circumstances, *Coyle v. U.S.*, 415 F.2d 488 (4th Cir. 1968), indicates that the unrecouped Marcus stock basis should be allocated to the basis of the subsidiary (Garibaldi) stock she still holds.

**Answer "C" is incorrect.** The § 302(b)(1)-(3) tests (§ 302(b)(4) is inapplicable in the § 304 context) are performed with respect to Cori's ownership of the issuing corporation's (i.e., Marcus) stock. § 304(b)(1).

145.    **The best answer is "A."** Marcus will recognize gain under § 311(b)(1).

**Answer "B" is a correct statement and, therefore, not the right answer.** As discussed in "A" of the prior question, when a parent corporation buys subsidiary stock from the parent's shareholder, the brother-sister rules of § 304(a)(1) apply. Where the brother-sister rules apply, if the transaction fails to qualify for "sale or exchange" treatment, the model for the analysis is: 1) Cori constructively exchanged the Garibaldi stock actually sold for additional Marcus stock in a § 351 transaction, 2) after which Marcus constructively redeemed the stock just issued. Under that model, the basis of the Garibaldi stock sold becomes the basis of the Marcus of stock deemed received in the constructive § 351 transaction. To the extent the succeeding constructive redemption is not accorded "sale or exchange" treatment under § 302(a), and therefore is characterized under § 301, the unrecouped constructive Marcus stock basis is allocated to other Marcus stock actually owned by Cori. § 1.304-2(c) Ex. 1.

**Answer "C" is a correct statement and, therefore, not the right answer.** As noted in "B," the basis in the Garibaldi stock is allocated to the Marcus stock actually owned by Cori. The fact that Cori owns no Garibaldi stock after the sale is irrelevant.

**Answer "D" is a correct statement and, therefore, not the right answer.** Cori will be eligible for "sale or exchange" treatment under § 302(b)(3) only if, after the sale, she does not constructively own any Marcus stock. The only possibility of such constructive ownership on these facts is through Garibaldi. Since Cori does not own at least 50% of the Garibaldi stock, so she is not deemed to own any of the Marcus stock owned by Garibaldi. § 318(a)(2)(C).

Therefore, Cori satisfies the requirements of § 302(b)(3) and is entitled to "sale or exchange" treatment under § 302(a).

146. The constructive ownership rules of § 318 apply. § 304(c)(3)(A). Taxpayer constructively owns the 36 shares owned by his daughter. § 318(a)(1)(A)(ii). Therefore, Taxpayer is deemed to own 51 shares (15 actually owned + 36 constructively owned). Control is defined for § 304 purposes as the ownership of stock holding at least 50% of the voting power or at least 50% of the total stock value. § 304(c)(1). Therefore, Taxpayer controls Parent.

147. Taxpayer is deemed to own the stock owned by his wife. § 318(a)(1)(A)(i). Taxpayer is not deemed to own the stock owned by his wife's mother because § 318(a)(5)(B) precludes applying the family attribution rules twice consecutively (i.e., from wife's mother to wife and then from wife to Taxpayer). Since Taxpayer is deemed to own 51% of Parent, Taxpayer is deemed to constructively own 28.05 (51% x 55) shares of the Subsidiary stock owned by Parent. Therefore, Taxpayer is deemed to own 71.05 shares of Subsidiary (28 actually owned + 15 constructively owned from spouse + 28.05 constructively owned from Parent), which constitutes control.

Note: § 304(c)(3)(B) modifies the "to/from corporation" attribution rules of § 318(a), reducing the threshold percentage from 50% to 5%, but this modification is not germane on these facts. It is relevant in "C," which follows.

148. Parent is deemed to own the stock owned by Taxpayer since Taxpayer owns at least 5% of Parent's stock. § 304(c)(3)(B) (modifying § 318(a)(3)(C)). Therefore, Parent is deemed to own 98 shares of Subsidiary (55 actually owned + 43 actually and constructively owned by Taxpayer). Therefore, Parent controls Subsidiary.

149. Taxpayer controls both Parent and Subsidiary, so the brother-sister rules of § 304(a)(1) could apply. But Parent also controls Subsidiary and Subsidiary is buying Parent stock from Taxpayer, so the parent-subsidiary rules of § 304(a)(2) could apply. Section 304(a)(1) expressly yields to § 304(a)(2), so the parent-subsidiary rules will apply.

150. This is a brother-sister transaction. § 304(a)(1). Since none of the relevant tests under § 302(b) are satisfied, the distribution is governed by § 301. § 302(d). The amount of the distribution to Taxpayer is $130,000. § 301(b)(1). The earnings and profits of Issuing and Acquiring are both available to determine the amount of the distribution that will be characterized as a dividend, with the earnings and profits of acquiring corporation being deemed distributed prior to those of the issuing corporation. § 304(b)(2). The combined earnings and profits are $60,000 ($10,000 + $50,000), which is less than the amount of the distribution. Therefore, $60,000 is characterized as a dividend. § 301(a), (c)(1). Next Taxpayer recovers the $100,000 basis in his Issuing stock from the remaining $70,000 of the distribution ($130,000 − $60,000). § 301(c)(2). As a result, $30,000 of Taxpayer's Issuing stock basis ($100,000 − $70,000) is left unrecovered. Since Taxpayer no longer owns any Issuing stock, this $30,000 is allocated to his Acquiring stock basis under § 1.304-2(c) Ex. 1, increasing it to $105,000 ($75,000 + $30,000).

151. Acquiring recognizes no gain or loss on the transaction under § 311(a)(2). Its earnings and profits are reduced to zero ($10,000 − $130,000). § 312(a)(1). Acquiring takes a $100,000 basis in the Issuing stock because the transaction is deemed governed by § 351. Acquiring

constructively acquired the Issuing stock from Taxpayer in exchange for new Acquiring stock. In such a transaction Acquiring takes a carryover basis from Taxpayer under § 362(a)(1), along with a six-year tacked holding period under § 1223(2).

152.   Issuing reduces its earnings and profits to zero [$50,000 − ($130,000 − $10,000)]. § 312(a)(1).

153.   This is a parent-subsidiary transaction. § 304(a)(2). Since none of the relevant tests under § 302(b) are satisfied, the distribution is governed by § 301. § 302(d). The amount of the distribution to Taxpayer is $130,000. § 301(b)(1). The earnings and profits of Issuing and Acquiring are both available to determine the amount of the distribution that will be characterized as a dividend, with the earnings and profits of acquiring corporation being deemed distributed prior to those of the issuing corporation. § 304(b)(2). The combined earnings and profits are $60,000 ($10,000 + $50,000), which is less than the amount of the distribution. Therefore, $60,000 is characterized as a dividend. § 301(a), (c)(1). Next Taxpayer recovers the $100,000 basis in his Issuing stock from the remainder of the distribution, which is $70,000 ($130,000 − $60,000). § 301(c)(2). As a result, $30,000 of Taxpayer's Issuing stock basis ($100,000 − $70,000) is unrecovered. This $30,000 would have been allocated to his remaining Issuing stock had Taxpayer still held any such stock. Because Taxpayer now holds no Issuing stock, the $30,000 is allocated to his Acquiring stock under *Coyle v. U.S.*, 415 F.2d 488 (4th Cir. 1968), increasing its basis to $105,000 ($75,000 +$30,000).

154.   Acquiring recognizes no gain or loss on the transaction. § 311(a)(2). Its earnings and profits are reduced to zero ($10,000 − $130,000). § 312(a)(1). Acquiring takes a $130,000 basis in the Issuing stock with a new holding period. Rev. Rul. 80-189, 1980-2 C.B. 106.

155.   Issuing reduces its earnings and profits to zero [$50,000 − ($130,000 − $10,000)]. § 312(a)(1).

156. **The best answer is "A."** Section 306(c)(1)(A) expressly so states.

   **Answer "B" is incorrect.** If a corporation has no earnings and profits at the time a § 305(a) distribution occurs, the distributed stock cannot be § 306 stock. § 306(c)(2).

   **Answer "C" is incorrect.** Stock rights are subject to § 306. § 306(d)(1).

   **Answer "D" is incorrect.** Section 306 does not restrict its application to preferred stock.

157. **The best answer is "B."** Section 306(a)(1) applies to such a sale.

   **Answer "A" is incorrect.** Section 306(a) does not apply if, in the same transaction, the shareholder disposes of all of its stock in the corporation. § 306(b)(1)(A).

   **Answer "C" is incorrect.** Section 306(a) does not apply if all of the stock with respect to which the § 306 stock was received has previously been disposed of. § 1.306-2(b)(3).

   **Answer "D" is incorrect.** Section 306(a) does not apply if the taxpayer establishes that the initial distribution of the § 306 stock and its subsequent disposition were not pursuant to a plan having as one of its principal purposes tax avoidance. § 306(b)(4). The disposition of § 306 stock by a minority shareholder is generally considered to satisfy these requirements. § 1.306-2(b)(3).

158. **The best answer is "C."** The distributing corporation never reduces its earnings and profits as a result of the disposition of § 306 stock unless the disposition is accomplished by a redemption. § 1.306-1(b)(1).

   **Answer "A" is a correct statement and, therefore, not the right answer.** The distribution of the preferred stock was governed by § 305(a), under which Natalie recognized no gain or loss with respect to the stock distribution.

   **Answer "B" is a correct statement and, therefore, not the right answer.** Natalie's preferred stock basis is determined by allocating the common stock basis between the two classes in proportion to their relative fair market values. § 307(a); § 1.307-1(a). The preferred stock was worth $10 per share; the common stock was worth $30 per share. Therefore, the common stock basis is allocated 1/4 to the preferred stock and 3/4 to the common stock. Her preferred stock basis is thus $40,000 (25% x $160,000). The common stock basis is reduced to $120,000 ($160,000 − $40,000, or 75% x $160,000).

   **Answer "D" is a correct statement and, therefore, not the right answer.** Stock distributed under § 305(a) is § 306 stock. § 306(c)(1)(A).

159. **The best answer is "B."** Natalie sold her § 306 stock. In such cases, § 306(a)(1) results in the following tax consequences:

1) The amount realized is characterized as ordinary income to the extent of the redeemed stock's pro rata share of the corporation's earnings and profits on the date of the distribution.

2) The remainder of the amount realized is offset by the basis of the redeemed stock, producing either a realized gain or loss.

a) Any realized gain is recognized as a capital gain.

b) Realized losses are not recognized. § 306(a)(1)(C). The unrecovered stock basis "jumps" to the redeeming shareholder's basis in the stock with respect to which the § 306 stock was distributed. § 1.306-1(b)(2) Ex. 2.

On the date the § 306 stock was distributed, Melbourne had $8,000,000 of earnings and profits. The value of the preferred stock distributed was $10,000,000 (1,000,000 shares x $10 per share). Therefore, each share of preferred stock is allocated $8 of earnings and profits.

Natalie sold 10,000 shares of preferred stock for $13 per share, receiving $130,000. The earnings and profits allocated to this stock is $80,000. Therefore, $80,000 is treated as ordinary income under the above rules. However, § 306(a)(1)(D) characterizes such ordinary income as dividends, making them eligible for the preferential tax rate on net capital gain under § 1(h).

The remainder of the amount realized, $50,000 ($130,000 − $80,000) is treated as the amount realized with respect to a sale of the stock. As noted above, the preferred stock has a basis of $40,000, resulting in a $10,000 long-term capital gain ($50,000 − $40,000).

**Answer "A" is incorrect.** The distributing corporation never reduces its earnings and profits unless the § 306 stock is redeemed. § 1.306-1(b)(1).

**Answer "C" is incorrect.** This proposed answer tests the student's understanding that the earnings and profits relevant to a non-redemption disposition are those in existence at the time of the distribution, not those in existence at the time of the disposition. At the time of the disposition the earnings and profits are $3,000,000. That would have led to $30,000 of earnings and profits allocated to the redeemed preferred stock and therefore $30,000 of ordinary income (characterized as a dividend).

**Answer "D" is incorrect.** As noted above, the long-term capital gain is $10,000.

160.  **The best answer is "B."** Natalie would have received $85,000 for the stock ($8.50 per share x 10,000 shares). The earnings and profits allocable to the redeemed shares is still $80,000. Therefore the amount realized for the purpose of determining gain or loss is $5,000 ($85,000 − $80,000). Her $40,000 basis exceeds this amount by $35,000, resulting in a realized loss. However, losses are not recognized. § 306(a)(1)(C). Instead of the $35,000 of excess of basis "jumps" to Natalie's common stock, bringing the common stock basis to $155,000 ($120,000 allocated in the § 305(a) transaction plus the $35,000 which "jumps" from the disposed preferred stock to her common stock).

**Answer "A" is incorrect.** As noted above, realized losses are not recognized.

**Answer "C" is incorrect.** The holding period in the preferred stock includes the holding period in the common stock with respect to which it was distributed. § 1223(4). Therefore, upon acquisition in Year 3, the preferred stock began with a holding period of two years.

**Answer "D" is incorrect.** Section 306(a) is inapplicable if all of a shareholder's stock is sold as part of the same transaction. § 306(b)(1)(A).

161. **The best answer is "D."** The disposition of § 306 stock is not governed by § 306(a) if the stock with respect to which the § 306 stock was distributed has already been disposed of. § 1.306-2(b)(3). Such dispositions are deemed to satisfy the § 306(b)(4) requirement that there is no tax avoidance purpose for the distribution or disposition the § 306 stock.

**Answer "A" is a correct statement and, therefore, not the right answer.** The redemption of § 306 stock is treated as a § 301 distribution. § 306(a)(2). Thus, the amount of the distribution is first characterized as a dividend to the extent of the earnings and profits allocated to the distribution. Any excess amount distributed reduces the redeemed stock's basis. Any further amount distributed is characterized as a capital gain. § 301(a), (c)(1)-(c)(3)(A). The relevant earnings and profits are those at the time of the redemption, $3,000,000. Since this is Melbourne's only distribution during the year, the $120,000 paid for the stock ($12 per share x 10,000 shares) is compared against the $3,000,000 of available earnings and profits. All of the distribution is characterized as a dividend. The redeemed stock's basis "jumps" (back) to the stock with respect to which the § 306 stock was distributed. § 1.306-1(b)(2) Ex. 2. Thus, the $40,000 of unrecovered preferred stock basis "jumps" to the common stock, bringing its basis to $160,000 ($120,000 allocated as part of the § 305(a) transaction plus $40,000 of unrecovered preferred stock basis).

**Answer "B" is a correct statement and, therefore, not the right answer.** Melbourne reduces its earnings and profits by the amount of earnings and profit allocated to the distribution. The earnings and profits allocated to the distribution is the amount of the distribution, but not more than the redeemed stock's proportionate share of earnings and profits. § 312(a)(1), (n)(7). Therefore, the maximum earnings and profits reduction is $100,000; so the minimum balance of earnings and profits is $2,880,000 ($3,000,000 − $120,000).

**Answer "C" is a correct statement and, therefore, not the right answer.** Section 306(a) overrides § 302(b)(1)-(3).

162.   **The best answer is "D."** A corporation that is subject to the personal holding company tax cannot be subject to the accumulated earnings tax in the same taxable year. § 535(b)(1).

**Answer "A" is a correct statement and, therefore, not the right answer.** Section 532(a) states: "The accumulated earnings tax . . . shall apply to every corporation . . . formed or availed of for the purpose of avoiding the income tax with respect to its shareholders . . . by permitting earnings and profits to accumulate instead of being . . . distributed."

**Answer "B" is a correct statement and, therefore, not the right answer.** Section 531 imposes the accumulated earnings tax at the same rate at which dividends would be taxed had they been distributed, presently 15% (for individual shareholders).

**Answer "C" is a correct statement and, therefore, not the right answer.** Section 535(a) provides that, in computing the accumulated earnings tax base, a deduction is allowed for the accumulated earnings credit (which is actually a deduction, not a credit). Most corporations are entitled to a "credit" of $250,000. If the corporation is a service corporation (health, law, accounting, consulting, etc), it is entitled to a "credit" of only $150.000. § 535(c)(2).

163.   **The best answer is "A."** Reserves to meet "uncertain or vague" needs are not included in the reasonable needs of a corporation's business. § 1.537-1(b)(1). Within that category are "unrealistic hazards." § 1.537-2(c)(5).

**Answer "B" is a correct statement and, therefore, not the right answer.** Section 533(a) expressly so states. The presumption is, however, rebuttable.

**Answer "C" is a correct statement and, therefore, not the right answer.** Section 535(b)(3) expressly so states. The dividends-received deduction is based on policy; there is no corresponding outflow of assets.

**Answer "D" is a correct statement and, therefore, not the right answer.** Section 535(b)(1) expressly so states. The deduction is available to both cash- and accrual-method corporations. § 1.535-2(a)(2).

164.   **The best answer is "D."** Section 535(c)(4) expressly so states. The purpose is to reconcile the fact that, under § 563(a), the prior taxable year was treated as the year of payment of such dividends for the purpose of determining such prior year's AET base. Failing to exclude it from the current year's accumulated earnings credit computation would constitute double-counting.

**Answer "A" is incorrect.** Section 532(a) states: "The accumulated earnings tax . . . shall apply to every corporation . . . formed or availed of for the purpose of avoiding the income tax with respect to its shareholders . . . by permitting earnings and profits to accumulate instead of being . . . distributed." Where there are no earnings and profits, there cannot be the prohibited accumulation.

**Answer "B" is incorrect.** Under § 535(b)(2), the AET base is reduced by the full amount of the current year's charitable contribution without regard to any deferral of the deduction for taxable income purposes. As a result, charitable contribution carryovers are ignored in determining the AET base.

**Answer "C" is incorrect.** A corporation's dividends paid deduction is the sum of its "dividends paid during the taxable year" and its consent dividends. § 561(a)(1)-(2). Under § 563(a), dividends paid during the taxable year include those actually paid during the taxable year, as well as those paid during the first 2½ months of the following taxable year. Therefore, the dividends paid deduction is $1,380,000.

165. Section 346(a) states that "a distribution shall be treated as in complete liquidation of a corporation if the distribution is one of a series of distributions in redemption of all of the stock of the corporation pursuant to a plan." So long as the intention to completely liquidate is clear from the corporation's and shareholders' actions, no formal plan of liquidation is required. *Kennemer v. Comm'r*, 96 F.2d 177 (5th Cir. 1938). A corporation is in complete liquidation status when it ceases to be a going concern and begins winding up its affairs, regardless of whether the corporation is legally dissolved under state law. § 1.332-2(c).

Under § 336(a) the corporation is treated as though it sold all of its assets at their fair market values. By its terms § 267(a)(1) does not apply to disallow related-party losses in the complete liquidation scenario. This could have impacted the corporation's ability to recognize loss with respect to in-kind distributions to the majority shareholder, R. The result for C is:

| | Receivables | Inventory | Equipment | Factory-Building | Factory-Land |
|---|---|---|---|---|---|
| Amount realized | $2,400,000 | $3,100,000 | $4,000,000 | $27,200,000 | $2,000,000 |
| Adjusted basis | (3,100,000) | (3,400,000) | (8,200,000) | (10,700,000) | (2,000,000) |
| Realized gain/(loss) | ($700,000) | ($300,000) | ($4,200,000) | $16,500,000 | $0 |

All recognized

| | | | | | |
|---|---|---|---|---|---|
| Character: | Ordinary | Ordinary | § 1231 | $260,000 Ordinary § 291[fn] | N/A |
| | | | | $16,240,000 § 1231 | |

[fn] *§ 291 treats 20% of the depreciation recapture as ordinary income = 20% x ($12,000,000 cost - $10,700,000 basis); rest of gain is § 1231*

| § 1231: | Gain on Factory-Building | $16,240,000 | |
|---|---|---|---|
| | Loss on Equipment | (4,200,000) | $12,040,000 |
| | | | |
| Ordinary: | § 291 on Factory-Building | $260,000 | |
| | Receivables | (700,000) | |
| | Inventory | (300,000) | (740,000) |
| Taxable income | | | $11,300,000 |
| Tax (35%) | | | $3,955,000 |
| Cash: | Beginning | $5,700,000 | |
| | Tax | (3,955,000) | |
| | Available for distribution | $1,745,000 | |

166. The distribution results in sale or exchange treatment to the shareholders. § 331(a). The shareholders take fair market bases in the distributed assets under § 334(a), with new holding periods. The results are:

|  |  | Q (40%) | R (50%) |
|---|---|---|---|
| Cash | $1,745,000 | $698,000 | $1,047,000 |
| Receivables | $2,400,000 | 960,000 | 1,440,000 |
| Inventory | $3,100,000 | 1,240,000 | 1,860,000 |
| Equipment | $4,000,000 | 1,600,000 | 2,400,000 |
| Factory-Building | $27,200,000 | 10,880,000 | 16,320,000 |
| Factory-Land | $2,000,000 | 800,000 | 1,200,000 |
|  |  | $16,178,000 | $24,267,000 |
|  |  |  |  |
| Amount realized |  | $16,178,000 | $24,267,000 |
| Basis in stock |  | (10,700,000) | (12,000,000) |
| Realized gain/(loss) |  | $5,478,000 | $12,267,000 |
|  |  |  |  |
| All recognized |  |  |  |
|  |  |  |  |
| Character |  | LTCG | LTCG |

167. There are two tax consequences associated with this change in facts. First, § 336(d)(2)(A) states that, "[f]or purposes of determining the amount of loss recognized by any liquidating corporation on any . . . distribution of property described in subparagraph (B), the adjusted basis of such property shall be reduced (but not below zero) by the excess (if any) of — (i) the adjusted basis of such property immediately after its acquisition by such corporation, over (ii) the fair market value of such property as of such time." In other words, the basis of "property described in subparagraph (B)" is reduced by the built-in loss in such property on the date the corporation acquired it.

Section 336(d)(2)(B)(i) states that "property is described in this subparagraph if — (I) such property is acquired by the liquidating corporation in a transaction to which section 351 applied . . . , and (II) the acquisition of such property . . . was part of a plan a principal purpose of which was to recognize loss . . . with respect to such property in connection with the [complete] liquidation." Under § 336(d)(2)(B)(ii) property acquired within two years of the date the plan of complete liquidation is adopted is presumed to have been acquired for such a purpose.

Assuming the corporation is unable to rebut this presumption, the following results occur:

| Basis at contribution | $10,500,000 |
|---|---|
| Value at contribution | (8,000,000) |
| Built-in loss | $2,500,000 |
|  |  |
| Basis at liquidation | $8,200,000 |
| Built-in loss | (2,500,000) |
| Revised basis | $5,700,000 |
|  |  |
| Amount realized | $4,000,000 |
| Revised basis | ( 5,700,000) |

| | |
|---|---|
| Revised realized loss | ($1,700,000) |

Thus, C's realized loss on the Equipment has been reduced from ($4,100,000) to ($1,700,000).

The second tax consequence partially reinstates the prohibition in § 267(a)(1) on related party losses. Section 336(d)(1)(A)(ii) states that "[n]o loss shall be recognized to a liquidating corporation on the distribution of any property to a related person (within the meaning of section 267) if such property is disqualified property." "Disqualified property" is "any property . . . acquired by the liquidating corporation in a transaction to which section 351 applied . . . during the 5-year period ending on the date of the distribution [in complete liquidation]." The Equipment is, thus, "disqualified property." R is related to C under § 267(b)(2). Therefore, 60% of C's loss (the portion attributable to the in-kind distribution of the Equipment to R) is disallowed. This loss disallowance occurs after taking into account the built-in loss rule considered above. Therefore, C's recognized loss with respect to the Equipment is:

| | |
|---|---|
| Realized loss | ($1,700,000) |
| Disallowed (60%) | 1,020,000 |
| Recognized loss | ($680,000) |

The two loss disallowances will impact the taxable income computation and the amount of cash available for distribution as follows:

| | | | |
|---|---|---|---|
| § 1231: | Gain on Factory-Building | $16,240,000 | |
| | Loss on Equipment | (680,000) | $15,560,000 |
| | | | |
| Ordinary: | § 291 on Factory-Building | $260,000 | |
| | Receivables | (700,000) | |
| | Inventory | (300,000) | (740,000) |
| Taxable income | | | $14,820,000 |
| Tax (35%) | | | $5,187,000 |
| Cash: | Beginning | $5,700,000 | |
| | Tax | (5,187,000) | |
| | Available for distribution | $513,000 | |

168. **The best answer is "D."** In this situation the subsidiary is insolvent. Section 1.332-2(b) states that § 332 does not apply unless the parent receives at least partial payment for its equity interest. It further states that the parent will recognize a loss under § 165(g). Since the value received by the parent from the subsidiary was less than the outstanding balance of the parent's loan to the subsidiary, all of the consideration received was in partial satisfaction of that obligation and none of the consideration received was related to the parent's equity interest in the subsidiary. Therefore, § 332 does not apply and the tax consequences are governed by § 331. The parent will recognize a loss of $1,300,000 on the worthless subsidiary stock. § 165(g). The parent will take a $600,000 fair market value basis in the raw land received in partial satisfaction of its $1,000,000 loan. It will have a bad debt loss of $400,000. § 166.

**Answer "A" is a correct statement and, therefore, not the right answer.** Under § 381(a)(1) the parent succeeds to the subsidiary's tax attributes as a result of the § 332 distribution.

**Answer "B" is a correct statement and, therefore, not the right answer.** Rev. Rul. 74-54,

1974-1 C.B. 76, so holds.

**Answer "C" is a correct statement and, therefore, not the right answer.** Section 1.332-7, which is related to § 337(b)(1), expressly so states.

169. **The best answer is "A."** Section 332 does not apply to the portion of the liquidating distributions made to minority shareholders. § 1.332-5. The minority shareholders will be deemed to have redeemed their stock under § 302(b)(3) (complete termination of interest). The following amount of Subsidiary's earnings and profits will be extinguished as a result of this redemption under § 312(a)(1) and (n)(7):

Lesser of: (Amount distributed in redemption of minority shareholder's stock *or* portion of earnings and profits allocable to redeemed stock)

= Lesser of ($100,000 net value of Raw Land Parcel 1 *or* [10% x $700,000])

= Lesser of ($100,000 *or* $70,000) = $70,000

Therefore: Parent will only succeed to $630,000 ($700,000 - $70,000) of Subsidiary's earnings and profits. § 381(c)(2).

**Answer "B" is a correct statement and, therefore, not the right answer.** Section 332 applies because a subsidiary corporation is liquidating and a parent corporation owns at least 80% (by vote and value) of the subsidiary stock. §§ 332(a)-(b)(1); 1502(a)(2). Therefore, the liquidating distribution by Subsidiary to Parent is a nonrecognition transaction under § 337(a).

**Answer "C" is a correct statement and, therefore, not the right answer.** In a § 332 transaction, the parent corporation takes a carryover basis in the property it receives from the subsidiary. § 334(b).

**Answer "D" is a correct statement and, therefore, not the right answer.** Where the transferee takes a basis in property determined by reference to the basis of the transferor, the transferee's holding period includes the holding period the transferor. § 1223(2).

170. **The best answer is "D."** Section 332 does not apply to liquidating distributions to minority shareholders. § 1.332-5. Therefore, Subsidiary recognizes a gain on the distribution of Raw Land Parcel 1 to Unrelated Individual under § 336(a) as follows:

| | |
|---|---|
| Amount realized | $2,300,000 |
| Adjusted basis | (1,000,000) |
| Gain | $1,300,000 |

Subsidiary will have a federal income tax liability on this gain of $442,000. § 11(b). This leaves only $400,000 ($842,000 - $442,000) of cash available to distribute to Parent. For this reason, **Answer "A" is incorrect.**

**Answer "B" is incorrect.** Because, as noted above, § 332 does not apply to distributions to minority shareholders, Unrelated Individual will recognize a loss on the liquidating distribution under § 331(a) as follows:

| | | |
|---|---|---|
| Amount realized: | Value of Raw Land Parcel 1 | $2,300,000 |

| Adjusted basis: | Mortgage on Raw Land Parcel 1[fn] | ($2,200,000) | |
| | Basis in Subsidiary stock | 250,000 | (2,450,000) |
| Realized and recognized loss: | | | ($150,000) |

[fn]: *Treated as cash paid*

**Answer "C" is incorrect.** Since the transaction was fully taxable, Unrelated Individual takes a fair market value basis in Raw Land Parcel 1. Because the basis in the parcel is not determined by reference to Subsidiary's basis therein, Subsidiary's holding period is not included in Unrelated Individual's holding period (i.e., no provision of § 1223 applies).

171.   **The best answer is "A."** A partnership is a "business entity" under § 301.7701-2(a). A
business entity with two or more members that is not a "corporation" is a partnership for tax
purposes by default. §§ 301.7701-2(c)(1), 301.7701-3(b)(1)(i). A business entity that would
otherwise be taxed as a partnership can be taxed as a "corporation" by electing association
status under § 301.7701-3(a). Once association status has been elected, the business entity
can also elect to be taxed as an S corporation. Rev. Rul. 2009-15, 2009-21 I.R.B. 1035.

**Answer "B" is incorrect.** The definition of partnership for federal income tax purposes is
broader than that for state law purposes. As given by § 101 of the Revised Uniform
Partnership Act, a partnership is "an association of two or more persons to carry on as co-
owners of a business for profit." For federal income tax purposes (ignoring the "check-the-
box" rules) a partnership "includes a syndicate, group, pool, joint venture, or other
unincorporated organization through or by means of which any business, financial operation,
or venture is carried on, and which is not, within the meaning of this title, a corporation or
a trust or estate." § 761(a). This broad language was deliberate to ensure that all
partnership-like financial ventures were subject to the partnership tax law, even if such
ventures were deliberately designed to avoid partnership status under state law. *See*, HR
REP. NO. 72-708 (1932); S. REP. NO. 72-665 (1932).

**Answer "C" is incorrect.** Section 1.701-2(a) provides that "Subchapter K is intended to
permit taxpayers to conduct joint business (including investment) activities through flexible
economic arrangement without incurring an entity-level tax. Implicit in the intent of
subchapter K [is that] the tax consequences . . . to each partner . . . must accurately reflect
the partners' economic agreement and clearly reflect the partner's income." "[E]ven though
the transaction may fall within the literal words of a particular statutory or regulatory
provision, the Commissioner can determine . . . that to achieve tax results that are
consistent with the intent of subchapter K [the] claimed tax treatment should . . . be
adjusted." § 1.704-1(b). Similarly, § 1.704-1(a)(1)(i) states that if "the partnership agreement
provides for the allocation of income [or] deduction . . . to a partner but such allocation does
not have substantial economic effect, then the partner's distributive share of such income [or]
deduction . . . shall be determined in accordance with such partner's interest in the
partnership." Thus, Subchapter K seeks the economic substance of the partners' economic
relationship and, except where expressly intended by the Code or Regulations (*see, e.g.*,
§ 1.701-2(a)(3)), does not permit tax results to be determined by mechanical, literal
interpretations of the law.

**Answer "D" is incorrect.** Section 761(a) provides that "the Secretary may, at the election of
all the members of an unincorporated organization, exclude such organization from the
application of [Subchapter K] if it is availed of — (1) for investment purposes only and not
for the active conduct of a business [or] for the joint production, extraction, or use of
property, but not for the purpose of selling services or property produced or extracted[,] if
the income of the members . . . may be adequately determined without the computation of

partnership taxable income."

Thus, the co-owners of a parcel of raw land adjacent to a county fairgrounds who rent parking spaces when activities are held on the fairgrounds could elect out of Subchapter K treatment since determining their individual incomes from the property would be straightforward.

172.    There is no depreciation recapture when X initially contributes the machine to Z. § 1245(b)(3). The recapture potential carries over to Z. § 1.1245-2(c)(2)(i), (2)(ii)(b).

For book purposes the depreciation each year should be $40,000 ($80,000/2). Of this, $33,333 (5/6) should be allocated to Q and $6,667 (1/6) should be allocated to X. The tax depreciation available for each year is, however, only $30,000 ($60,000/2), so all of it is allocated to Q and none of it is allocated to X under the "ceiling rule." § 1.704-3(b)(1), (b)(2) Ex. 1(ii).

On January 1, Year 3 the machine has a book value of $40,000 ($80,000 - $40,000). It has an adjusted basis of $30,000 ($60,000 - $30,000). The book gain on the disposition of the machine is $50,000 ($90,000 - $40,000). The tax gain is $60,000 ($90,000 - $30,000). The book-tax difference of the machine on January 1, Year 3 is $10,000 ($40,000 book value - $30,000 adjusted basis), which is allocated to X. § 704(c). The remaining $50,000 tax gain ($60,000 - $10,000) is allocated 1/6 to X ($8,333). The total gain allocated to X is thus $18,333 ($10,000 + $8,333). Under § 1.1245-1(e)(2)(i) and (ii)(A), the amount of depreciation recapture allocated to the property contributor is the lesser of the total *depreciation* taken by or allocated to the contributor ($40,000, all taken prior to X's contribution of the machine to the partnership) and the total *gain* allocated to the contributor ($18,333). Therefore, the § 1245 ordinary income to X is $18,333 — all of X's gain.

173.    **The best answer is "D."** Under § 709(b)(1) the organizational cost deduction for Year 1 is $3,544, computed as follows:

Bonus amount = $5,000 - ($52,000 - $50,000) = $3,000

Regular amortization for Year 1 = [($52,000 - $3,000)/180 months] x 2 months = $544

Total amount = $3,000 + $544 = $3,544.

**Answer "A" is a correct statement and, therefore, not the right answer.** Section 2 of Rev. Proc. 93-27, 1993-2 C.B. 343, defines a capital interest as "an interest that would give the holder a share of the proceeds if the partnership's assets were sold at fair market value and then the proceeds were distributed in a complete liquidation of the partnership." A profits interest is defined as "a partnership interest other than a capital interest," which means the right to share in future profits.

**Answer "B" is a correct statement and, therefore, not the right answer.** Rev. Proc. 93-27, 1993-2 C.B. 343, expressly so states and Rev. Proc. 2001-43, 2001-2 C.B. 191, makes clear that § 83 does not change this result. However, the receipt of a capital interest in exchange for future services is a taxable event under § 1.721-1(b)(1) subject to § 83.

**Answer "C" is a correct statement and, therefore, not the right answer.** A partner recognizes no gain on a partnership distribution until the amount of cash distributed exceeds the partner's basis in its interest. Such gain is characterized as a sale or exchange of the partnership interest, which is a capital asset. § 731(a)(1).

174.    **The best answer is "B."** Only the final sentence is false. A partner recognizes no gain on a

partnership distribution unless the cash distributed exceeds the partner's basis in its interest. A partner's adjusted basis in property distributed by a partnership is generally its basis to the partnership, here $30,000. §§ 731(a)(1), 732(a)(1). The ending basis of the partnership interest is $20,000 ($100,000 - $50,000 - $30,000). §§ 705(a)(2), 733.

**Answer "A" is a correct statement and, therefore, not the right answer.** Section 742 states that "[t]he basis of an interest in a partnership acquired other than by contribution shall be determined under part II of subchapter O." Subchapter O includes § 1012(a) which provides that the basis of property is its cost, unless otherwise provided by the Code.

**Answer "C" is a correct statement and, therefore, not the right answer.** This difference is express in § 1.704-1(b)(2)(iv)(c). Note that the partner's capital account does include any partnership liability that the partner expressly assumes. The liability assumption is characterized as a cash contribution by the partner to the partnership, which uses the contributed cash to retire the liability.

**Answer "D" is a correct statement and, therefore, not the right answer.** Section 1.704-1(b)(2)(iv)(f) so provides.

175. **The best answer is "C."** The assumption of a partner's liability by a partnership is considered a constructive distribution of cash to the partner. § 752(b). An increase in a partner's share of the partnership's liabilities is considered a constructive cash contribution by the partner to the partnership. § 752(a). Cash contributions increase a partner's basis. § 722. Cash distributions to a partner reduce the partner's basis under § 733(1) and cash distributions require the partner to recognize gain if the cash distributed exceeds the partner's basis. § 731(a)(1). However, § 1.752-1(f) provides that "[i]f, as a result of a single transaction, a partner incurs both an increase in the partner's share of the partnership liabilities . . . and a decrease in . . . the partner's individual liabilities . . . , only the net decrease is treated as a distribution from the partnership." Therefore, the partner is deemed to have received a net cash distribution of $275,000 (a $550,000 constructive cash distribution to reflect the fact that the partnership has assumed the partner's personal liability, plus a $275,000 constructive cash contribution to reflect the fact that the partner has become obligated for that amount of the partnership's new $550,000 liability). The $275,000 constructive cash distribution exceeds the partner's $200,000 basis (which arises from the basis of the contributed property under § 722) by $75,000, requiring the partner to recognize a capital gain in that amount. The partner's basis in its interest is zero.

**Answer "A" is a correct statement and, therefore, not the right answer.** See the analysis above.

**Answer "B" is a correct statement and, therefore, not the right answer.** Section 1.752-2(a) expressly so states.

**Answer "D" is a correct statement and, therefore, not the right answer.** Section 752(c) and § 1.752-1(e) so provide.

176. Nonrecourse liabilities are allocated in three tiers under § 1.752-3, as follows:

Tier I: The total Tier I allocation is the excess on the date being measured of the balance of the nonrecourse liability encumbering the asset over the book value of the encumbered asset, a quantity known as the "partnership minimum gain." The excess is: $200,000 - $250,000 = $0. Therefore, there is no Tier I allocation. The amount of the nonrecourse liability yet to be allocated is $200,000.

Tier II: The Tier II allocation is the lesser of: 1) the amount of the nonrecourse liability yet to be allocated, and 2) the amount of gain that would be recognized by the contributing partner under § 704(c) if the encumbered asset were sold for an amount equal to the outstanding balance of the nonrecourse liability encumbering it.

Z's § 704(c) gain potential on this date is: $250,000 (book value of Raw Land on this date) - $230,000 (basis of Raw Land on this date) = $20,000. Since this amount is less than the unallocated nonrecourse liability ($200,000), $20,000 is allocated to Z. The amount of the nonrecourse liability yet to be allocated is $180,000 ($200,000 - $20,000).

Tier III: Partnerships have several options in the methodology used to allocate Tier III recourse liabilities. One such methodology is specified in the facts as required by the partnership agreement.

All of Z's § 704(c) gain potential was accounted for in Tier II. Therefore, the remaining unallocated liability of $180,000 is allocated in proportion to the partners' profit-sharing ratios (20:70:10), as follows:

| Partner | Profit-sharing Ratio | Tier III Allocation of Nonrecourse Liability |
|---------|---------------------|---------------------------------------------|
| X | 20% | $36,000 |
| Y | 70% | 126,000 |
| Z | 10% | 18,000 |
| | 100% | $180,000 |

The total allocation of the nonrecourse liability is:

| Partner | Tier I | Tier II | Tier III | Total |
|---------|--------|---------|----------|-------|
| X | $0 | $0 | $36,000 | $36,000 |
| Y | 0 | 0 | 126,000 | 126,000 |
| Z | 0 | 20,000 | 18,000 | 38,000 |
| | $0 | $20,000 | $180,000 | $200,000 |

177. Under § 1.752-2 recourse liabilities are allocated using a constructive liquidation model. With one exception all of the partnership's assets, including cash, are deemed to be worth nothing and are deemed to be sold for that amount. The exception is that any asset securing a nonrecourse liability is deemed to be worth the amount of the nonrecourse liability it secures. Thus, the amount realized for all of the partnership's assets is: zero plus total amount of nonrecourse liabilities. A loss will result. This loss is allocated among the partners in accordance with the partnership agreement, which changes their capital account balances. The final balances of the capital accounts, given that state law requires partners with deficits to make capital contributions sufficient to bring the deficits to zero, measure the economic risk of loss to the partners and therefore represent the amounts of the recourse liabilities that should be allocated to them.

Applying the stated rules to these facts, the deemed amount realized is: $0 + $200,000 (relief from nonrecourse liability) = $200,000. From the balance sheet the total book value of the assets is $1,430,000. Therefore, the deemed loss is: $200,000 (amount realized) - $1,430,000 (aggregate book value of assets) = ($1,230,000). This is allocated among the partners in proportion to their partnership interests (20:70:10), resulting in the following ending capital account balances:

| Partner | Capital Account before Constructive Liquidation | Allocation of Constructive Loss | Capital Account after Constructive Liquidation |
|---|---|---|---|
| X | $6,000 | ($246,000) | ($240,000) |
| Y | 21,000 | (861,000) | (840,000) |
| Z | 3,000 | (123,000) | (120,000) |
| | $30,000 | ($1,230,000) | ($1,200,000) |

The balance sheet of the partnership immediately after the constructive sale is:

| Liabilities: | | Accounts Payable | $400,000 | |
|---|---|---|---|---|
| | | Recourse note-Equipment | 800,000 | $1,200,000 |
| Capital Accounts: | | X | ($240,000) | |
| | | Y | (840,000) | |
| | | Z | (120,000) | ($1,200,000) |
| | | | | $0 |

The ending balances in the capital accounts (e.g., ($240,000) for X) reflect the extent to which the partners bear the economic risk of loss with respect to the recourse liabilities. For that reason, the recourse liabilities are allocated to the partners in those amounts. Note that § 1.752-2(b)(6) conclusively presumes that all of the partners will actually fulfill their payment obligations.

178.

| Partner | Basis before Allocation of Liabilities | Partnership "Assumption" of Nonrecourse Liability | Allocation of Nonrecourse Liability | Allocation of Recourse Liabilities | Basis after Allocation of Liabilities |
|---|---|---|---|---|---|
| X | $6,000 | | $36,000 | $240,000 | $282,000 |
| Y | $21,000 | | $126,000 | $840,000 | $987,000 |
| Z | $183,000 | ($200,000) | $38,000 | $120,000 | $141,000 |

179. The allocation of the recourse liabilities determined above, which includes $400,000 of Accounts Payable, is repeated below:

| X | $240,000 |
|---|---|
| Y | 840,000 |
| Z | 120,000 |
| | $1,200,000 |

If Z guarantees the Accounts Payable, then neither X nor Y bear the economic risk of loss with respect to them. Therefore, neither of those partners should be allocated any of the

Accounts Payable. § 1.752-2(b)(3)(i), (b)(5). The revised allocation of recourse liabilities follows:

| Partner | Original Allocation of Recourse Liabilities | Reallocation of Risk of Loss re: Accounts Payable | Computation | Revised Allocation of Recourse Liabilities |
|---|---|---|---|---|
| X | $240,000 | ($80,000) | 20% x $400,000 | $160,000 |
| Y | 840,000 | (280,000) | 70% x $400,000 | 560,000 |
| Z | 120,000 | 360,000 | 90% x $400,000 | 480,000 |
| | $1,200,000 | $0 | | $1,200,000 |

180. The allocation of the recourse liabilities determined above, which includes $400,000 of Accounts Payable, is repeated below:

| | |
|---|---|
| X | $240,000 |
| Y | 840,000 |
| Z | 120,000 |
| | $1,200,000 |

There would be no change because the partners are conclusively presumed to perform. Thus, the guarantee would never be called upon. § 1.752-2(b)(6).

If Z indemifies X and Y with respect to the accounts payable, then neither X nor Y bear the economic risk of loss with respect to them. Even if they perform (as they are conclusively presumed to do), they will be entitled to reimbursement by Z. Therefore, neither of those partners should be allocated any of the accounts payable. § 1.752-2(b)(3)(i), (b)(5). The revised allocation of recourse liabilities follows:

| Partner | Original Allocation of Recourse Liabilities | Reallocation of Risk of Loss re: Accounts Payable | Computation | Revised Allocation of Recourse Liabilities |
|---|---|---|---|---|
| X | $240,000 | ($80,000) | 20% x $400,000 | $160,000 |
| Y | 840,000 | (280,000) | 70% x $400,000 | 560,000 |
| Z | 120,000 | 360,000 | 90% x $400,000 | 480,000 |
| | $1,200,000 | $0 | | $1,200,000 |

181. The liability becomes recourse with respect to X. § 1.752-2(a)(1), (b)(3)(i), (f) Ex.5.

182. **The best answer is "C."** Section 703(a) expressly requires a partnership to calculate its taxable income.

**Answer "A" is a correct statement and, therefore, not the right answer.** As to the former proposition, § 701 expressly so states. As to the second, § 702(a) requires the partners to take into account their distributive shares of the partnership's tax items.

**Answer "B" is a correct statement and, therefore, not the right answer.** Under § 702(b) the character of any partnership tax item allocated to a partner is "determined as if such item were realized directly from the source."

**Answer "D" is a correct statement and, therefore, not the right answer.** Section 703(b) expressly so states.

183. **The best answer is "C."** There is no exhaustive statement of the partnership tax items that require separate statement. Section 702(a)(1)-(6) lists some such items; § 1.702-1(a)(8)(i)-(ii) lists additional items. Section 1.702-1(a)(8)(ii) sets forth the policy that "[e]ach partner must . . . take into account separately the partner's distributive share of any partnership item which, if separately taken into account by any partner, would result in an income tax liability for that partner, or for any other person, different from that which would result if that partner did not take the item into account separately."

**Answer "A" is a correct statement and, therefore, not the right answer.** Section 703(a)(2)(C) expressly so states.

**Answer "B" is a correct statement and, therefore, not the right answer.** A partnership creates a Schedule K in the process of preparing its tax return. The various items on that schedule are disaggregated and allocated to the partners in accordance with the partnership agreement, etc. Section 6031(b) requires the partnership to send each partner a statement indicating that partner's distributive shares of each partnership tax item. That statement is called a Schedule K-1.

**Answer "D" is a correct statement and, therefore, not the right answer.** A partner takes into its tax return its distributive share of the partnership's tax items for the partnership's taxable year "ending within or with the taxable year of the partner." § 706(a). The partnership's taxable year ends October 31, Year 1. That year-end occurs within the partner's taxable year running from April 1 of Year 1 to March 31 of Year 2 (the following calendar year).

184. **The best answer is "D."** Section 704(a) sets forth this general rule, overriding it only if the allocation does not have substantial economic effect. § 704(b)(2).

**Answer "A" is incorrect.** The partnership must first seek a "majority interest year." § 706(b)(1)(B)(i). Such a year exists if partners owning more than 50% of the partnership interests have that year. § 706(b)(4)(A). No such year exists here.

The partnership must then seek a taxable year used by all of the principal partners under § 706(b)(1)(B)(ii). A principal partner is one owning at least a 5% interest in the partnership. § 706(b)(3). All of the partners are 4.17% partners, so no principal partners exist.

The partnership must then seek a taxable year that minimizes the "aggregate deferral of income." § 1.706-1(b)(3)(i) (promulgated under the authority of § 706(b)(1)(B)(iii)). Since the partnership interests are evenly distributed across the year, none of the 12 possible taxable year's minimizes the aggregate deferral of income.

At this point the partnership will be on the calendar year under § 706(b)(1)(B)(iii) unless it can demonstrate a business purpose under Rev. Rul. 87-57, 1987-2 C.B. 117, or it elects a taxable year under § 444. *See,* § 706(b)(1)(C). The statement that this partnership "must adopt" a calendar year overstates the case.

**Answer "B" is incorrect.** Section 1.6031(a)-1(e)(2) requires partnership returns to be filed on or before the fifteenth day of the fourth month following the close of the partnership's taxable year. Therefore, the return is due on April 15. The rule as stated applies to corporations.

**Answer "C" is incorrect.** The substantial economic effect rules are used to test whether the allocation of a partnership tax item under the partnership agreement has sufficient economic substance to be respected. When the partnership agreement is silent about the allocation of a tax item, that item is allocated in accordance with the partners' interests. § 704(b)(1).

185.   **The best answer is "A."** Under § 1.704-1(b)(2)(iii)(a) "the economic effect of an allocation . . . is substantial if there is a reasonable possibility that the allocation . . . will affect substantially the dollar amounts to be received by the partners from the partnership, *independent* of tax consequences." (Emphasis added.) Thus, the tax benefits from an allocation cannot be taken into account in determining whether the economic effect of the allocation is substantial.

   **Answer "B" is a correct statement and, therefore, not the right answer.** Section 1.704-1(b)(1)(i) so provides.

   **Answer "C" is a correct statement and, therefore, not the right answer.** Section 1.704-1(b)(2)(ii)(b)(1) so provides.

   **Answer "D" is a correct statement and, therefore, not the right answer.** Section 1.704-1(b)(2)(ii)(a) so provides.

186.   **The best answer is "A."** Section 1.704-1(b)(4)(ii) states that "[a]llocations of tax credits . . . are [generally] not reflected by adjustments to the partners' capital accounts[.] Thus, such allocations cannot have economic effect and the tax credits . . . must be allocated in accordance with the partners' interests in the partnership[.]"

   **Answer "B" is a correct statement and, therefore, not the right answer.** The book depreciation taken on an asset must be proportional to the tax depreciation taken. § 1.704-1(b)(2)(iv)(g)(3).

   **Answer "C" is a correct statement and, therefore, not the right answer.** Section 1.704-2(b)(1) so provides.

   **Answer "D" is a correct statement and, therefore, not the right answer.** Section 1.704-1(b)(3)(ii)(a), (c) and (d) includes these factors as part of a non-exhaustive enumeration.

187.   **The best answer is "D."** Janice will take into income her distributive shares of the four partnership tax items under § 702(a)(1) (short-term capital loss), § 702(a)(2) (long-term capital gain), § 702(a)(7) and § 1.702-1(a)(8)(i) (§ 212 expenses), and § 702(a)(8) (ordinary operating income).

   **Answer "A" is incorrect.** The partnership can also use the pro rata method (i.e., allocate a pro rata amount of each partnership tax item to each day of the partnership's taxable year and then allocate those amounts in proportion to the partnership interests outstanding on each such day). § 1.706-1(c)(2)(ii).

   **Answer "B" is incorrect.** Under § 704(e)(2) allocations to the donee of a gifted partnership interest must reflect reasonable compensation for services rendered by the donor. The IRS would likely argue that that $80,000 of the $200,000 of partnership income should first be allocated to Parent, with the remaining $120,000 ($200,000 - $80,000) being allocated equally to Parent and Child. This would reduce Child's allocation from $100,000 to $60,000. *See, e.g., Weller v. Brownell*, 240 F. Supp. 201 (M.D. Pa. 1965).

   **Answer "C" is incorrect.** The basis adjustment ordering rules are provided by § 1.704-1(d).

Kevin's pre-distribution basis is $140,000 ($50,000 beginning balance + $90,000 interest income). § 705(a)(1)(A). The interest income will be included on his personal tax return under § 702. Then he will subtract the $125,000 distribution, reducing his basis to $15,000. § 705(a)(2), 733(1). No gain is recognized on the distribution under § 731(a)(1) because there is sufficient basis. Then Kevin will attempt to subtract the two capital losses from his remaining basis under § 705(a)(2)(A). These losses cannot drive his basis below zero and he is not permitted to take into account on his personal return the excess losses. § 704(d). Under § 1.704-1(d) the excess losses are carried forward proportionately and are treated as deductions allocable to the following taxable year as follows:

| Loss | Amount | Percent | Allowed | Suspended |
|---|---|---|---|---|
| Long-term capital loss | $30,000 | 60% | $9,000 | $21,000 |
| Short-term capital loss | 20,000 | 40% | 6,000 | 14,000 |
| | $50,000 | 100% | $15,000 | $35,000 |

188. **The best answer is "B."** Section 706(c)(2)(A) expressly so provides.

**Answer "A" is incorrect.** The liquidation of a 10% partnership interest is not a "termination" under § 708(b)(1)(B) both because 10% fails to satisfy the minimum 50% requirement and because liquidations are not considered "sales or exchanges" for these purposes. § 1.708-1(b)(2). Therefore, the liquidation of the interest closes only the taxable year of the deceased, liquidated partner. § 706(c)(1), (2)(A).

**Answer "C" is incorrect.** Such a sale constitutes a termination under § 708(b)(1)(B), resulting in the closing of the partnership taxable year for all partners. § 706(c)(1).

**Answer "D" is incorrect.** The disposition constituted only 12% (60%/5) of the partnership interests and is therefore not a termination. § 708(b)(1)(B). Nor did the partner sell his entire interest. Therefore, the partnership's taxable year closes for no one. § 706(c)(2)(B).

189. **The best answer is "A."** A termination under § 708(b)(1)(B) requires a sale or exchange of at least 50% of the capital interests *and* at least 50% of the profits interests. § 1.708-1(b)(2).

**Answer "B" is incorrect.** Roy's provision of services to the partnership is not in his capacity as a partner. Therefore, the money received for his accounting services is not an allocation of partnership income. § 707(a)(1); § 1.707-1(a).

**Answer "C" is incorrect.** Jim is receiving a guaranteed payment under § 707(c). The partnership deducts the $60,000 in arriving at its § 702(a)(8) ordinary taxable income. Nonetheless, the guaranteed payment is considered part of Jim's distributive share of partnership ordinary income. Jim's total allocation is $102,000 ($60,000 + $42,000).

**Answer "D" is incorrect.** Les is not receiving a guaranteed payment because it is not determined without regard to partnership income. (He receives the first $60,000. If the partnership does not have $60,000 of income in any particular year, Les will not receive $60,000.) Rev. Rul. 67-158, 1967-1 C.B. 188.

190. **The best answer is "D."** The partnership's § 702(a)(8) amount is an ordinary loss of $10,000 ($30,000 - $40,000). Guy is allocated 20% of this loss ($2,000). Guy's guaranteed payment is considered a distributive share of partnership ordinary income. His total allocation is $38,000 ($40,000 - $2,000). § 1.707-1(c) Ex. 3.

**Answer "A" is a correct statement and, therefore, not the right answer.** Frances' gain is $220,000 ($700,000 - $480,000). Section 707(b)(2) provides that the gain is ordinary since, in the hands of the partnership, the lots will have the status of inventory and Frances owns more than 50%. § 707(b)(1)(A). This provision is analogous to § 1239.

**Answer "B" is a correct statement and, therefore, not the right answer.** The transaction is characterized as part-sale and part-contribution to capital. The sale portion is 60% ($420,000/$700,000). Sixty percent of the basis ($126,000) is allocated to the sale portion. Terry's gain is $294,000 ($420,000 cash received from the partnership - $126,000). The remaining $84,000 of basis in the machine ($210,000 - $126,000) increases the basis in her partnership interest as a contribution to capital. § 722.

**Answer "C" is a correct statement and, therefore, not the right answer.** Section 707(b)(1)(A) gives this related-party loss essentially the same treatment as would result under § 267(a)(1) and (d). The original transferor, Elaine, will not be allowed to recognize the $300,000 realized loss. The original transferee, the partnership, will not have to recognize the first $300,000 of gain (which exceeds the actual realized gain of $50,000) upon the later sale of the property to an unrelated party.

191. **The best answer is "D."** The partner's assumption of the partnership recourse liability ($120,000) is treated as a cash contribution to the partnership and the relief enjoyed by the partner in his capacity as such in being relieved of one third of that liability ($40,000: 1/3 x $120,000) is treated as a cash distribution from the partnership. § 752(a), (b). Under § 1.752-1(f) these two amounts are netted, resulting in an $80,000 increase (constructive cash contribution) in the partner's basis account under § 722. Therefore, the partner's pre-distribution basis is $90,000 ($10,000 + $80,000).

Under § 732(a)(1) the partner's basis in the distributed property is tentatively the same as the partnership's basis, $100,000. However, § 732(a)(2) limits that basis to the partner's basis in its interest, which is only $90,000. Therefore, the crane takes a basis of $90,000. The partner's basis in his interest is reduced to zero ($90,000 - $90,000). § 733(2).

**Answer "A" is a correct statement and, therefore, not the right answer.** Section 731(b) expressly so states.

**Answer "B" is a correct statement and, therefore, not the right answer.** Section 731(c)(1) so provides.

**Answer "C" is a correct statement and, therefore, not the right answer.** A draw is not treated as a distribution until the last day of the taxable year. § 1.731-1(a)(1)(ii). Since there is no distribution with respect to this draw (it was repaid by the end of the year), gain cannot be recognized.

192. **The best answer is "A."** The distribution is governed by § 737(a). Gain will be recognized by the contributing partner equal to the lesser of: 1) the partner's net pre-contribution gain or 2) the excess of the value of the non-cash property received over the contributing partner's basis in its partnership interest.

Partner 1's net pre-contribution gain is, in essence, the remaining § 704(c) gain potential in the contributed asset. § 737(b). That amount here is $7,000 ($21,000 current book value of contributed asset - $14,000 current basis of contributed asset).

The excess of the value of the non-cash property received over the contributing partner's basis in its partnership interest is $10,000 ($30,000 value of raw land - $20,000 basis in partner's interest).

The lesser of these two, $7,000, is the recognized gain. § 1.737-1(e) Ex. 1. The character of the gain is determined by reference to the contributed property. § 737(a). Because the original cost ($35,000) exceeded the basis of the property on the date of contribution ($20,000), the first $15,000 ($35,000 - $20,000) of gain recognized is § 1245 ordinary income.

Had this rule not applied, Partner 1 would have taken a $20,000 basis (the lesser of the partnership's basis in the property or the partner's basis in its partnership interest) in the distributed property under § 732(a)(1), which would have reduced the basis in its partnership interest to $0. § 733(2). No gain would have been recognized. § 731(a)(1).

**Answer "B" is a correct statement and, therefore, not the right answer.** As indicated in the answer to "A," Partner 1 will recognize a gain of $7,000. Section 704(c)(1)(B) parallels the outcome of § 737(a). Example 2 in § 1.704-4(a)(5) is fundamentally identical to Example 1 in § 1.737-1(e), referenced above.

**Answer "C" is a correct statement and, therefore, not the right answer.** Theresa will receive $15,000 ($50,000 x 30%), which will yield a loss of $55,000 ($70,000 - $15,000). The loss will be characterized as a sale or exchange of her partnership interest, which is a capital asset. § 731(a)(2)(A).

**Answer "D" is a correct statement and, therefore, not the right answer.** Under § 731(a)(1) gain is not recognized unless cash (and possibly marketable securities) is distributed. Loss is not recognized unless only cash, "hot" assets (unrealized receivables and inventory items under § 751) and possibly marketable securities are distributed. § 731(a)(2). Neither is true in this case.

193.  **The best answer is "B."** The wage payable with respect to the key employee is an "allocable cash basis item." § 706(d)(2)(B)(iii). Therefore, the $30,000 of compensation must be allocated equally to each day during the period to which it relates. § 706(d)(2)(A). This results in an allocation of $1,000 per day ($30,000/30 days). The measurement of ownership occurs at the end of the day. *Id.* Dan is allocated $20,000 ($1,000 x 20 days) of the compensation expense.

**Answer "A" is a correct statement and, therefore, not the right answer.** Section 737(d)(1) expressly so states.

**Answer "C" is a correct statement and, therefore, not the right answer.** A partner generally takes the partnership's basis in the distributed property. § 732(a)(1). When a person's basis in property is determined by reference to another person's basis in the same property, the transferee's holding period includes the holding period the transferor. §§ 735(b), 1223(2).

**Answer "D" is a correct statement and, therefore, not the right answer.** Although the $370,000 ($600,000 cost - $230,000 adjusted basis) of depreciation recapture would be ordinary income under § 1245 in any case, the remaining $100,000 of gain ($470,000 total gain - $370,000 depreciation recapture) would normally be § 1231 gain. However, § 724(b) converts the § 1231 gain into ordinary income because the machine was inventory in Kelly's hands. §§ 724(d)(2), 751(d)(1).

194.    The implied value of goodwill is $380,000 ($960,000 from appraisal - $580,000 value of identifiable assets). Given that this is a service partnership, goodwill is included as a partnership asset only if the partners elect. The unrealized receivables (§ 751(c)(2)) are not treated as partnership property. § 736(b)(2), (3). Therefore, the partnership property eligible for § 736(b) treatment is:

| Asset | Value |
|-------|-------|
| Cash | $90,000 |
| Raw land | 320,000 |
| Goodwill | 380,000 |
| | $790,000 |

Keith's share is $263,333 ($790,000 x 1/3), which is his total § 736(b) amount, recognized evenly over the four years ($65,833 per year). § 1.736-1(b)(5)(i). Since the total amount he will receive is $320,000 (4 x $80,000), the total § 736(a) payments are $56,667 ($320,000 total payments - $263,333 payment for partnership property). The § 736(a) payments will be recognized at the rate of $14,167 ($56,667/4) per year. *Id.*

The § 736(b) payments are governed by § 731 such that no gain is recognized until Keith's basis is fully recovered. § 1.731-1(a)(1)(i). The § 736(a) payments are guaranteed payments under § 707(c) since they are not determined by reference to partnership income. The tax consequences are:

| | | Year 2 | Year 3 | Year 4 | Year 5 | Total |
|---|---|--------|--------|--------|--------|-------|
| § 736(b) | Payment | $65,833 | $65,833 | $65,833 | $65,834 | $263,333 |
| | Basis | (65,833) | (34,167) | (0) | (0) | (100,000) |
| | | $0 | $31,666 | $65,833 | $65,834 | 163,333 |
| § 736(a) | | $14,167 | $14,167 | $14,167 | $14,166 | 56,667 |

195.    The Inventory comprises "inventory items." § 751(d)(1). It has "appreciated substantially" because its value is 200% of its basis ($120/$60), which exceeds the 120% threshold. § 751(b)(3)(A). Section 751(b)(1)(A)(ii) applies because X's interest in the partnership's Inventory is increasing while X's interest in the partnership's Land is decreasing, as demonstrated below:

Before the distribution of the Inventory, X has a one third interest in the partnership ($120 X's capital account/$360 total partnership capital). After the distribution of Inventory worth $60, XYZ's balance sheet is:

| | | Book Value | |
|---|---|-----------|---|
| Assets: | Inventory | $60 | (120 - 60) |
| | Land | 240 | |
| | | $300 | |
| | | | |
| Capital: | X | $60 | (120 - 60) |
| | Y | 120 | |
| | Z | 120 | |
| | | $300 | |

Therefore, after the distribution of the Inventory, X has a one fifth interest in the partnership ($60/$300).

Before the distribution of the Inventory, X's interest in the partnership's assets is:

| | | |
|---|---|---|
| Inventory | $40 | (1/3 interest before distribution x $120 book value) |
| Land | 80 | (1/3 x $240) |
| | $120 | |

After the distribution of the Inventory, X's interest in the partnership's assets is:

| | | |
|---|---|---|
| Inventory | $12 | (1/5 x $60) |
| Land | 48 | (1/5 x $240) |
| | $60 | |

Keeping in mind that, after the distribution of the Inventory, X also has a direct personal property interest in the Inventory (since some Inventory has been distributed to X), the *change* in X's *total* interest in the Land and Inventory is:

| | | Inventory | | Land | |
|---|---|---|---|---|---|
| Post-distribution interest: | Personal | $60 | | $0 | |
| | Through XYZ | 12 | $72 | 48 | $48 |
| Pre-distribution interest: | Through XYZ | | (40) | | (80) |
| Change in interest | | | $32 | | ($32) |

Interpretation: X is deemed to have exchanged (given up) an interest in the Land worth $32 for an interest in the Inventory of $32. Where did X get the $32 worth of Land that is being given up? XYZ is deemed to have distributed that amount of Land to X. Therefore, we have the following sequence of constructive events:

1) XYZ distributes $32 worth of Land to X;

2) XYZ and X engage in a taxable exchange wherein X returns the $32 worth of Land distributed to X in 1), receiving $32 worth of Inventory in consideration;

3) Since X ultimately has Inventory worth $60, XYZ must distribute an additional $28 of Inventory ($60 ultimately held by X - $32 deemed acquired in the taxable exchange in 2).

The tax analysis of these steps follows:

## 1) XYZ distributes $32 worth of Land to X

*Tax consequences to X*: X recognizes no gain or loss on the distribution of $32 worth of Land. § 731(a)(1). X takes a basis in the distributed Land of $24 ($32 distributed/ $240 book value x $180 basis). § 732(a)(1). The adjusted basis in X's partnership interest is reduced to $56 ($80 - $24). § 733(2).

*Tax consequences to XYZ*: XYZ recognizes no gain or loss on the distribution. § 731(b). Its basis in the Land is reduced to $156 ($180 - $24). Its book value in the land is reduced to $208 ($240 - $32).

## 2) XYZ and X engage in taxable exchange of $32 worth of Land for $32 worth of Inventory

*Tax consequences to X*: X recognizes a capital gain of $8 on the exchange [$32 amount realized (value of Inventory received) - $24 (basis in Land distributed in prior step)]. X takes a basis in the Inventory just received of $32. § 1012(a).

*Tax consequences to XYZ*: XYZ recognizes an ordinary gain of $16 on the exchange [$32 amount realized (value of Land received) - $16 (basis in Inventory given up; basis is 50% of value)]. XYZ now has a basis in the Land of $188 ($156 after the distribution to X, above, plus $32 § 1012(a) cost basis resulting from taxable exchange).

The $16 gain just recognized is allocated to all of the partners *other than* X in proportion to their relative profit-sharing ratios. § 1.751-1(b)(2)(ii). This increases the bases in Y's and Z's partnership interests to $88 ($80 beginning balance + $16/2 proportionate share of gain). There is no change in either Y's or Z's capital accounts because, for book purposes, XYZ is simply exchanging Inventory with a book value of $32 for Land with a book value of $32 — no gain or loss.

## 3) XYZ distributes $28 worth of Inventory to X

*Tax consequences to X*: Ultimately, X has $60 worth of Inventory. After the preceding steps, X only has $32 worth of Inventory. Therefore, X must receive the remaining $28 worth of Inventory as a distribution from XYZ. Under the authority previously given, X recognizes no gain or loss on the distribution. X takes a basis in the newly distributed Inventory of $14 (basis is 50% of value), bringing X's aggregate basis in the Inventory to $46 ($32 from Inventory acquired in taxable exchange + $14 from Inventory distributed in this step). The basis of X's partnership interest is reduced to $42 ($56 balance before this step - $14 assigned to Inventory just distributed).

*Tax consequences to XYZ*: Again under authority previously given, XYZ recognizes no gain or loss on the distribution. Its basis in the Inventory declines to $30 ($44 balance before the step - $14 in Inventory just distributed).

The partnership's ending balance sheet, accompanied by basis accounts, is:

|  |  | Book Value | Adjusted Basis |
| --- | --- | --- | --- |
| Assets: | Inventory | $60 | $30 |
|  | Land | 240 | 188 |
|  |  | $300 | $218 |
| Capital: | X | $60 | $42 |
|  | Y | 120 | 88 |
|  | Z | 120 | 88 |
|  |  | $300 | $218 |

196.  **The best answer is "D."** Because a § 754 election is in place, there will be a basis adjustment under § 743. It will apply only to W. § 743(b).

The basis adjustment is as follows: W's basis in her partnership interest - W's share of the basis to the partnership of the partnership's assets. § 1.743-1(b).

W's basis in her partnership interest under § 1.743-1(c) is: $66,000 (cost basis under § 742) + $10,000 ($30,000/3 share of liabilities under § 752) = $76,000.

W's share of the basis to the partnership of the partnership's assets is: W's interest in the partnership's previously taxed capital + W's share of the partnership liabilities.

W's interest in the partnership's previously taxed capital is (§ 1.743-1(d)(1)):

1) The amount of cash W would receive if all of the partnership's assets were sold at their fair market values and the partnership completely liquidated, plus

2) The tax loss that would be allocated to W on the constructive sale, minus

3) The tax gain that would be allocated to W on the constructive sale.

If the partnership engaged in such a sale, W would receive the value of her capital interest, $66,000 [($228,000 value of assets - $30,000 liabilities)/3]. A gain of $21,000 [($228,000 value of assets - $165,000 bases in assets)/3] would be allocated to her. Therefore, W's interest in the partnership's previously taxed capital is $66,000 (cash W would receive) - $21,000 (gain allocated to W) = $45,000.

W's share of the basis to the partnership of the partnership's assets is: $45,000 (W's interest in the partnership's previously taxed capital) + $10,000 (share of liabilities) = $55,000.

Therefore, the § 743(b) adjustment is: $76,000 (W's partnership interest basis) - $55,000 (W's share of the basis to the partnership of the partnership's assets) = $21,000.

The § 743(b) basis adjustment is allocated, in accordance with their respective gains and losses, between: 1) the capital and § 1231 assets, and 2) all other assets (ordinary income assets). Where there are multiple assets in one of these two classes, the allocation is intended to reduce the difference between the assets' values and bases. § 755(a), (b); § 1.755-1(b).

Of the ordinary income assets (Receivables and Inventory), only the Inventory has a built-in gain. W's share of that built-in gain is $1,000 [($63,000 - $60,000)/3]. Therefore, the § 743(b) adjustment to Inventory is $1,000.

There is only one capital asset. W's share of the built-in gain in that asset is $20,000 [($120,000 - $60,000)/3]. Therefore, the § 743(b) adjustment to the Capital Asset is $20,000.

**Answer "A" is incorrect.** Distributions in complete liquidation of a partnership interest are governed by § 732(b) and (c). The available partnership interest basis is first allocated to cash, reducing the available basis to $90 ($100 - $10). Basis is next allocated to unrealized receivables and inventory items equal to the amount of their bases to the partnership. This reduces the available basis to $70 [$90 - ($0 + $20)]. The aggregate bases of the three capital assets is $112, which exceeds the remaining basis of the partnership, $70. Therefore the bases of those three assets must be reduced by $42 ($112 - $70).

The bases of the assets with built-in losses are reduced first in proportion to their relative built-in losses; but the adjustments cannot reduce the bases below the assets' fair market values. The analysis follows:

| Capital Asset | Value | Basis to Part- nership | Built-in Loss | % | Tentative Adjust- ment | Maximum Adjust- ment | Revised Basis |
|---|---|---|---|---|---|---|---|
| 1 | $50 | $70 | $20 | 80% | $33.60 | $20 | $50 |
| 2 | $20 | $25 | 5 | 20% | 8.40 | 5 | 20 |
| 3 | $40 | $17 | 0 | 0% | 0.00 | 0 | 17 |
| | | | $25 | 100% | $42.00 | $25 | $87 |

The aggregate basis of the capital assets still needs to be reduced by $17 ($87 current aggregate basis - $70 remaining basis in partnership interest). At this point the bases of the three capital assets are simply reduced proportionately until the $17 excess disappears, as follows:

| Capital Asset | Revised Basis | % | Adjustment (rounded) | Final Basis |
|---|---|---|---|---|
| 1 | $50 | 57.47% | $10 | $40 |
| 2 | 20 | 22.99% | 4 | 16 |
| 3 | 17 | 19.54% | 3 | 14 |
| | $87 | 100.00% | $17 | $70 |

The ending basis in the partnership interest is zero [$70 - ($40 + $16 + $14)].

**Answer "B" is incorrect.** Under § 735(a)(1) the gain or loss on the unrealized receivables would be ordinary under all circumstances. However, under § 735(a)(2) the ordinary "taint" on the inventory items expires after five years.

**Answer "C" is incorrect.** Q first reduces her partnership interest basis by the cash received to $800,000 ($900,000 - $100,000). The remaining $800,000 of basis is allocated to Raw Land 2. § 732(b). This constitutes a "substantial basis reduction" under § 734(d)(1) because Q is taking a basis of $800,000 in an asset in which the partnership had a basis of only $500,000; the $300,000 differential surpasses the $250,000 threshold. As a result the partnership must reduce the basis in its properties by $300,000. § 734(b)(2).

Section 755(b) and § 1.755-1(c) require the partnership to reduce the bases in its capital assets since the asset distributed was a capital asset. Therefore, the partnership's basis in Raw Land 1 becomes $650,000 ($950,000 beginning basis - $300,000 § 734 adjustment).

197.  **The best answer is "D."** The partnership agreement is the document as comprised at the due date of the tax return (without extensions). § 761(b). Retroactive changes are therefore allowed. However, the retroactive allocations must be consistent with the partners' varying interests during the year per § 706. Further, pre-admission losses cannot be allocated to partners before their dates of admission (or to pre-existing partners with respect to the date of the increase in their interests). Rev. Ruls. 77-310, 1977-2 C.B. 217, and 77-119, 1977-1 C.B. 177.

**Answer "A" is incorrect.** For allocations to be respected as having economic effect, liquidating distributions must be in accordance with positive capital account balances. § 1.704-1(b)(2)(ii)(b)(2). This requirement, which is violated here, is intended to ensure that the allocation of partnership tax items "are consistent with the underlying economic arrangement of the partners." § 1.704-1(b)(2)(ii)(a).

**Answer "B" is incorrect.** The economic effect of the allocation of partnership tax items is not substantial unless "there is a reasonable possibility that the allocation (or allocations) will affect substantially the dollar amounts to be received by the partners from the partnership, independent of tax consequences." Present value concepts are taken into account in determining the economic impact of the allocations, as are the unique tax attributes of the individual partners (e.g., the availability of net operating loss or capital loss carryovers). § 1.704-1(b)(2)(iii)(a).

The economic effect of shifting (i.e., intra-year) allocations are not substantial "if, at the time the [allocations become] . . . . part of the partnership agreement, there is a strong likelihood that [t]he net increases and decreases that will be recorded in the partners' respective capital accounts for [the] taxable year will not differ substantially from [those] that would be recorded . . . if the allocations were not contained in the partnership agreement, and [t]he total tax liability of the partners . . . will be less than if the allocations were not contained in the partnership agreement." § 1.704-1(b)(2)(iii)(b).

These facts could raise substantiality issues. To illustrate, assume Partner #1 has available a $40,000 net operating loss carryover and that Partner #2 is in the 35% marginal tax bracket. Without the allocations the tax consequences would be:

|  | Partner #1 | Partner #2 | Total |
|---|---|---|---|
| Ordinary income | 15,000 | 15,000 | 30,000 |
| § 103 interest | 10,000 | 10,000 | 20,000 |
|  | 25,000 | 25,000 | 50,000 |
|  |  |  |  |
| Tentative taxable income | 15,000 | 15,000 |  |
| NOL carryforward | (40,000) | (0) |  |
| Taxable income | 0 | 15,000 |  |
|  |  |  |  |
| Federal tax liability | 0 | 5,250 | 5,250 |

With the allocations the tax consequences would be:

|  | Partner #1 | Partner #2 | Total |
|---|---|---|---|
| Ordinary income | 25,000 | 5,000 | 30,000 |
| § 103 interest | 0 | 20,000 | 20,000 |
|  | 25,000 | 25,000 | 50,000 |
|  |  |  |  |
| Tentative taxable income | 25,000 | 5,000 |  |
| NOL carryforward | (40,000) | (0) |  |
| Taxable income | 0 | 5,000 |  |
|  |  |  |  |
| Federal tax liability | 0 | 1,750 | 1,750 |

With or without the allocations, both partners' capital accounts would increase by the same amount, as follows:

Partner #1:          + 25,000 (whether it is 15,000 of ordinary income plus 10,000 of
                      § 103 interest, or 25,000 of only ordinary income)

Partner #2:              + 25,000 (whether it is 15,000 of ordinary income plus 10,000 of
                        § 103 interest, or 5,000 of ordinary income plus 20,000 of § 103
                        interest)Partner #1:

Therefore, these intra-year, or shifting, allocations lack substantiality.

**Answer "C" is incorrect.** These are transitory allocations per § 1.704-1(b)(2)(iii)(c) and therefore lack substantiality. The difference between shifting and transitory allocations is that the former relates to allocations within a single taxable year, whereas the latter relates to allocations occurring over two or more taxable years. The fundamental principle is the same: The allocations reduce the partners' aggregate tax liability while having no impact on the partners' ultimate capital account balances. As noted earlier, present value concepts are taken into account. Therefore, the $103,000 allocation arising in the second taxable year would be viewed as having a present value equal to the $100,000 allocation arising in the first taxable year (103,000 ÷ 1.03). As illustrated in the discussion of answer B, it is not difficult to envision circumstances in which the allocations would lower the aggregate tax liability while leaving the capital accounts unchanged.

198.   **The best answer is "B."** The general rule is that the gain or loss recognized by a partner on the sale or exchange of a partnership interest is capital. § 741. A partner does not recognize a loss upon the distribution by the partnership of property to the partner unless the distribution is in complete liquidation of the partner's interest (true here) and the partner's adjusted basis in its partnership interest exceeds the sum of the cash distributed and the bases to the partnership of the § 751 assets (unrealized receivables and inventory items; none here). Any such loss is treated as realized from the sale or exchange of the partner's interest. § 733(2). Therefore, Guy will recognize a capital loss of $40,000 ($60,000 basis in partnership interest - $20,000 cash received).

**Answer "A" is incorrect.** Had Fran still held the interest, the statement would have been true. Fran would have been allocated the built-in loss of $400,000 under § 704(c)(1)(A) and would have been allocated 25% of the remaining $100,000 loss under § 704(b). However, where a partner with a § 704(c)(1)(A) built-in loss sells or exchanges its interest, the built-in loss permanently disappears, depriving the successor partner of any benefit from the built-in loss. § 704(c)(1)(C). Therefore, Ned will be allocated only 25% of the remaining $100,000 loss, $25,000.

**Answer "C" is incorrect.** If an "unrealized receivable" is distributed by the partnership to a partner, the gain or loss recognized by the partner upon the later disposition of the receivable is ordinary. § 735(a)(1). This is an "unrealized receivable" because it arose from the sale of services and has not yet been included in the partnership's gross income (because the partnership uses the cash method). § 751(c)(2).

**Answer "D" is incorrect.** As discussed under B, unless § 751 assets are involved (not true here), the gain or loss recognized upon the sale or exchange of a partnership interest is capital.

199.   **The best answer is "C."** Section 755(b) divides partnership property into the following two classes: 1) capital assets *and § 1231 assets*, and 2) all other property.

**Answer "A" is a correct statement and, therefore, not the right answer.** A § 743 adjustment, which requires a § 754 election to be in effect (true here since there is, in fact, a § 743 adjustment), applies only to the acquiring partner. § 743(b)(1). For this reason, the

$100,000 gain allocated to Dale by the partnership, which is based on the basis of Asset #4 to the partnership (which does not reflect the § 743 adjustment), must be adjusted to take into account the fact that Dale's purchase price for the partnership interest included an extra $40,000 attributable to Asset #4 (Dale's § 743 adjustment with respect to this asset). Therefore, Dale reports a gain of $60,000 ($100,000 gain allocated to Dale by partnership — Dale's § 743 adjustment).

**Answer "B" is a correct statement and, therefore, not the right answer.** Cunningham received only one asset in the complete liquidation of his interest: raw land with a basis to the partnership of $600,000. Cunningham takes a basis in the raw land equal to the $1,000,000 basis of his interest less the cash distributed in the same transaction (here $0): $1,000,000. § 732(b). That amount is $400,000 more than the partnership's basis in that asset, resulting in a "substantial basis reduction." § 734(d)(1), (b)(2)(B). This requires the partnership to reduce the basis in its property by $400,000. § 734(a), (b)(2)(B). The adjustment is allocated among the partnership's assets under § 755. § 734(c).

**Answer "D" is a correct statement and, therefore, not the right answer.** This is the purpose of § 743 adjustments, as noted in the discussion of answer A.

200.   **The best answer is "D."** Under § 1362(b)(1), the S election form, Form 2553, would have to be filed by March 15 for the election to be effective as of the beginning of Fedor's first taxable year. March 30 is too late. If nothing was done to mitigate the late election, the corporation would have obtained S status on January 1 of the following year. § 1362(b)(3). However, § 1362(b)(5) authorizes the IRS to give an S election retroactive effect if it finds a "reasonable cause for the failure to timely make [the] election." The CPA's illness would likely constitute reasonable cause. *See, e.g.,* Priv. Ltr. Rul. 98-39-011.

    **Answer "A" is a correct statement and, therefore, not the right answer.** Michael, Sue and Michelle count as one shareholder. § 1361(c)(1). Art is a shareholder. A QSST such as the Polly Trust can be an S corporation shareholder under § 1361(d)(1)(A). However, where the beneficiary is a member of the family of another shareholder (true here because Polly is Art's wife), the family rules apply. § 1.1361-1(e)(3)(ii)(B). Therefore, the QSST and Art count as one shareholder. The Fisher Trust is a shareholder, eligible for that status under § 1361(c)(2)(A)(v); Pittsford College is a permissible beneficiary. §§ 1361(e)(1)(A)(i), 170(c)(2)(B). NYU is a permissible shareholder. § 1361(b)(1)(B), (c)(6). Claude and Mildred, as joint owners, are both shareholders. § 1.1361-1(e)(1). Finally, Gwendolyn is a shareholder. *Id.* Thus, there are seven shareholders.

    **Answer "B" is a correct statement and, therefore, not the right answer.** The tax consequences of a QSST are no different from other trusts that are required to pay out all of their income annually. The beneficiary treats the trust income like any other and the tax rate applied to the trust income is whichever rate is applicable under the circumstances. The tax rate on ESBTs is, however, always the highest rate of taxation under § 1(e). § 641(c)(2)(A).

    **Answer "C" is a correct statement and, therefore, not the right answer.** Section 1362(a)(2) expressly so states.

201.   **The best answer is "B."** The 20-year term loan comes within the "straight-debt" safe harbor to the debt-as-a-second-class-of-stock rule. § 1361(c)(5). It is in the form of debt, debt service is not contingent, it is not convertible, and the lender is an individual. The facts that the debt is subordinated and that the IRS has successfully recharacterized the note as equity are irrelevant. § 1.1361-1(l)(5)(ii), (iv).

    **Answer "A" is a correct statement and, therefore, not the right answer.** The periodic advances come within the "short-term unwritten advances" safe harbor under § 1.1361-1(l)(4)(ii)(B)(1) — i.e., less than $10,000 and repaid within a reasonable period of time.

    **Answer "C" is a correct statement and, therefore, not the right answer.** A grantor trust may be a shareholder. The deemed owner of the trust is treated as the actual shareholder. § 1361(c)(2)(A)(i), (B)(i).

    **Answer "D" is a correct statement and, therefore, not the right answer.** The issue with respect to the multiple-classes-of-stock rule is whether there are differences in the distribution rights. *See* S. REPT. No. 97-640, at 8. There are no such differences. Differences in voting rights are irrelevant. § 1361(c)(4).

202.   **The best answer is "A."** Section 1361(b)(1)(C) prohibits nonresident alien shareholders. Section 1.1361-1(g)(1)(i) extends this prohibition to spouses of S corporation shareholders who have a "current ownership interest" in the stock. The regulation states that such an interest exists when a nonresident alien spouse has rights in the stock under community property laws. Note that if both spouses elect under § 6013(g), a nonresident alien spouse will be treated as a U.S. resident for all income tax purposes, thereby removing the jeopardy to S status.

**Answer "B" is incorrect.** An estate can be an S corporation shareholder. § 1361(b)(1)(B). This includes a bankruptcy estate. § 1361(c)(3).

**Answer "C" is incorrect.** A testamentary trust can be an S corporation shareholder, but only for two years. § 1361(c)(2)(A)(iii).

**Answer "D" is incorrect.** The both-spouses-comprise-one-shareholder rule under § 1361(c)(1)(A)(i) does not apply to divorced spouses. § 1.1361-1(e)(2). Therefore, the S corporation now has 100 shareholders, but that does not deprive it of "small business corporation" status. § 1361(b)(1)(A).

203.   **The best answer is "B."** A new S corporation which has never been a C corporation will not generate any earnings and profits. § 1371(c)(1).

**Answer "A" is a correct statement and, therefore, not the right answer.** Subchapter C governs Subchapter S corporations except to the extent Subchapter S expressly states to the contrary and except to the extent applying Subchapter C to an S corporation would be inconsistent with Subchapter S principles. § 1371(a).

**Answer "C" is a correct statement and, therefore, not the right answer.** Section 1363(c)(1) expressly so states, with limited exceptions.

**Answer "D" is a correct statement and, therefore, not the right answer.** Section 1363(a) expressly so states. The exceptions are the built-in gains tax under § 1374 and the tax on excess net passive income under § 1375.

204.   **The best answer is "D."** Section 1363(b)(1) requires that, in computing the taxable income of an S corporation, "the items described in section 1366(a)(1)(A) . . . be separately stated[.]" Section 1366(a)(1)(A) states that, "[i]n determining the tax . . . of a shareholder . . . , there shall be taken into account the shareholder's pro rata share of the corporation's . . . items of income [and] deduction . . . the separate treatment of which could affect the liability for tax of any shareholder[.]"

**Answer "A" is incorrect.** Section 1363(b)(2) states that, in computing an S corporation's taxable income, "the deductions referred to in section 703(a)(2) shall not be allowed[.]" Section 703(a)(2)(C) lists charitable contributions as one of the prohibited deductions.

**Answer "B" is incorrect.** Certain distributions reduce stock basis under § 1367(a)(2)(A).

**Answer "C" is incorrect.** Certain cash distributions can reduce stock basis. § 1367(a)(2)(A). To the extent such a distribution does not exceed the shareholder's stock basis, no gain is recognized under § 1368(b)(1). However, if the distribution exceeds the stock basis, the excess is treated as a gain from the constructive sale or exchange of the stock. § 1368(b)(2).

205. **The best answer is "A."** Section 1.1366-1(a)(2)(vi) and the flush language of subparagraph (2), respectively, expressly so state.

**Answer "B" is incorrect.** The Code contains relatively few express enumerations of separately stated items. The Regulations provide a semi-comprehensive list, but expressly caveat their enumerations with "include, but are not limited to." *See,* § 1.1366-1(a)(2).

**Answer "C" is incorrect.** Section 1363(b)(3) expressly allows § 248 deductions.

**Answer "D" is incorrect.** The correct document is Schedule K-1.

206. Gwen recognizes no gain on the transfer of the raw land to Babylon. § 351(a). She takes a basis in her Babylon stock of $300,000 ($300,000 basis in the raw land). § 358(a)(1). Her holding period in the stock is five years. § 1223(1).

Since Gwen was a shareholder for the entire year, she is allocated 20% of the corporation's tax items under § 1377(a)(1) as follows:

Non-separately computed income:

| | |
|---|---:|
| Sales | $10,000,000 |
| Cost of sales | (6,000,000) |
| Marketing expense | (1,000,000) |
| Administration expense | (500,000) |
| Personal injury loss | (2,250,000) |
| Nonseparately computed income | $250,000 |
| Gwen's share | 20% |
| Amount allocated to Gwen | $50,000 |

Separately stated items (§ 1366(a); § 1.1366-1(a)(2)):

| | | Total | Gwen (20%) |
|---|---|---:|---:|
| Income: | § 1231 gain | $80,000 | $16,000 |
| | Exempt interest | $10,000 | $2,000 |
| Nondeductible: | Penalties | ($5,000) | ($1,000) |
| Deductible: | § 179 amount | ($100,000) | ($20,000) |
| | Short-term capital loss | ($120,000) | ($24,000) |

Gwen's share of the December 31 distribution is $360,000 ($1,800,000 x 20%).

Gwen adjusts her stock basis per § 1367(a). The following stock basis adjustment ordering rules of § 1.1367-1(f) apply:

First, basis is increased by all income items (whether or not excluded from your income);

Second, basis is decreased by all distributions;

Third, basis is decreased by all nondeductible, non-capitalizable expense items;

Fourth, basis is decreased by all deductible expense items.

Thus, Gwen makes the following adjustments to her stock basis:

| | | | |
|---|---|---:|---:|
| Beginning basis under § 358 | | | $300,000 |
| Income items: | § 1231 gain | $16,000 | |
| | Exempt interest | 2,000 | |
| | Nonseparately computed income | 50,000 | 68,000 |
| | | | 368,000 |
| Distribution | | | (360,000) |
| | | | 8,000 |
| Nondeductible/non-capitalizable items: Penalties | | | (1,000) |
| | | | 7,000 |
| Deductible items: | § 179 amount | 20,000 | |
| | Short-term capital loss | 24,000 | (44,000) |
| Negative balance — not permitted | | | ($37,000) |

Gwen's stock basis cannot go below zero. § 1367(a)(2). She can take losses supported by her stock basis only to the extent thereof. § 1366(d)(1)(A). Therefore only a portion of the deductible items can be taken into account at this stage, as follows:

| Item | Amount | % | Subtracted from Basis | Remaining |
|---|---:|---:|---:|---:|
| § 179 amount | $20,000 | 45.45% | $3,182 | $16,818 |
| Short-term capital loss | 24,000 | 54.55% | 3,818 | 20,182 |
| | $44,000 | 100.00% | $7,000 | $37,000 |

The result is that Gwen's stock basis is reduced to zero.

If distributions and expense items have driven its stock basis to zero, an S corporation shareholder can use its loan basis to take into account further expense items under §§ 1366(d)(1)(B) and 1367(b)(2)(A), as follows:

| | | | |
|---|---|---:|---:|
| Basis in debt | | | $35,000 |
| Deductible items: | § 179 amount | $16,818 | |
| | Short-term capital loss | 20,182 | (37,000) |
| Negative balance — not permitted | | | ($2,000) |

Gwen's debt basis cannot be reduced below zero, so only a portion of the expense items can be taken into account, as follows:

| Item | Amount | % | Subtracted from Basis | Remaining |
|---|---:|---:|---:|---:|
| § 179 amount | $16,818 | 45.45% | $15,909 | $909 |
| Short-term capital loss | 20,182 | 54.55% | 19,091 | 1,091 |
| | $37,000 | 100.00% | $35,000 | $2,000 |

The result is that Gwen's debt basis is reduced to zero. The remaining $2,000 of expense items are treated as incurred in the succeeding taxable year. § 1366(d)(2)(A).

On her personal tax return Gwen will show the following tax items:

| | |
|---|---:|
| § 1231 gain[fn1] | $16,000 |
| Exempt interest | $2,000 |

| | | |
|---|---|---|
| Ordinary income[fn2] | $50,000 | |
| § 179 amount[fn3] | $19,091 | ($3,182 + $15,909) |
| Short-term capital loss[fn4] | $22,909 | ($3,818 + $19,091) |

[fn1] *Will be combined with other § 1231 gains and losses and ultimately characterized as capital gain or ordinary gain*
[fn2] *Nonseparately computed income is always ordinary*
[fn3] *Allowable to the extent of available business income shown on Gwen's return*
[fn4] *Allowable to the extent of capital gains (plus $3,000)*

207. Gwen's share of this ordinary income is $40,000 ($200,000 x 20%). First, Gwen must restore her basis in the debt under § 1367(b)(2)(B); second, she must restore her basis in the stock under § 1367(a)(1). Thus, the first $35,000 of ordinary income restores Gwen's loan basis to its original amount. The other $5,000 increases Gwen's stock basis to that amount.

Now that there is positive stock and loan basis, the $2,000 of suspended expense items from the prior year are released as follows:

| | | |
|---|---|---|
| Stock basis after restoration | | $5,000 |
| § 179 amount | $909 | |
| Short-term capital loss | 1,091 | (2,000) |
| | | $3,000 |

On her personal tax return for Year 2 Gwen will show the following tax items:

| | |
|---|---|
| Ordinary income | $5,000 |
| § 179 amount | $909 |
| Short-term capital loss | $1,091 |

208. **The best answer is "B."** When a shareholder has made multiple loans to an S corporation, loan basis is reduced by expense items in proportion to the relative loan bases at the end of the year. § 1.1367-2(b)(3). If an allocation of S corporation income is available to restore the bases of multiple loans made by the same shareholder, that income is allocated among the loans in proportion to the relative cumulative amount of basis reduction each loan has suffered. § 1.1367-2(c)(2).

In Year 1 the shareholder reduced the first loan of $10,000 by $8,000 to $2,000. In Year 2, there were two loans, the original with a basis of $2,000 and the new with a basis of $6,000. The loan bases are in the ratio of 2,000:6,000 or 1:3. Thus, the loan bases are reduced by the $2,000 of remaining expense items in the respective amounts of $500 and $1,500; their respective balances at the end of Year 2 are $1,500 ($2,000 - $500) and $4,500 ($6,000 - $1,500).

In Year 3 $5,000 is available to restore loan basis. The cumulative amount by which the first loan has been reduced is $8,500 ($10,000 original loan - $1,500 basis at the end of Year 2); the cumulative amount by which the second loan has been reduced is $1,500 ($6,000 - $1,500). These reductions are in the ratio of 85:15. Therefore, the $5,000 of income in Year 3 restores the basis of the first loan by $4,250 (85% x $5,000) to $5,750 ($1,500 beginning-of-year basis + $4,250 restoration). The amount allocated to the second loan is $750 (15% x $5,000), bringing its basis to $5,250 ($4,500 + $750).

**Answer "A" is incorrect.** Courts uniformly hold that a loan guarantee, alone, provides no basis against which losses can be deducted. The shareholder must make an economic investment to create such basis. No economic investment is made unless the shareholder is required to perform on its guarantee. *Maloof v. Comm'r*, 456 F.3d 645 (6th Cir. 2006).

**Answer "C" is incorrect.** Suspended losses are personal to the shareholder and cannot be transferred along with the shareholder's stock. The only exception is inter-spousal transfers under § 1041. § 1.1366-2(a)(5)(i), (ii).

**Answer "D" is incorrect.** Just because an S corporation shareholder has sufficient stock and/or loan basis to allow a deduction to be taken into account, that does not mean the shareholder is entitled to take the deduction presently on the shareholder's personal income tax return. In the context of capital losses the shareholder must still have sufficient capital gains to allow the capital loss deduction under § 1211. For example, if this is the only capital loss and there are no capital gains, the shareholder would be limited to a $3,000 deduction on its personal tax return.

209.  **The best answer is "C."** Normally an exclusion would be allowed. However, § 119 is available only if the taxpayer is classified as an employee. Section 1372(a) states that, "[f]or the purpose of applying the provisions of this subtitle which relate to employee fringe benefits — (1) the S corporation shall be treated as a partnership, and (2) any 2-percent shareholder of the S corporation shall be treated as a partner[.]" Partners are not classified as employees with respect to their partnership. Lauren is a "2-percent shareholder." § 1372(b). Therefore, Lauren is ineligible for the benefits of § 119.

**Answer "A" is a correct statement and, therefore, not the right answer.** Section 1.1368-1(g) expressly so provides.

**Answer "B" is a correct statement and, therefore, not the right answer.** Each S corporation tax item is allocated pro rata to each day of the taxable year. Then the amount allocated to each day is divided by the number of shares outstanding on that day. This is the "per-day, per-share" rule of § 1377(a)(1). Here the $365,000 of ordinary income is allocated $1,000 per day.

On March 1 there were 1,000 shares outstanding, resulting in an allocation of $1 of ordinary income per share. The shareholder held 10 shares on this day, resulting in an allocation of $10 ($1 x 10 shares). On March 2 there were 2,000 shares outstanding, resulting in an allocation of $.50 of ordinary income per share. The shareholder held 11 shares on this day, resulting in an allocation of $5.50 ($.50 x 11 shares). The total allocation to the shareholder for the taxable year is $15.50.

**Answer "D" is a correct statement and, therefore, not the right answer.** Section 1377(a)(2) expressly permit this procedure. Section 1.1377-1(b) elaborates.

210.  **The best answer is "C."** Section 1368(e)(1)(B) requires the AAA to be reduced by the redeemed stock's pro rata share thereof.

**Answer "A" is a correct statement and, therefore, not the right answer.** Section 1366(e) authorizes the IRS to reallocate S corporation income among family shareholders where a family-member shareholder is undercompensated for services rendered or capital provided. If Father is allocated an additional $20,000 of taxable income, $50,000 would remain to be divided, resulting in an allocation to Daughter of $25,000 ($50,000 x 50%). § 1.1366-3(b) Ex. 1.

**Answer "B" is a correct statement and, therefore, not the right answer.** A shareholder is required to take its allocation of S corporation tax items onto the shareholder's return in the shareholder's taxable year with or within which the taxable year of the corporation ends. § 1366(a)(1); § 1.1366-1(a)(1). Here the taxable year of the corporation ends April 30, Year 1. That year ends within the shareholder's taxable year ending December 31 of Year 1, the return for which will be due in April of Year 2.

**Answer "D" is a correct statement and, therefore, not the right answer.** Section 1.1368-1(f)(3) expressly provides for such a "deemed dividend" followed by a "deemed capital contribution."

211. Section 1378(a) requires S corporations to use as their taxable year a "permitted year," defined by § 1378(b) as: "(1) . . . a year ending December 31, or (2) . . . any other [annual] accounting period for which the corporation establishes a business purpose."

Section 1.1378-1(a) (and virtually all tax authorities) refers to § 1378(a)(1)'s "a year ending December 31" as the "required taxable year." The "required taxable year" is the default. Affirmative action is required to adopt a different taxable year.

Section 1.1378-1(a) expands the term "permitted year" to include a taxable year elected under § 444. That section allows an S corporation to elect a taxable year other a "required taxable year" or a year for which a business purpose is established. The primary limitation comes from § 444(b)(1), which prohibits a "deferral period" of more than three months. Keeping in mind that normally an S corporation is required to use the calendar year, the three-month deferral limit basically means that the proposed taxable year cannot end earlier than September 30 (the deferral period is exactly three months: from the end of September to the end of December).

Because an election under § 444 could cause a deferral of tax receipts, the taxpayer must participate in so-called "§ 7519 payments." These payments are fundamentally deposits with the IRS which increase and decrease over time. At any given time, the balance of the deposit is intended to eliminate the adverse time-value-of-money impact on the government resulting from the corporation's elected fiscal year.

Rev. Proc. 2006-46, 2006-2 C.B. 859, identifies when a "business purpose" has been established, stating: "a business purpose [exists] if the requested [taxable year] coincides with the taxpayer's . . . ownership taxable year . . . or [its] natural business year." An ownership taxable year is "the taxable year (if any) that . . . constitutes the taxable year of . . . shareholders . . . holding more than 50-percent of the corporation's . . . outstanding shares." A natural business year exists if, in essence, at least 25% of the year's gross receipts are recognized in the last two months of such year.

Thus, the four possible years are: 1) calendar, 2) § 444, 3) ownership taxable year, and 4) business purpose taxable year.

212. **The best answer is "B."** Although § 1371(c)(1) precludes the creation of earnings and profits while the corporation is governed by Subchapter S, a corporation which was previously a C corporation may have had a balance in earnings and profits on the day S status began. Distributions to shareholders by the S corporation could then carry out earnings and profits

and, therefore, be characterized as dividends. § 1368(c).

An S corporation's accumulated adjustments account (AAA) tracks all of the income and losses recognized while the corporation holds S status, as well as all of the distributions out of its cumulative post-election income. So long as the AAA has a positive balance, no earnings and profits are carried out by S corporation distributions to shareholders. If the AAA has a zero balance, however, any additional distribution by the S corporation to its shareholders during the year will carry out earnings and profits (to the extent thereof), which distribution would then be characterized as a dividend.

**Answer "A" is a correct statement and, therefore, not the right answer.** Section 1363(d)(1) expressly so states. Under FIFO, the oldest inventory is deemed sold first, leaving the newer (usually more costly) inventory on the balance sheet. Under LIFO, the newest inventory is deemed sold first, leaving the oldest (usually least expensive) inventory on the balance sheet. The LIFO adjustment will be positive.

**Answer "C" is a correct statement and, therefore, not the right answer.** Section 1371(b)(1), as modified by § 1374(b)(2) so states.

**Answer "D" is a correct statement and, therefore, not the right answer.** The AAA adjustments for corporate tax items and distributions are very similar to the adjustments shareholders make in their stock bases for those tax items and distributions, but they are not identical. Among the differences are: 1) the AAA is not adjusted upward for exempt income (§ 1368(e)(1)(A)), 2) the AAA can have a negative balance (§ 1.1368-2(a)(3)(ii)), and 3) some or all of the corporation's deductible and nondeductible items reduce the AAA before reductions in that account for distributions (§ 1.1368-2(a)(5)(ii), (iii)).

213.   Picard's accumulated adjustments account (AAA) begins with a zero balance. § 1.1368-2(a)(1). None of the earnings and profits (E&P) will be carried out by corporate distributions unless the AAA is zero (or negative). § 1368(c). The AAA is adjusted in the following order under § 1.1368-2(a)(5):

Step 1:   The AAA is adjusted upward by all items of corporate income (other than exempt income) for the year;

Step 2:   The AAA is adjusted downward by all items of corporate expense (whether deductible or not) for the year, but not in excess of the amount by which the AAA was increased in Step 1 (the excess of the corporation's expense items over its income items for the current year is called the "net negative adjustment" (NNA), which comes into play in Step 4);

Step 3:   The AAA is adjusted downward by distributions to shareholders (but only to the extent the AAA begins Step 3 with a positive balance) — distributions beyond the positive balance in the AAA are deemed sourced from E&P to the extent thereof;

Step 4:   The AAA is adjusted downward by the NNA; and

Step 5:   The AAA is adjusted downward for redemptions occurring during the year (not relevant here).

In Year 1 the AAA (which begins with a zero balance) is first increased by the $250,000 of ordinary income and then decreased by the $100,000 of ordinary deductions, resulting in a pre-distribution balance of $150,000. The $120,000 distribution reduces the AAA to $30,000. Since there was a sufficient amount in the AAA to take into account all of the distributions during the year, none of the E&P was carried out. § 1368(b).

In Year 2, the AAA is increased by $300,000 of ordinary income to $330,000. The tentative negative adjustment to the AAA for the year resulting from the short-term capital loss is

$700,000, but the pre-distribution negative adjustments to the AAA cannot exceed the year's positive income adjustments. Therefore, the AAA is reduced by only $300,000 of the $700,000 to a balance of $30,000. The remaining $400,000 of short-term capital loss constitutes a NNA. Only $30,000 of the $100,000 distribution can be sourced from the AAA, bringing its balance to zero. The remaining $70,000 is deemed sourced from E&P. Since the balance in E&P is $200,000, all of the $70,000 is characterized as a dividend and the E&P balance is reduced to $130,000. § 312(a)(1). Finally, the AAA is adjusted downward by the NNA to a negative balance of ($400,000).

In Year 3, the AAA is increased by the $100,000 of ordinary income to a negative balance of ($300,000). Since the tentative negative adjustment to the AAA resulting from the long-term capital loss of $400,000 exceeds the positive income-related adjustment of $100,000, only $100,000 of the long-term capital loss is deducted in this step. The remaining $300,000 is an NNA. The pre-distribution balance of the AAA is negative, ($400,000). Since the AAA does not have a positive balance, none of the $150,000 distribution can be absorbed by the AAA. All of the distribution is deemed sourced from E&P to the extent thereof. Since the balance in E&P is only $130,000, only that amount of the $150,000 distribution is characterized as a dividend. The balance in E&P is now zero. Since the corporation no longer has any E&P, there is no longer any need to maintain the AAA.

214. **The best answer is "B."** The net unrealized built-in gain (NUBIG) is determined by subtracting the aggregate bases of all corporate assets from the aggregate value of such assets at the last moment the corporation is a C corporation. § 1374(d)(1). This definition is modified by § 1.1374-3(a), which is intended to put cash-method corporations on the same footing as accrual-method corporations. Specifically, it allows a cash-method corporation to deduct, in determining its NUBIG, the amount of its liabilities that would, if paid, generate a deduction. (Accrual-method corporations have already had the benefit of these deductions.)

The cumulative value of the corporation's assets is $1,150,000 ($500,000 Factory +$300,000 Receivables +$350,000 Inventory). Their aggregate basis is $1,000,000 ($900,000 Factory +$0 Receivables +$100,000 Inventory). The NUBIG would appear to be $150,000 ($1,150,000 aggregate value - $1,000,000 aggregate basis). However, the cash-method corporation is also permitted to deduct the Accounts Payable, resulting in an NUBIG of $50,000 ($150,000 - $100,000).

**Answer "A" is a correct statement and, therefore, not the right answer.** If a C corporation distributes appreciated property it recognizes gain. § 311(a)(2). If it could convert to S status prior to disposing of those assets, it could sidestep the double-taxation regime by eliminating the corporate-level tax. (An S corporation would also recognize the gains under § 311(a)(2), but no tax would be imposed on the S corporation as a result.) The BIG tax was enacted to thwart this scheme.

**Answer "C" is a correct statement and, therefore, not the right answer.** Recognized built-in gain is any gain recognized on the disposition of an asset by an S corporation during the recognition period unless either the corporation did not own the asset on the date of S conversion or the gain recognized exceeds the gain potential in the asset on the date of S conversion. § 1374(d)(3). This asset had no gain potential on the date of S conversion (it had a built-in loss). Therefore, the gain recognized on it by the S corporation is not part of the built-in gains tax base.

**Answer "D" is a correct statement and, therefore, not the right answer.** The economic performance requirement is set forth in § 461(h)(2)(C)(ii) and § 1.461-4(g)(2). In the determination of the NUBIG § 1.1374-4(b)(2) waives the economic performance requirement for liabilities such as those described here, bringing the corporation back into the "pure" accrual method upon which the built-in gains tax is based.

215. **The best answer is "D."** The shareholder is also allocated the $35,000 built-in gains tax paid by the corporation. The $35,000 will be characterized as a long-term capital loss. § 1366(f)(2).

**Answer "A" is a correct statement and, therefore, not the right answer.** Had the corporation sold the land prior to becoming an S corporation, the corporate-level tax would have been $12,500. § 11(b). The built-in gains tax is imposed at a rate of 35%, resulting in a tax liability of $24,500. § 1374(b)(1).

**Answer "B" is a correct statement and, therefore, not the right answer.** Section 1.1374-2(a)(2) expressly so states. Any excess of the tentative amount subject to the built-in gains tax for the year over the taxable income for such year is called a "recognized built-in gain carryover" and is treated as a recognized built-in gain in the succeeding taxable year. § 1374(d)(2)(B).

**Answer "C" is a correct statement and, therefore, not the right answer.** Section 1374(b)(3)(B) expressly so states.

216. **The best answer is "A."** If an S corporation has earnings and profits from its prior existence as a C corporation and if its passive investment income exceeds 25% of its gross receipts, a corporate-level tax is imposed. § 1375. If the S corporation, in three consecutive years, has passive investment income that exceeds 25% of its gross receipts, its S status is terminated. § 1362(d)(3)(A)(i)(II).

**Answer "B" is incorrect.** The proceeds from such assets are not offset by their bases. § 1.1362-2(c)(4)(i). This is not true for capital assets. §§ 1375(b)(3), 1362(d)(3)(B).

**Answer "C" is incorrect.** Royalties and rents derived from the active conduct of business are excluded from passive investment income. § 1.1362-2(c)(5)(ii)(A)(2), (B)(2). They are not "passive."

**Answer "D" is incorrect.** The amount of the tax is correct, but the amount the shareholder reports as rental income is not. Under § 1375(a), the tax is computed as: 35% x Excess net passive income. "Excess net passive income" is defined as:

$$\text{Net passive income x } \frac{[\text{Passive investment income - (25\% x Gross receipts)}]}{\text{Passive investment income}}$$

§ 1375(b)(1)(A); § 1.1375-1(b)(1)(i).

"Passive investment income" is defined as "gross receipts from royalties, rents, dividends, interest and annuities." §§ 1375(b)(3), 1362(d)(3)(C)(i). "Net passive income" is the aggregate of all passive investment income less all of the deductions directly connected with generating such income. § 1375(b)(2).

Here the passive investment income is $1,015,000 ($350,000 rentals + $665,000 interest). The net passive income is $975,000 [$1,015,000 passive investment income - ($25,000 expenses related to rentals + $15,000 expenses related to interest)].

The excess net passive income is:

$$\frac{\$975,000 \times [\$1,015,000 - (25\% \times \$3,821,000)]}{\$1,015,000} = \$57,395$$

The tax under § 1375 is: 35% x \$57,395 = \$20,088

Section 1366(f)(3) characterizes the tax as a loss. Section 1.1366-4(c) allocates that loss among the components of passive investment income in proportion to their respective net passive incomes. The answer incorrectly allocates the tax in proportion to their respective gross passive investment incomes (not their net passive incomes). The correct allocation is:

| Item | Net Passive Income | % | Allocation of Tax | Net Passing to Shareholder |
|---|---|---|---|---|
| Rental income | \$325,000 | 33.33 | \$6,696 | \$318,304 |
| Interest income | 650,000 | 66.67 | 13,392 | 636,608 |
| | \$975,000 | 100.00 | \$20,088 | \$954,912 |

217. **The best answer is "D."** An "S termination year" arises only if the first year following the loss of S status begins on other than the first day of the taxable year. § 1362(e)(1); § 1.1362-3(a).

**Answer "A" is a correct statement and, therefore, not the right answer.** Voluntary termination with the consent of the majority of shares (i.e., revocation) is provided for under § 1362(d)(1). Ceasing to be a small business corporation involuntarily terminates the S election. § 1362(d)(2)(A). The involuntary termination associated with excess passive income results from § 1362(d)(3)(A)(i).

**Answer "B" is a correct statement and, therefore, not the right answer.** If an S election has been terminated, a corporation "shall not be eligible to make [another S] election . . . for any taxable year before its 5th taxable year which begins after the 1st taxable year for which such termination is effective." § 1362(g). On these facts, the "5th taxable year" is Year 17. (Year 12 is the "first taxable year for which such termination is effective.")

**Answer "C" is a correct statement and, therefore, not the right answer.** Section 1362(f) empowers the IRS to waive such involuntary terminations. Expedited relief may be available (possibly through a process as simple as filing a late election form flagged as a request for relief). Rev. Proc. 2003-43, 2003-1 C.B. 998. Where that revenue procedure does not apply, relief may be obtained through the private letter ruling process. § 1.1362-4(c). To be eligible for a waiver the following conditions must be satisfied:

1) Within a reasonable time after discovering the circumstances resulting in the termination, steps were taken to cure the problem;

2) The IRS determines that the circumstances resulting in the termination were inadvertent; and

3) The corporation and all of its shareholders agree to whatever adjustments the IRS may require to ensure that the tax consequences reported by the corporation and the shareholders since the terminating event are consistent with S status.

218. By having a second class of stock with different distribution rights Galactica ceased being a "small business corporation." § 1361(a)(1), (b)(1)(D). The loss of that status causes the loss of S status. Galactica became a C corporation on August 3, Year 6. § 1361(a)(1), 1362(d)(2).

219. Because the first year as a C corporation did not begin on the first day of Galactica's taxable

year, Galactica has an "S termination year." § 1362(e)(4). This results in an S short taxable year (January 1–August 2, Year 6) and a C short taxable year (August 3–December 31, Year 6). § 1362(e)(1). Because Galactica does not make any accounting elections, all of its tax items (here only ordinary income) are allocated between the short years on a daily basis. § 1362(e)(2). Since there are 215 days in the S short year and 151 days in the C short year, the ordinary income is allocated $645,000 to the S short year ($1,098,000 x 215/366) and $453,000 to the C short year ($1,098,000 x 151/366).

220. The taxable income for the C short year must be annualized. § 1362(e)(5)(A). The annualized taxable income is $1,098,000 ($453,000 x 366/151). The tax liability on that taxable income is $373,320. § 11(b). The short year tax liability is $154,020 ($373,320 x 151/366).

221. Since Galactica will not request an extension, the tax returns for both the S short year and the C short year are due on the same day the C short year return is due, March 15, Year 7. §§ 1362(e)(6)(B), 6072(b).

222. The post-termination transition period (PTTP) begins on August 13, Year 6 (the first day of the C short year) and ends on the later of August 13, Year 7 (one year later) or March 15, Year 7 (the due date of the S short year return, including extensions (of which there are none here)). Thus, the PTTP ends on August 13, Year 7.

223. Cori's suspended deductions are deemed incurred on August 13, 20X7 (the last day of the PTTP). § 1366(d)(3)(A). To the extent she has stock basis on that date, those suspended deductions are released. Cori's $500,000 contribution to capital on August 11, Year 7 provides $500,000 of basis. Therefore, all $300,000 of the suspended ordinary deductions will be released to Cori's tax return for Year 7. The basis of her stock is reduced by $300,000 to $200,000. § 1366(d)(3)(C).

224. Cash distributions during the PTTP are treated as other than dividends (which is relevant only where earnings and profits (E&P) exist) to the extent of the accumulated adjustments account (AAA). § 1371(e)(1). This treatment is available only to those who were shareholders on the last day of the S short year. § 1.1377-2(b). Thus, this treatment is not available to Starbuck.

The distribution to Cori is $300,000. Galactica has a balance in its AAA of $150,000. Cori's basis account is $200,000. Therefore, the first $150,000 of the $300,000 distribution to Cori reduces the AAA to zero (§ 1368(e)(1)(A); § 1.1368-2(a)(5)(iii)) and reduces Cori's stock basis to $50,000 ($200,000 - $150,000) (§§ 1367(a)(2)(A), 1368(c)). Now the regular Subchapter C rules apply. The remaining amount of the distribution is $450,000 ($600,000 total distribution - $150,000 deemed sourced from the AAA). Since the E&P ($700,000) exceeds this amount, both the $150,000 remaining distribution to Cori and the entire $300,000 distribution to Starbuck are deemed sourced from E&P and are therefore dividends. §§ 316(a), 301(c)(1). Galactica's E&P is reduced to $250,000 ($700,000 - $450,000). § 312(a)(1).

225. **The best answer is "C."** If association status is elected, the LLC is taxed like a C corporation. C corporations are not able to allocate their tax items among their equity holders.

**Answer "A" is a correct statement and, therefore, not the right answer.** Section 301.7701-3(b)(1)(i) expressly so states. This is the default rule for LLCs with two or more members. The default rule for one-member LLCs is that it is a disregarded entity. If the member is an individual, the tax treatment is determined like a sole proprietorship. If the member is a corporation, the LLC is treated as a department within the corporation.

**Answer "B" is a correct statement and, therefore, not the right answer.** The members of an LLC have no personal liability for the LLC's obligations and, therefore, have no economic risk of loss. Each member's liability is limited to the loss of its investment.

**Answer "D" is a correct statement and, therefore, not the right answer.** Once "association" status has been elected, the business entity can also elect to be taxed as an S corporation. Rev. Rul. 2009-15, 2009-21 I.R.B. 1035.

226. **The best answer is "A."** Partnerships and S corporations are not subject to the alternative minimum tax. §§ 701, 1363(a).

**Answer "B" is incorrect.** Only individuals and certain closely held C corporations are subject to the at-risk rules. § 465(a)(1).

**Answer "C" is incorrect.** The death of a shareholder has no impact on the taxable year of a C corporation. The disposition of a partnership interest as a result of death does not terminate the partnership's taxable year under § 708(b)(1)(B). § 1.708-1(b)(2). An S corporation's taxable year could terminate if the new shareholder is ineligible under § 1361(b)(1). § 1362(e)(1).

**Answer "D" is incorrect.** This is true only for partnerships and S corporations. §§ 752(a), 1367(b)(2)(A). Since C corporations are separate taxable entities, they are unable to pass losses through to their shareholders. § 172(a). Shareholder loans to C corporations do not change this feature.

227. **The best answer is "B."** Section 731(b) expressly so states.

**Answer "A" is incorrect.** All capital contributions to partnerships are tax-free per § 721(a).

**Answer "C" is incorrect.** Partners include their share of any partnership debt in their outside basis, which increases the opportunity to take deductions. §§ 722, 752(a). Guarantees by partners can sometimes increase the amount of such liabilities includable in their basis by making them recourse. § 1.752-2. S corporation shareholders are entitled to use their bases in loans made by them to the corporation to allow losses, but guarantees are not treated as the equivalent of a loan until the guarantor is called upon to perform. *See, e.g., Maloof v.*

*Comm'r*, 456 F.3d 645 (6th Cir. 2006). Liabilities of S corporations other than shareholder loans do not increase the ability of shareholders to take entity-level losses.

**Answer "D" is incorrect.** An LLC with only one member will be characterized as a disregarded entity and taxed like a sole proprietorship (or corporate department). § 301.7701-3(b)(1)(ii).

228.  **The best answer is "A."** All entities must compute their taxable income. §§ 6012(a)(2), 6031(a). All entities must generally file a tax return. § 11(a), 702(a), 1363(b).

**Answer "B" is incorrect.** Only C corporations are subject to double taxation. The tax items of S corporations and partnerships pass through to their shareholders and partners. §§ 11(a), 701, 702, 1366.

**Answer "C" is incorrect.** Deductions for organizational expenses are available to all of these entities. §§ 248, 709.

**Answer "D" is incorrect.** An employer-employee relationship is required for a service provider to get the benefits of § 119. Section 1372(a) states that, "[f]or the purpose of applying the provisions of this subtitle which relate to employee fringe benefits — (1) the S corporation shall be treated as a partnership, and (2) any 2-percent shareholder of the S corporation shall be treated as a partner." Partners are not classified as employees with respect to their partnership. Therefore, no partner and no shareholder with more than 2% of an S corporation's stock can benefit from § 119. Shareholder-employees of C corporations are eligible for gross income exclusion under § 119.

229.  **The best answer is "A."** Both C and S corporations are subject to § 267(a)(1). Partnerships (and the described LLCs) are subject to § 707(b)(1), which is very similar to § 267(a)(1).

**Answer "B" is incorrect.** Only partnerships are subject to this risk because of the possible existence of unrealized receivables and inventory items. § 751(b).

**Answer "C" is incorrect.** Only partnerships with § 754 elections in effect may adjust the bases of their non-cash property as a result of distributions made to partners. § 734.

**Answer "D" is incorrect.** To be an S corporation, the corporation must qualify as a "small business corporation." S status precludes nonresident alien shareholders and significantly limits the kinds of trusts that may hold S corporation stock. § 1361. No other entity faces these restrictions.

230.  **The best answer is "B."** Because C corporations are taxable entities, C corporation losses are trapped at the entity level. § 172. To the extent of available basis, entity-level losses pass through to partners and S corporation shareholders. §§ 702(a), 704(d), 1366(a), 1367.

**Answer "A" is incorrect.** Only C corporations are allowed charitable deductions. §§ 170, 703(a)(2)(C), 1363(b)(2).

**Answer "C" is incorrect.** Only S corporations that have earnings and profits from their prior existence as a C corporation have an accumulated adjustments account. § 1368(e).

**Answer "D" is incorrect.** Entities subject to Subchapter K must allocate pre-contribution gain to the contributing partner under § 704(c)(1). While the amount of gain potential can change over time (e.g., through depreciation adjustments that bring book value and tax basis into alignment), until that gain potential is gone the tax consequences associated with it will be allocated to the contributing partner.

231. **The best answer is "D."** This is true for partnerships and S corporations. §§ 705(a), 1367(a). The bases of C corporation shareholders never change simply because the corporation recognizes items of gross income, deduction, etc.

**Answer "A" is a correct statement and, therefore, not the right answer.** An entity taxed like a C corporation determines the character of its income, deductions, etc., at the entity level. When its income is distributed to its equity holders, the character is determined under § 301(c): dividend, recovery of capital, or gain from constructive sale or exchange. In passthrough entities like partnerships and S corporations, the character of the income, deductions, etc., passing through to the equity holder is preserved as though realized directly from the source. §§ 702(b), 1366(b).

**Answer "B" is a correct statement and, therefore, not the right answer.** Allocations in the partnership agreement will be respected unless they do not have substantial economic effect. § 704(b)(2).

**Answer "C" is a correct statement and, therefore, not the right answer.** Unlike § 708(b)(1)(B) with respect to partnerships, the taxable year of a corporation never closes simply because a large portion of its stock changes hands.

232. **The best answer is "A."** Section 83(a) expressly so states.

**Answer "B" is incorrect.** Rev. Proc. 93-27, 1993-2 C.B. 343, expressly states to the contrary and Rev. Proc. 2001-43, 2001-2 C.B. 191, makes clear that § 83 does not change this result. However, the receipt of a capital interest is a taxable event and is subject to § 83. § 1.721-1(b)(1).

**Answer "C" is incorrect.** The fact that a partnership becomes taxed like a corporation (whether governed by Subchapter C or Subchapter S) has no impact on state law. Therefore, the partnership still has unlimited liability to the extent specified in the laws of its state of domicile.

**Answer "D" is incorrect.** Due to the fact that C corporations are subject to double taxation, placing appreciating assets in them exposes that appreciation to two rounds of taxation. Partnerships and S corporations, which are not subject to the double-taxation regime, tax the appreciation on the property only once. In this context partnerships (or LLCs taxed like partnerships) have the advantage because the distribution of appreciated property to the partners is not a taxable event, whereas the distribution of such property by an S corporation to its shareholders is a taxable event (although taxation is triggered only at the shareholder level).

233. **The best answer is "D."** C corporations have the most discretion in the selection of the taxable year. With rare exception, a C corporation can select any taxable year provided for by the Code. Partnerships and S corporations are subject to strict taxable year rules. §§ 706(b), 1378. A small amount of flexibility is provided under the "business purpose" and § 444 alternatives, but nothing compares to the flexibility of a C corporation in this regard.

**Answer "A" is a correct statement and, therefore, not the right answer.** C corporations will have an earnings and profits account. S corporations that had a prior existence as a C corporation (or that were involved in a reorganization that included a C corporation) could have an earnings and profits account. Partnerships and LLCs that elect association status could also have an earnings and profits account.

**Answer "B" is a correct statement and, therefore, not the right answer.** An LLC taxed like a partnership has a great deal more flexibility in allocating entity tax items to its members as compared to an S corporation. The lack of limitations on the number and types of shareholders and on the number of classes of equity interests makes using an LLC much less confining than an S corporation. The lack of limited liability with respect to partnerships very often makes using that form of business entity foolhardy. The only advantage of C corporations in this context is their comparative immunity from factors that impact their shareholders personally.

**Answer "C" is a correct statement and, therefore, not the right answer.** The exceptional flexibility in crafting economic arrangements that is the hallmark of the partnership term means that there are an extraordinary number of contingencies to plan for, tax consequences to anticipate and allocate, etc. The tax aspects of partnerships are vastly more complex than those of the other common forms of business entity.

# PRACTICE FINAL EXAM: ANSWERS

1. **The best answer is "A."** Fayette has a net long-term capital loss of $700,000 - $1,100,000 = ($400,000). It has a net short-term capital gain of $900,000 - $800,000 = $100,000. Therefore Fayette has a net capital loss of $100,000 - $400,000 = ($300,000). § 1222(5), (8), (10). Section 1211(a) allows a deduction for capital losses only to the extent of capital gains. The excess loss carries back three and then forward five years as a short-term capital loss. § 1212(a)(1). Under § 1231 the $50,000 loss is treated as ordinary and is therefore deductible. Thus, Fayette's taxable income is $1,950,000 ($2,000,000 - $50,000).

   **Answer "B" is incorrect** because it takes a deduction for the $300,000 net capital loss.

   **Answer "C" is incorrect** because it takes a deduction for the $300,000 net capital loss and ignores the $50,000 § 1231 ordinary loss.

   **Answer "D" is incorrect** because it ignores the $50,000 § 1231 ordinary loss.

2. **The best answer is "C."** Although stock received for services does not enjoy nonrecognition under § 351, per § 351(d)(1) such stock does count for purposes of measuring control if the service-providing shareholder also receives stock in exchange for property. § 1.351-1(a)(2) Ex. 3. This rule applies only if the stock received for the property is not "of relatively small value" as compared to the stock received for services. § 1.351-1(a)(1)(ii). As a rule of thumb, the former must be at least 10 percent of the latter. Rev. Proc. 77-37, 1977-2 C.B. 568, § 3.07.Therefore, for purposes of measuring control, the shareholder is deemed to have received 105 shares. The tax consequences for the stock acquired in exchange for services will be governed by § 83.

   **Answer "A" is incorrect.** Section 351 is a deferral nonrecognition transaction. It does not provide for permanent nonrecognition. When the stock received is later disposed of in a taxable transaction, any deferred gain or loss will be recognized.

   **Answer "B" is incorrect.** To have control under § 368(c), as required by § 351(a), the transferring shareholder (or shareholders if there is a control group) must own stock representing at least 80% of the voting power and must also own at least 80% of the number of nonvoting shares. If there are multiple classes of nonvoting shares, the shareholder (or control group) must own 80% of each class. Rev. Rul. 59-259, 1959-2 C.B. 115.

   **Answer "D" is incorrect.** The test for whether a liability has been assumed by the corporation in a § 351 transaction is different for recourse and nonrecourse liabilities. With respect recourse liabilities, the corporate assumption will be respected only if the corporation is expected to satisfy the liability. Thus, the assumption of a shareholder's liability by an insolvent corporation would likely not be treated as an assumption for § 351 purposes. § 357(d)(1)(A).

   With respect to nonrecourse liabilities, the general rule is that a corporation taking an asset subject to such a liability is deemed to have assumed the entire liability (even if the value of the asset is less than the amount of the liability). § 357(d)(1)(B). If the nonrecourse liability also encumbers other assets which are not transferred to the corporation, the amount of the liabilities deemed assumed by the corporation is reduced by the lesser of: 1) the value of such other assets, or 2) the amount the owner of such other assets has agreed and is expected to satisfy. § 357(d)(2).

Assume a shareholder transfers Asset 1 (worth $100,000) to Corporation B and transfers Asset 2 (worth $300,000) to Corporation C. The shareholder had previously obtained, for bona fide business purposes, a $500,000 nonrecourse loan secured by both of these assets, which had been worth considerably more than $500,000 when the loan was originated.

Under the default rule both corporations will be deemed to have assumed the entire $500,000 nonrecourse liability (i.e., the same liability is deemed assumed twice). If Corporation B agrees to pay $200,000 of the liability (and is expected to do so), the amount deemed assumed by Corporation C would be: $500,000 (gross liability) − *lesser of* [$100,000 (value of asset transferred to Corporation B) or $200,000 (amount Corporation B agrees to and is expected to pay)] = $500,000 - $100,000 = $400,000. If at the same time Corporation C has not agreed to pay any of the liability, Corporation B will still be deemed to have assumed the entire $500,000 liability.

3.    **The best answer is "A."** The parent takes a carryover basis in all of the assets received from the subsidiary under § 334(b)(1). The parent's basis in its subsidiary stock disappears in a § 332 liquidation. *See, e.g.,* Priv. Ltr. Rul. 2007-01-019.

**Answer "B" is incorrect.** Section 337(a) only applies if the distribution qualifies under § 332. A series of liquidating distributions cannot qualify under § 332 unless the last distribution in the series occurs not later than the end of the third taxable year following the year during which the first distribution in the series was made. § 332(b)(3). If the last distribution in the series occurs after this date, all of the distributions within the series are fully taxable under § 336(a). § 1.332-4(b).

**Answer "C" is incorrect.** The payment by Lori on behalf of Wagoner must be characterized under the doctrine of *Arrowsmith v. Comm'r*, 344 U.S. 6 (1952). Had Wagoner paid the $900,000 in damages prior to its liquidating distribution, Lori's long-term capital gain would have only been $100,000 ($1,000,000 - $900,000). Therefore, Lori must treat the payment as a long-term capital loss, resulting in an overall capital gain of $100,000 ($1,000,000 originally reported long-term capital gain - $900,000 partial reversal of that gain resulting from payment of claim against Wagoner for damages). She reports the $900,000 long-term capital loss in the year paid; she does not file an amended return for the stock disposition year.

**Answer "D" is incorrect.** Rupert is entitled to use the cost recovery method with respect to the distributions. Rev. Rul. 85-48, 1985-1 C.B. 126. Under the cost recovery method Rupert would treat the first $50,000 received as a recovery of stock basis. Thus, at the end of Year 1, Rupert's basis in his Earnest stock would be $10,000 ($60,000 original basis - $50,000 distribution during Year 1). Thus, he will report no gain as a result of the liquidating distribution in Year 1.

4.    **The best answer is "B."** Section 1.704-1(b)(2)(iii)(a) provides that "the economic effect of an allocation . . . is not substantial if, at the time the allocation becomes part of the partnership agreement, (1) the after-tax economic consequences of at least one partner may, in present value terms, be enhanced compared to such consequences if the allocation . . . were not

contained in the partnership agreement, and (2) there is a strong likelihood that the after-tax economic consequences of no partner will, in present value terms, be substantially diminished compared to such consequences if the allocation . . . were not contained in the partnership agreement."

**Answer "A" is a correct statement and, therefore, not the right answer.** Section 1.704-1(b)(2)(ii)(b)(2), (3) so requires.

**Answer "C" is a correct statement and, therefore, not the right answer.** This is a "shifting" allocation under § 1.704-1(b)(2)(iii)(b). Its economic effect is not substantial. § 1.704-1(b)(5) Ex. 6.

**Answer "D" is a correct statement and, therefore, not the right answer.** This is a "transitory" allocation under § 1.704-1(b)(2)(iii)(c). Its economic effect is not substantial. § 1.704-1(b)(5) Ex. 7.

5. There are three formulations of the step-transaction doctrine: the interdependence test, the end-result test and the binding-commitment test. *Andantech, L.L.C. v. Comm'r*, 83 T.C.M. (CCH) 1476 (2002). Here, the IRS' argument will be upheld under both the interdependence test and the-end result test. The interdependence test applies when, based on the objective facts, the steps taken were so interdependent that none would have been undertaken except in contemplation of undertaking the others. Courts often look to how independent parties would have shaped the transaction. Here it appears objectively unlikely that the creation of the Patrick Corp. followed by the quick Patrick stock sale to Heavy Construction would have been undertaken by independent parties. The incorporation, stock sale and liquidation steps were interdependent.

The end-result test applies when it appears that the various steps undertaken were parts of a single transaction intended from the outset to achieve the specific end result actually accomplished. The taxpayer's subjective intent is important and may be inferred from the facts and circumstances. The manner in which these events unfolded appears to provide clear evidence of Robert's intent from the very beginning to achieve the result of converting ordinary income into long-term capital gain.

The binding-commitment test is inapplicable here because all of the events took place within three days this test only applies when a significant period of time (generally more than one year) elapses between steps.

6. **The best answer is "D."** The amount of gain to be recognized is not determined by comparing the boot received with the net gain determined by subtracting the total basis of all assets transferred from the total value of such assets. Instead, the amount of realized gain or loss on each contributed asset is separately determined. Then the boot is allocated to each contributed asset in proportion to its value. No loss is recognized on any asset. The realized gains on the assets are individually recognized, but not in excess of the amount of the boot allocated to each such asset. § 351(b); Rev. Rul. 68-55, 1968-1 C.B. 140.

**Answer "A" is a correct statement and, therefore, not the right answer.** Transfers within the control group do not affect § 351 eligibility since, regardless of which member of the control group ultimately holds the stock, the stock ownership of the control group as a whole is unchanged. Rev. Rul. 79-194, 1979-1 C.B. 145.

**Answer "B" is a correct statement and, therefore, not the right answer.** A corporation never recognizes gain or loss when it issues its stock in exchange for property. § 1032(a).

**Answer "C" is a correct statement and, therefore, not the right answer.** Section 1001(a) provides the general rule that the disposition of property (which includes an exchange) triggers the measurement of realized gain or loss. Section 1001(c) states that, as a general rule, any realized gain or loss is recognized. However, that provision begins with the phrase: "Except as otherwise provided." Section 351 provides an exception to the general rule of § 1001(c). § 1.1002-1(c). Where § 351 fails to apply to a capitalization transaction, all shareholders transferring property are subject to the general rule and must recognize any realized gains or losses.

7.      If Goliad owns 8% of Lipscomb, Goliad is entitled to a 70% dividends-received deduction under § 243(a)(1). Therefore its taxable income increases as a result of the dividend by $30,000 ($100,000 − (70% x $100,000)).

Where a corporation owns at least 20% of the stock (by vote and value) of the distributing corporation, but less than 80%, an 80% deduction is substituted for the 70% deduction illustrated above. § 243(c). Therefore, if Goliad owns 25% of Lipscomb, its taxable income increases as a result of the dividend by $20,000 ($100,000 − (80% x $100,000)).

Under § 243(b)(1), a "qualifying dividend" exists if the distributing and receiving corporations are part of the same affiliated group. An affiliated group exists for these purposes if one of the corporations owns at least 80% (by vote and value) of the other corporation. §§ 243(b)(2)(A), 1504(a)(1)-(2). In the case of qualifying dividends, a 100% dividends-received deduction is allowed. § 243(a)(3). Therefore, if Goliad owns 98% of Lipscomb, its taxable income does not increase as a result of the dividend.

8.      **The best answer is "A."** Both dividends and sales or exchanges are subject to the same tax rates for corporate taxpayers. However, a redemption qualifying for sale or exchange treatment has the advantage of offsetting the stock basis against the amount distributed. It also has the advantage that it can be offset by current and carried-over capital losses. However, dividends have the advantage of being subject to a 70%, 80% or 100% dividends-received deduction under § 243. In general, corporations prefer dividend to sale or exchange characterization because of the dividends-received deduction.

**Answer "B" is a correct statement and, therefore, not the right answer.** The primary and original test for whether a redemption is accorded sale or exchange treatment is found in § 302(b)(1): sale or exchange treatment results if "the redemption is not essentially equivalent to a dividend." The Supreme Court in *U.S. v. Davis*, 397 U.S. 301 (1970), held that this requires a meaningful reduction in the redeeming shareholder's interest in the corporation. Because these standards are ambiguous, two safe harbors were enacted. First, under § 302(b)(2) a redemption satisfies the "not essentially equivalent to a dividend" test if: 1) after the redemption the redeeming shareholder does not have control, 2) the redeeming shareholder's voting power has contracted by more than 20%, and 3) the value of the redeeming shareholder's overall common stock ownership (whether voting or non-voting) has contracted by more than 20%. The more than 20% contraction, accompanied by the lack of control, is deemed to evidence a meaningful reduction in the redeeming shareholder's interest in the corporation. Second, under § 302(b)(3) if a shareholder completely terminates its interest in the corporation, that is also deemed to evidence a meaningful reduction in the redeeming shareholder's interest in the corporation.

**Answer "C" is a correct statement and, therefore, not the right answer.** *Johnston*, 77 TC 679 (1981); Rev. Rul. 75-502, 1975-2 C.B. 111.

**Answer "D" is a correct statement and, therefore, not the right answer.** Section 302(b)(2)(D) requires the substantially disproportionate redemption tests to be performed after all of a planned series of redemptions are completed.

For example, assume unrelated individuals X, Y and Z own the following respective number of a corporation's 100 outstanding shares of common stock (only class): 60, 30 and 10. If X redeems half of her stock the transaction constitutes a substantially disproportionate redemption as follows:

$$\text{Voting power after redemption} = (60 - 30)/(100 - 30) = 30/70 < 50\%$$
$$\text{(no longer has control)}$$

$$\text{Voting power after redemption/Voting power before redemption} = (30/70)/(60/100) = .71, \text{ which is less than}$$
$$80\% \text{ (contraction in voting power exceeds 20\%)}$$

However, if this transaction is part of a series in which Y also redeems 2/3 of his stock (i.e., 20 shares), the tests with respect to X fail as follows:

$$\text{Voting power after redemption} = (60 - 30)/(100 - 30 - 20) = 30/50 > 50\% \text{ (still has control)}$$

$$\text{Voting power after redemption/Voting power before redemption} = (30/50)/(60/100) = 1, \text{ which is greater}$$
$$\text{than } 80\% \text{ (demonstrating that, in fact, no contraction of voting power has occurred)}$$

9A.    P recognizes no gain or loss. § 721(a). It takes a carryover basis in the Raw Land and the Equipment under § 723, with tacked holding periods under § 1223(2). P will succeed to the method of depreciation used by D with respect to the Equipment. § 168(i)(7)(A), (B).

9B.    C recognizes no gain or loss. § 721(a). C's basis in his partnership interest is the same as his basis in the Raw Land, $50,000. § 722. His holding period in the interest includes the 24-year holding period in the Raw Land. § 1223(1).

9C.    For book purposes (that is, under the accounting rules required to maintain the partners' capital accounts under the § 704(b) regulations), there should be $400,000 of depreciation with respect to the Equipment in its final year. However, the Equipment only has a basis of $30,000. Because there is not sufficient basis to provide the correct amount of book depreciation to all the partners, and because D contributed the Equipment, D will receive none of the tax depreciation under the "ceiling rule." § 1.704-3(b)(1), (b)(2) Ex. 1(ii). Although B should get $50,000 of tax depreciation (12.5% x $400,000) and C should get $250,000 (62.5% x $400,000), there is only $30,000 of tax depreciation available. The depreciation is allocated only to B and C as follows:

| Partner | Partnership Interest | Relative Percentage | Depreciation Allocation |
|---------|---------------------|---------------------|-------------------------|
| B | 12.5% | 16.67% | $5,000 |
| C | 62.5% | 83.33% | 25,000 |
|   | 75.0% | 100.00% | $30,000 |

9D.    For book purposes the Equipment now has a carrying value of zero ($400,000 original entry

- $400,000 of book depreciation). The Equipment has a tax basis of zero ($30,000 original basis to P - $30,000 of tax depreciation taken by P). Thus, there is no longer any book-tax difference upon which to base an allocation to D under § 704(c). Therefore, under § 704(a), the gain of $300,000 ($300,000 amount realized - $0 basis) is allocated in accordance with the partnership interests as follows:

| Partner | Partnership Interest | Gain Allocation |
|---|---|---|
| B | 12.5% | $37,500 |
| C | 62.5% | 187,500 |
| D | 25.0% | 75,000 |
| | 100.0% | $300,000 |

10. **The best answer is "D."** Section 306(a) overrides § 302(a).

**Answer "A" is incorrect.** Section 306(a) is inapplicable in the context of a complete liquidation. § 306(b)(2).

**Answer "B" is incorrect.** Section 306(a) is inapplicable in the context of a partial liquidation qualifying under § 302(b)(4). § 306(b)(1)(B).

**Answer "C" is incorrect.** Stock is not § 306 stock if at the time it was distributed the distributing corporation had no earnings and profits. § 306(c)(2).

11. For tax purposes, all distributions are deemed sourced from earnings and profits to the extent thereof. § 316(a). Here there is sufficient earnings and profits ($2,800,000) to cover the entire distribution ($2,000,000). The board's decision to source the dividends from additional paid-in capital (i.e., to return invested capital for financial accounting purposes) is irrelevant since, under the Supremacy Clause, state law does not govern in the federal tax area. The Supreme Court said in *Burnet v. Harmel*, 287 U.S. 103 (1932) that "[s]tate law may control only when the federal taxing act, by express language or necessary implication, makes its own operation dependent upon state law." Therefore, all of the distribution to Angus will be characterized as a dividend and his stock basis will be reset to $1,300,000.

12. Despite the fact that Barbara is the 100% shareholder of Essex, these are not expenses incurred in *her* business; they are Essex' business expenses. The corporation is a separate legal entity and a separate taxpayer. *Moline Properties, Inc. v. Comm'r*, 319 U.S. 436 (1943). Section 162(a) allows a business expense deduction only to the taxpayer in whose business the cost was incurred. Therefore, Barbara cannot take a business deduction on her personal tax return for these expenses.

The tax law will recharacterize these events into a constructive capital contribution by Barbara to Essex of $13,000, followed by Essex's constructive payment of the business expenses. Essex will receive a deduction under § 162(a). Barbara will increase the basis of her Essex stock by $13,000 to reflect the capital contribution. *Deputy v. Du Pont*, 308 U.S. 488 (1940).

13A. Under § 1.752-2 nonrecourse liabilities are allocated in three tiers, as follows:

Tier I: The total Tier I allocation is the excess, at the time of computation (here January 1), of the balance of the nonrecourse liability encumbering the asset over the book value of the encumbered asset, a quantity known as the "partnership minimum gain." The excess here is: $600,000 - $1,000,000 = $0. Therefore there is no Tier I allocation. The amount of the nonrecourse liability yet to be allocated is $600,000.

Tier II: The Tier II allocation (an allocation involving only the contributing partner) is the lesser of: 1) the amount of the nonrecourse liability yet to be allocated and 2) the amount of gain that would be recognized by the contributing partner under § 704(c) if the encumbered asset were sold for an amount equal to the outstanding balance of the nonrecourse liability encumbering it.

R's § 704(c) gain potential on January 1 is: $1,000,000 (book value of machine on this date) - $50,000 (basis of machine on this date) = $950,000. Since this amount exceeds the unallocated nonrecourse liability ($600,000), the entire $600,000 unallocated nonrecourse liability is allocated to R.

Tier III: Since the entire $600,000 nonrecourse liability has been allocated, there is no Tier III allocation.

13B. A partner's basis in its partnership interest acquired by the contribution of property begins with the basis of the property contributed. § 722. That basis is adjusted under § 705(a) (in conjunction with the ordering rules of § 1.704-1(d)) as follows:

> Upward for the partner's additional contributions to capital and distributive share of the partnership's income (including exempt income), then
>
> Downward for distributions under § 733 (amount of cash and basis of non-cash property received), then
>
> Downward for the partner's distributive share of: 1) partnership deductions, and 2) partnership nondeductible and non-capitalizable items (such as fines and 50% of meals)

Q's partnership interest basis begins with his $100,000 contribution. § 722. Q's basis is then adjusted for his share of the nonrecourse liabilities (a constructive cash contribution under § 752(a)), which is zero as of January 1. Therefore, Q's basis on this date is $100,000.

R's basis begins with her $50,000 basis in the machine. From this basis is subtracted the amount of liabilities from which R is relieved (a constructive cash distribution under § 752(b)). The partnership is deemed to assume the nonrecourse liability encumbering the machine, so R's basis is reduced by $600,000. In addition, her basis is adjusted upward by the amount of the nonrecourse liability just allocated to her (a constructive cash contribution), also $600,000. Note that the basis reduction for liability relief and the basis increment for allocated liabilities are deemed to occur simultaneously since they both derive from the same transaction, with only the net amount (here, zero) taken into account. § 1.752-1(f). Therefore, R's basis on January 1 is $50,000.

13C. During the year, the book value of the machine was reduced by $500,000 (50% x $1,000,000) of depreciation to $500,000 ($1,000,000 - $500,000). The machine's basis was reduced by $25,000 (50% x $50,000) to $25,000 ($50,000 - $25,000).

Tier I: In essence, the partnership minimum gain tracks the amount of deductions taken by the partners attributable to basis sourced from nonrecourse liabilities. Here, the partnership minimum gain is: $600,000 (balance of encumbrance on December 31) - $500,000 (book value on December 31) = $100,000. The partnership minimum gain is allocated between the partners in proportion to the manner in which the deductions (here depreciation) causing the partnership minimum gain to arise are allocated. This ratio is

20:80, so Q is allocated $20,000 (20% x $100,000) of the partnership minimum gain; R is allocated $80,000. The amount of the nonrecourse liability yet to be allocated is $500,000 ($600,000 - $100,000).

Tier II: R's § 704(c) gain potential on December 31 is: $500,000 (book value of machine on this date) - $25,000 (basis of machine on this date) = $475,000, which is less than the $500,000 of unallocated liability. Therefore, R is allocated $475,000. The amount of the nonrecourse liability yet to be allocated is $25,000 ($500,000 - $475,000).

Tier III: If R's § 704(c) gain potential had not been fully addressed in Tier II, the remaining $25,000 of unallocated liability would first be allocated to R to the extent of her remaining § 704(c) gain potential. Since that is not the case, the remaining $25,000 is allocated using the partners' profit-sharing ratio (20:80). Therefore, Q will be allocated $5,000 (20% x $25,000) of the liability; R will be allocated $20,000.

In summary, the partners are allocated the following amounts of the $600,000 nonrecourse liability:

| Tier | Q | R |
|------|------|------|
| I | $20,000 | $80,000 |
| II | 0 | 475,000 |
| III | 5,000 | 20,000 |
| | $25,000 | $575,000 |

13D.  Q's basis on January 1, without taking into account his allocation of the nonrecourse liability, was $100,000. To this is added his share of the $300,000 pre-depreciation expense taxable income, $60,000 (20% x $300,000). Book depreciation was $500,000. This is allocated $100,000 (20% x $500,000) to Q's capital account and $400,000 (80% x $500,000) to R's capital account. This is the amount of depreciation each partner should get to correctly reflect their underlying 20:80 economic arrangement. Unfortunately, there is only $25,000 of tax depreciation. Neither partner can be allocated an amount of tax depreciation equal to their book depreciation allocations. Under the "ceiling rule", and using the traditional method, the available tax depreciation is first allocated to the non-contributing partner to the extent possible to achieve that partner's book allocation of depreciation. If any depreciation remains, it is allocated to the contributing partner. This "penalty" on the contributing partner is part of the logic of § 704(c). In summary, Q is allocated $25,000 of tax depreciation (since there was not enough to give him his $100,000 book allocation). R is allocated no tax depreciation.

Q's basis on December 31, prior to the adjustment for his allocation of the nonrecourse liability, is $135,000 ($100,000 + $60,000 - $25,000). Including his share of the nonrecourse liability, his basis is $160,000 ($135,000 + $25,000).

R's basis on January 1, without taking into account her allocation of the nonrecourse liability, was $50,000. To this is added her share of the $300,000 pre-depreciation expense taxable income, $240,000 (80% x $300,000). As noted above, R is allocated no tax depreciation. Inclusive of the allocation to R of her share of the nonrecourse liability, R's basis in her partnership interest on December 31 is $265,000, determined as follows:

| Basis on Jan. 1, without liability allocation | $50,000 |
|---|---|
| Allocation of pre-depreciation taxable income | 240,000 |
| Allocation of tax depreciation | (0) |
| Relief from nonrecourse liability | (600,000) |
| Allocation of nonrecourse liability | 575,000 |
| | $265,000 |

13E. The capital account balances for the partners on December 31 are determined as follows:

| | Q | R |
|---|---|---|
| Contribution of cash | $100,000 | |
| Contribution of machine (net of liability) | | $400,000 |
| Allocation of pre-depreciation book income (same as taxable income) | 60,000 | 240,000 |
| Allocation of book depreciation | (100,000) | (400,000) |
| | $60,000 | $240,000 |

14. Giving each of the two transactions (redemption followed by sale) separate effect, the redemption of Georgia's stock would not be eligible for "sale or exchange" treatment under § 302(a) because the redemption would fail to meet any of the four tests of § 302(b). There was no partial liquidation under § 302(b)(4) since there was no contraction of the corporation's business as a result of the distribution (all of the distributed assets were unrelated to Ashland's business). *Blaschka v. U.S.*, 393 F.2d 983 (Ct. Cl. 1968). There was no complete termination of interest under § 302(b)(3) because, after the redemption, Hillary still owned 100% of the outstanding stock. For the same reason, there was no substantially disproportionate redemption under § 302(b)(2). Nor did the redemption satisfy the "not essentially equivalent to a dividend" test of § 302(b)(1), which requires no control after the redemption. *Johnston*, 77 T.C. 679 (1981); Rev. Rul. 75-502, 1975-2 C.B. 111. Therefore, the distribution would be treated as a dividend to the extent of Ashland's earnings and profits, which are substantial. §§ 302(d), 301(a), 316(a).

However, in *Zenz v. Quinlivan*, 213 F.2d 914 (6th Cir. 1954), it was held that a redemption followed by a sale, the combined effect of which was the complete termination of the redeeming shareholder's interest in the corporation, would be respected as a § 302(b)(3) transaction. The IRS acquiesced in Rev. Rul. 55-745, 1955-2 C.B. 223. Therefore, Georgia will receive "sale or exchange" treatment with respect to the redeemed stock.

15. **The best answer is "B."** The acquisition of stock with cash consideration is a purchase, not an exchange. § 1.1002-1(d). No gain or loss is recognized on a purchase since the basis in the cash remitted equals its value. The acquiror takes a cost basis in the stock. § 1012(a). Thus § 351, which defers realized gain or loss on the exchange of property for stock, is inapplicable.

Nonetheless, if the acquiror is a member of the control group, the stock acquired for cash is included in determining whether the group has control. *George M. Holstein III*, 23 T.C. 923 (1955), interpreting the predecessor to § 351 under the Internal Revenue Code of 1939.

**Answer "A" is incorrect.** Stock received for services is never considered to have been received in exchange for property. § 351(d)(1). However, such stock is included for the purpose of determining whether control exists if property (in excess of a "relatively small" amount per § 1.351-1(a)(1)(ii)) is also transferred by the service-providing shareholder. § 1.351-1(a)(2) Ex. 3.

**Answer "C" is incorrect.** Courts have held that the face amount of a personal note (assuming the note carries an appropriate rate of interest) contributed to a corporation creates stock basis that can help avoid the "liabilities-in-excess-of-basis" forced gain rule of § 357(c)(1)(A). *Peracchi v. Comm'r*, 143 F.3d 487 (9th Cir. 1998). However, the IRS disagrees. Rev. Rul. 68-629, 1968-2 C.B. 154. Therefore, a taxpayer cannot assume the use of a personal note will avoid gain recognition.

**Answer "D" is incorrect.** Where a shareholder receives multiple classes of stock in a § 351 transaction, the stock basis to be allocated is assigned to the classes in proportion to their relative values. § 358(b)(1); § 1.358-2(b)(2).

16. **The best answer is "B."** An S corporation cannot have a nonresident alien shareholder. § 1361(b). An *alien* is a non-U.S. citizen or national. Bainbridge's representative in China is a resident of China, not the U.S., and is a Chinese citizen.

**Answer "A" is incorrect.** Members of a family are treated collectively as one shareholder. A family consists of a common ancestor and all of the ancestor's lineal descendents (and their spouses) so long as the common ancestor is not more than six generations removed from the youngest generation of shareholders. Great-grandfather Roy and his descendents (and their spouses) satisfy the definition of family. § 1361(c). Therefore there are deemed to be only 28 shareholders (the Roy family + 27 unrelated employees), which satisfies the "not more than 100 shareholder" rule of § 1361(b)(1)(A).

**Answer "C" is incorrect.** The focus of the "second class of stock" rule is on whether the shares of stock each have identical rights to liquidation and distribution proceeds (differences in voting rights are irrelevant). The fact that shareholder loans, which are made in proportion to their equity holdings, lose their status as "indebtedness" and becomes "equity" such that interest deductions are disallowed under debt-equity characterization principles does not establish a second class of stock. § 1.1361-1(*l*).

**Answer "D" is incorrect.** Subchapter S status can be re-elected as of the beginning of the fifth taxable year that begins after the first taxable year for which the termination is effective. § 1362(g). The first year for which the termination was effective for Bainbridge is the short Subchapter C year December 29 through December 31, 2002. Therefore, Bainbridge could re-elect Subchapter S status as of January 1, 2007 (the beginning of the fifth year following the first year that Bainbridge was a Subchapter C corporation). Re-election on January 1 of the upcoming year poses no problem.

17A. Yes. Chan has a realized gain of $60,000 ($70,000 value - $10,000 basis). § 1001(a).

17B. Chan will not recognize this gain. § 721(a). His basis in the partnership interest will be his basis in the raw land, $10,000. § 722. Chan's holding period in his partnership interest includes, or "tacks," his holding period in the raw land, four years. § 1223(1).

17C. Chan will be required to recognize the $60,000 of realized gain because he does not control X immediately after the contribution. § 351(a). For these purposes, control is defined as the ownership of stock having at least 80% of the voting power (Chan has only 20%). § 368(c).

Chan's tax cost basis in the stock will be his basis in the raw land ($10,000) plus the gain recognized ($60,000) or $70,000. § 1012(a). Chan's holding period in the stock does not include the holding period in the raw land because no provision of § 1223 applies.

17D. Now Chan has control of X immediately after the contribution, which makes this a nonrecognition transaction under § 351(a). Chan's basis in the stock will carry over from his basis in the raw land ($10,000). § 358(a). His holding period in the stock will include his holding period in the raw land (four years). § 1223(1).

18A. To be eligible for sale or exchange treatment under § 302(b)(1) the redemption must satisfy the "not essentially equivalent to a dividend" test. That test requires a meaningful reduction in the shareholder's interest in the corporation. *U.S. v. Davis*, 397 U.S. 301 (1970). A shareholder's interest is comprised of three rights: the rights to participate in control, in earnings, and in assets upon liquidation. *Himmel v. Comm'r*, 338 F.2d 815 (2d Cir. 1964). Control is the key right under the meaningful reduction analysis. *Johnston*, 77 T.C. 679 (1981); Rev. Rul. 75-502, 1975-2 C.B. 111.

Before the redemption Louise had control of Nesnong (80% voting power). After the redemption she had 2/3 of the voting power [(80 - 40)/(100 - 40)]. Since control has not been lost, Louise fails the "not essentially equivalent to a dividend" test. The IRS takes the view that the mere loss of "super-majority" control is not sufficient. Rev. Rul. 78-401, 1978-2 C.B. 127.

18B. As noted above, Louise fails to fall below 50% voting power as a result of the redemption. This is sufficient to prevent sale or exchange treatment under § 302(b)(2). Further, Louise's voting power only contracted by 16.7% (1 – (2/3 ÷ 80%)), which is less than the required more-than-20%.

18C. Louise did not completely terminate her interest in the corporation.

19. **The best answer is "A."** A shareholder who owns at least 50% of the value of a corporation's stock is deemed to own the stock owned by such corporation in proportion to the shareholder's ownership interest. § 318(a)(2)(C). Since Dan owns less than 50% by value, he is deemed to own none of the stock owned by Ryan.

**Answer "B" is a correct statement and, therefore, not the right answer.** A partner is deemed to own a proportionate amount of the stock owned by the partnership. § 318(a)(2)(A).

**Answer "C" is a correct statement and, therefore, not the right answer.** A trust is deemed to own all of the stock owned by its beneficiaries. § 318(a)(3)(B)(i).

**Answer "D" is a correct statement and, therefore, not the right answer.** Section 318(a)(5)(A) expressly so states. The exceptions are re-attribution within a family under § 318(a)(5)(B) and re-attribution to another equity holder of stock constructively owned by an entity by virtue of attribution from a different equity holder under § 318(a)(5)(C).

20. **The best answer is "B."** There can be no dividend unless there are earnings and profits. § 316(a). An S corporation which has never been a C corporation (and which has never been involved with a reorganization involving a C corporation) has no earnings and profits. § 1371(c)(1).

**Answer "A" is a correct statement and, therefore, not the right answer.** Section 6037(c)(1) expressly so states.

**Answer "C" is a correct statement and, therefore, not the right answer.** Subchapter C governs unless Subchapter S expressly states otherwise or unless applying Subchapter C would be inconsistent with Subchapter S principles. § 1371(a). Therefore, § 351 is fully applicable to the capitalization of an S corporation. Section 351 applies on these facts.

**Answer "D" is a correct statement and, therefore, not the right answer.** Section 1367(a)(1)(A) requires stock basis to be increased by the stockholder's share of the corporation's separately stated income items under § 1366(a)(1)(A). The latter expressly includes exempt income. Section 1367(a)(2)(D) reduces stock basis by "any expense of the corporation not deductible in computing its taxable income and not properly chargeable to capital[,]" which includes the nondeductible meals.

21.    **The best answer is "C."** Earnings and profits are reduced by the amount of the distribution, but not below zero. § 312(a)(1).

**Answer "A" is a correct statement and, therefore, not the right answer.** Section 311(a)(2) expressly so states with respect to property. Property includes cash. § 317(a).

**Answer "B" is a correct statement and, therefore, not the right answer.** Section 301(a) and (c)(1) require dividends to be included in gross income. Section 316(a) states that all distributions are sourced from earnings and profits to the extent thereof and that such distributions constitute dividends.

**Answer "D" is a correct statement and, therefore, not the right answer.** Corporate shareholders are generally entitled to a dividends-received deduction under § 243. The amount of the dividends-received deduction is 70%, 80% or 100%. § 243(a)(1), (a)(3), (b)(1)(A)-(B), (c).

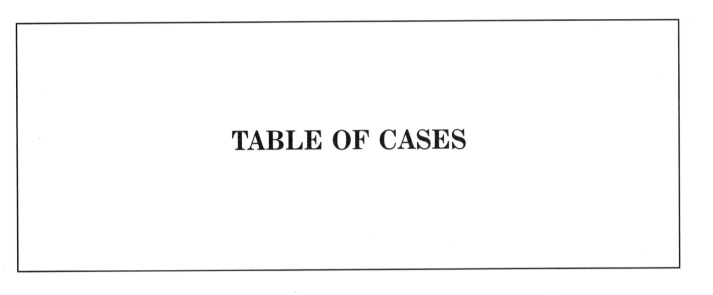

# TABLE OF CASES

# TABLE OF CASES

[1] Question numbers preceded with an "E" indicate a Practice Exam Question.

# TOPIC INDEX

# TOPIC INDEX

---

[1] Question numbers preceded with an "E" indicate a Practice Exam Question.

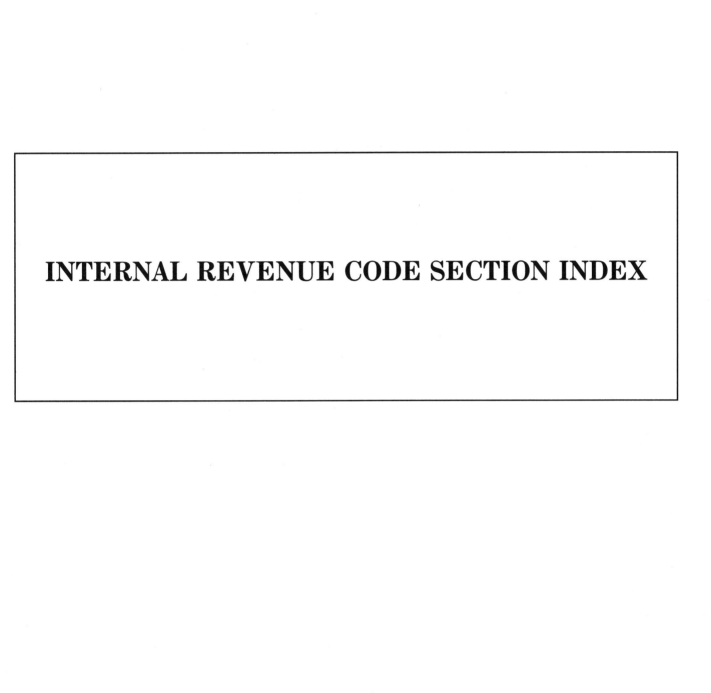

# INTERNAL REVENUE CODE SECTION INDEX

# INTERNAL REVENUE CODE SECTION INDEX

---

[1] Question numbers preceded with an "E" indicate a Practice Exam Question.

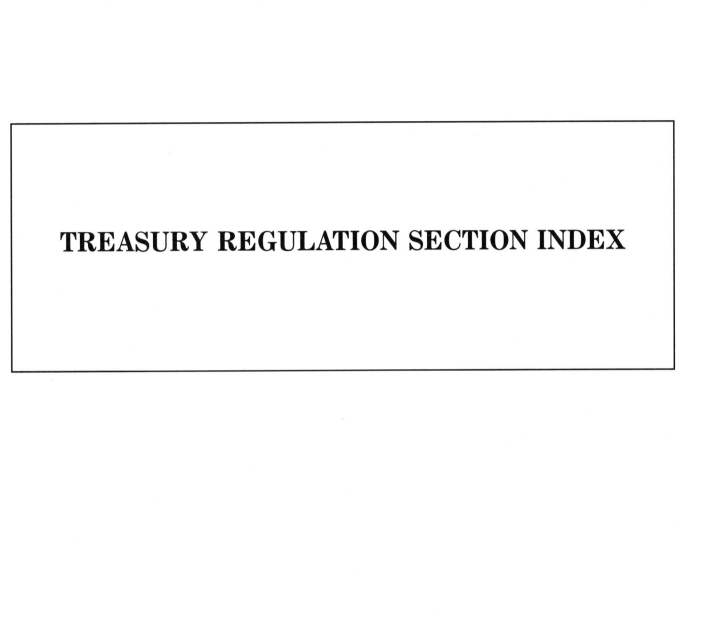

# TREASURY REGULATION SECTION INDEX

# TREASURY REGULATION SECTION INDEX

---

[1] Question numbers preceded with an "E" indicate a Practice Exam Question.